THE TRANSFORMATIONAL JOURNEY

To Dick, Scottie & Family
Enjoy the journey!

From Merry Christmas

Mark

I wish for you a life of wealth, health, and happiness; a life in which you give to yourself the gift of patience, the virtue of reason, the value of knowledge, and the influence of faith in your own ability to dream about and to achieve worthy rewards.

— **Jim Rohn**

THE TRANSFORMATIONAL JOURNEY

Receive Special Bonuses When Buying
The Transformational Journey Book

To access bonus gifts and to send us your testimonials and comments, please send an email to

gifts@TransformationalJourneybook.com

Published by
Kyle Wilson International
KyleWilson.com

Distributed by
Kyle Wilson International
P.O. Box 2683
Keller, TX 76244
info@kylewilson.com

The Transformational Journey
ISBN: 978-1-7357428-5-4

Printed in the United States of America

EXCERPTS FROM
THE TRANSFORMATIONAL JOURNEY

Don't tell them about it, show them by your actions. It's much better to walk your talk. A positive role model does more as a parent than any lecturing could possibly do.

— Denis Waitley, Iconic Speaker, Author of Seeds of Greatness

I realize I am one of the fortunate ones who escaped financial illiteracy. I had the privilege of learning valuable skills on the job that grew my knowledge, and ultimately, my financial stability and wealth. For those who have not been able to break the cycle, my life mission has shifted to provide them knowledge and opportunity.

— Gina Linette Shin, CEO, Shin Equity Partners, Investor, Board Member

We hadn't realized the difference between growing a business and scaling a business. In just under three years, we had accomplished growing our business so tall and so narrow that the slightest wind would have it tipping over and crumbling to its demise. Even worse, all of the other parts of my life were also on the brink of collapse. Something had to give, and it was our pride.

— Patrick Murray, Founder of Local Roots, Coach, Speaker

Five years post-graduation, I was debt-free, had a significant sum saved in the bank, was in a great romantic relationship, and was riding the consulting wave through Y2K and into the new millennium. Five years later, I had more debt than when I graduated college, the consulting market was dry in the wake of the 9/11/2001 terrorist acts, and I was quite ill.

— Bill Malchisky, Entrepreneur, Speaker, Solution Architect

I truly believe I am right where God wants me in this season in life. You only live once. I figure I might as well do something I enjoy doing.

— Landon Schlabach, Entrepreneur, Speaker, Real Estate Investor

Each time you pick up the phone to discuss your strategy for building wealth with your CPA and financial planner, your next call should be to your REALTOR®.

— Deanna Bone, CEO, Speaker, Investor, Real Estate Consultant

Life is never perfect at all times, in every area. Young, old, married, single, employee, entrepreneur, at all points of our life, we are all dealing with something. If we don't stop to look around us and appreciate all the people in our lives, our career journey, the family member that "if they only behaved this way, then I would really love them," we will never be happy!

— Steffany Boldrini, CEO of Monte Carlo Real Estate Investments

With this list, I created The Afghanistan Memory Wall, a project where I travel the United States, writing out these 7,000 words from memory on a wall. It takes about 10 hours to physically do it. The core message of the tribute is that they are not forgotten.

— Ron White, Speaker, Two-Time USA Memory Champion

The powerful truth is we can, repeatedly, decide. The root of the word decide is to cut. We remember and reassemble the past and our meaning we assign. Deciding and reassembling the past, we embrace the virtues and strengths from the crucible of our experience.

— Kimberly R. Faucher, Physician, Investor, Well-Being Strategist

Their mentorship not only accelerated my growth but also launched a desire in me to start passing on the lessons I've been privileged to learn. There was yet another level I was being pulled toward.

— Dale Young, Calling & Teamwork Coach and Speaker

In each trial we face, we have the opportunity to grow and transform, if that is what we choose. When you stand at the crossroad of misery or success—YOU pick!

— Shelly Slocum, Author, Speaker, Success Trainer

Life doesn't always work out the way you plan, but I decided to make the best life I could with the cards I was dealt. After I changed my mindset and no longer dwelled on the fact that I wasn't going to have kids, the anger, jealousy, and bitterness went away. I felt better than I had in years. This one life I have was turning into something amazing.

— Mandy Junge, Entrepreneur, Investor, Health Enthusiast

The more struggles I had, the darker I got, the more I drank, the more I didn't care about myself. I avoided riding my motorcycle because I was getting too involved in risk-taking—a direct symptom of PTSD. I felt a darkness, but I didn't know what it was. I wasn't suicidal, but I was terrified of what the stage after the darkness might be.

— Dustin Reichert, Author, Speaker, Hypnotist, Retired Deputy Sheriff

Outside of our careers, Randy and I worked on our real estate hobby: rental properties, remodels, and increasing our knowledge and experience. We decided early on that we didn't want to retire on a teacher's salary.

— Jana Hubbs, Master Educator, Asset Manager, Investor

If you have enthusiasm for what you do, the universe works in your favor. It's being grateful for the little things, because it's through gratitude that your character is revealed to the spiritual world.

— Latino, 20 #1 Hit Songs, Singer, Producer

As our mindset shifted to go bigger, Samantha and I built new businesses and ultimately expanded them across the United States. This required me to get on social media for the first time in 10 years. I needed to get out of my comfort zone and start showing the universe what was going on in my world. I've got a lot to offer!

— Dean Shupe, Serial Entrepreneur, Real Estate Developer

You fall now and then and scrape your knees, but it's the choice to stand back up and try again that makes the journey possible.

— Heather Roxburgh, CEO, Broker, Realtor®, The Roxburgh Group

I've discovered that you're never too old to pivot. It's just, "Are you fearless enough to do so?" Life is too short to never try. The worst thing that can happen is I will fail forward, get back up, and try again. I don't want to get down the road and "wish" for something. I want to turn my thoughts and aspirations into a reality and go for it.

— Robin Binkley, Entrepreneur, Podcast Host, Strategist

Through determination and a commitment to financial responsibility, I transformed my financial situation from overwhelming debt to a debt-free life.

— Adebayo Fasanya, MD, Real Asset Syndicator, Doctor, Speaker, Coach

Today, the world needs independent doctors more than ever. We need doctors who can deliver top-quality care to patients without devastating their households financially. We need doctors and staff who are themselves healthy, secure, and fulfilled.

— George C. Ozoude, MD, Orthopaedic Surgeon, CEO Time Health Capital

I try to live the example for people and tell people it's possible for them too. I want to empower because sometimes you can have all the education, but unless you are empowered to act, you're not going to be able to do it.

— Wagner Nolasco, Real Estate Developer, Investor, Volunteer

Pleasure is our birthright, and yet, so many are overworking, overthinking, overeating, over worrying, and a whole slew of other "overs" that have made us unsatisfied, unhealthy, and unhappy in staggering numbers. Did you know that you can have a life that is healthy, vibrant, and passionate? Embracing ALL parts of you and your story is essential to help you create that reality.

— Dr. Stormy Hill, OTR/L, Relationship Coach, Speaker, Podcaster

In one instant, it hit me: I am responsible. If I want my future to be different, I am responsible. If I don't want to repeat the mistakes and wreckage of the past, I am responsible.

— Dan Faulkner, Realtor, Youth Advocate, Real Estate Investor

Real estate investing gives me the flexibility to travel, network, connect with people, add value, continue my personal development, develop my fitness, and give back to the community I live in.

— Vish Muni, Lifestyle Investor, Commercial Real Estate

Instead of succumbing to adversity, I harnessed it as fuel to propel me towards success. The human spirit is resilient and I have seen how, through steadfast determination, our boundless potential can be unlocked.

— Ena Hull, Entrepreneur, Executive, Advisor, Private Equity

The true measure of a person's maturity and wisdom is determined by their ability to handle difficult emotions in trying times. This insightful chapter gives you a tool and doable practice to make it so.

— Greg Zlevor, Author, Speaker, Global Leadership Expert

Being willing to seek life and business improvements through well-calculated risk-taking keeps us sharp and ultimately enhances our chances of wildly successful outcomes.

— Steve Trent, Developer, Attorney, Preferred Choice Homes

If you have lost a child or loved one, I am hoping this story will bring you hope and will allow me to somehow walk by your side. I am wishing you a life where you embrace people who are still with you and share stories of loved ones who have passed. Where you experience joy along with sorrow, as they are both true, and where, rather than allowing the toxicity of unforgiveness to hold you hostage, you embrace the healing powers of mercy and forgiveness.

— Joell Mower, DomiNic's Place CEO, Youth Advocate

I always tell people, songwriting is 90% perspiration and 10% inspiration. But you've got to do the 90% to be there for that 10% when it happens. Those are the moments songwriters live for.
— Seth Mosley, Three-Time Grammy Winner, Songwriter, Producer

I look back now and realize I never doubted myself. Call it innocence or even naivete, but I knew my life would be different than anything I'd grown up with.
— Jackie Marushka, PR Expert, Inspirational Speaker

Despite my luck, I have realized I do not have 100% control over situations and their outcomes. We can be prepared for those moments and persist through the resistance of life to become transformed on the other end. Then, we must reflect with a critical eye to determine who that transformation makes us.
— Ben Buzek, Visionary, Trailblazer, Special Operations Veteran

By chasing your dreams, you are forced to become a better person by overcoming obstacles, including your own head trash and self-doubts. It's through all of the ups and downs along this pursuit of your best self and your best life that you will find transformation and happiness, not upon the completion of a specific goal.
— Pete Schnepp, Real Estate Investor, Entrepreneur, Family Man

I found peace and comfort in turning inwards during those early morning hours, and over time, I gained greater clarity on my life and my next steps, and I started asking better questions. With a shift in mindset, I realized the power to change my circumstances lay in my own hands. This shift unlocked resources I never knew I had. I recognized opportunities instead of doubting myself and letting them pass.
— Jin Wang, Former CPA & Auditor, Real Asset Investor

I understood that my brain, through repetition of the mantra "I love myself, I appreciate myself, thank you life," would eventually believe it and give me a whole new feeling. I understood that my brain doesn't differentiate between receiving that compliment from someone else and me repeating it to myself.
— Dominic Lagrange, Expert Advisor, Coach of Visionary Leaders

Looking back at my journey, I can see that physicians need to learn finance early in their career. Doctors need to make their money work for them and start building financial freedom along with building their career. The sooner physicians act, the better. Financial stability will allow physicians to practice on their terms.
— Lydia R. Essary, MD, Entrepreneur, Speaker, Real Estate Syndicator

Transformational success requires belief, faith, and hunger. It also requires massive action. I believe habits, routine, and behavior are the foundation.
— Tyler Vinson, CEO REtokens, Speaker, Real Estate Liquidity

Starting a venture capital fund was the most challenging and exciting experience of my life. I had always been an entrepreneur, but a venture capital fund was a whole new ballgame.

— Mark Hasebroock, Founder, VC Investor, Serial Entrepreneur, Advisor

I lead with gratitude. I am grateful for the simple things, which really are the big things—like waking up each morning, and the opportunities ahead. I am so grateful for the incredible people in my life who love, support, and challenge me. Every single setback and hardship I've faced has shaped who I am today.

— Cindy Aronstam, Real Estate Expert, Animal Advocate

If you can design your vision for your life so that the majority of your day is spent doing what you are very good at and what you enjoy, then it doesn't feel like work. This was a turning point for me.

— Derek Dombeck, Real Estate Investor, Speaker, Private Lender

That's exactly where I was going wrong. First, there was no team. It was me making every decision and me with all the responsibilities. I thought that was how it was supposed to be because it was my business. Finally, when it couldn't be like that anymore, I was forced to delegate, which was one of my dad's keys from day one.

— Chris Gronkowski, NFL Player, Shark Tank, Founder of Ice Shaker

When I look back on what brought me to where I am today, I see the transformation that had to happen in my heart and mind long before the opportunity came to make it all possible.

— Christie Frieg, Visionary, President, Alethia Software

The goal of many real estate professionals and investors is to replace one's active income with passive income to provide financial freedom. If an investor can do this, they can decide to work because they want to work, not because they have to work. I prefer to take this a step further and pursue true freedom, not just financial freedom.

— Chad Zdenek, Founder CSQ Properties, Real Estate Investor, TV Host

None of us want pain, challenges, and difficult life circumstances. In fact, we as humans tend to gravitate towards our comfort zone and security. But oftentimes, it's the things that push us out of our comfort zone that have a transformational impact on us.

— Kyle Wilson, Founder Jim Rohn International, Marketer, Strategist

TABLE OF CONTENTS

DISCLAIMER

The information in this book is not meant to replace the advice of a certified professional. Please consult a licensed advisor in matters relating to your personal and professional well-being including your mental, emotional and physical health, finances, business, legal matters, family planning, education, and spiritual practices. The views and opinions expressed throughout this book are those of the authors and do not necessarily reflect the views or opinions of all the authors or position of any other agency, organization, employer, publisher, or company.

Since we are critically-thinking human beings, the views of each of the authors are always subject to change or revision at any time. Please do not hold them or the publisher to them in perpetuity. Any references to past performance may not be indicative of future results. No warranties or guarantees are expressed or implied by the publisher's choice to include any of the content in this volume.

If you choose to attempt any of the methods mentioned in this book, the authors and publisher advise you to take full responsibility for your safety and know your limits. The authors and publisher are not liable for any damages or negative consequences from any treatment, action, application, or preparation to any person reading or following the information in this book.

This book is a collaboration between a number of authors and reflects their experiences, beliefs, opinions, and advice. The authors and publisher make no representations as to accuracy, completeness, correctness, suitability, or validity of any information in the book, and neither the publisher nor the individual authors shall be liable for any physical, psychological, emotional, financial, or commercial damages, including, but not limited to, special, incidental, consequential, or other damages to the readers of this book.

Dedication

To all the mentors who have shaped the lives of each author in this book. To our loved ones who fan our flames. To all those who read this book and are inspired to take the next step in their transformational journey!

Acknowledgments

A big thank you—

To Takara Sights, our writing coach, editor, and project manager extraordinaire, for your endless hours of work and passion in this book! Despite the complexities involved with a project like this, you keep the process a pleasure and always provide first-class results. A thousand praises! You are a rockstar!

To Claudia Volkman, Joe Potter, and Anne-Sophie Gomez, who have put countless hours into designing and formatting this book. Your thoughtful design allows readers to receive the wisdom in these pages! We are grateful!

To Dan Armstrong, Tammy Hane, Mark Hartley, Jo Hausman, Aaron Naninni, John Obenchain, Adrian Shepherd, and Jennifer Stewart for being our second eyes and proofreading the manuscript. We so appreciate it!

And to Brian Tracy, Tom Ziglar, Kevin Eastman, Bob Beaudine, Olenka Cullinan, Former Marine Colonel Tim Cole, Newy Scruggs, Former Navy SEAL TC Cummings, and Dr. Tom Burns, and ALL the amazing mentors and world-class thought leaders who took the time to read this book's manuscript and give their endorsements— thank you!

FOREWORD

by Brian Tracy

Welcome to *The Transformational Journey*. Put up your tray tables and put on your seat belts. You are about to become a different person, in a very positive way. In the pages ahead, you will learn some of the most important insights and truths about success and happiness ever discovered written by wise, diverse authors who were guided by editor Takara Sights and master teacher Kyle Wilson.

Kyle and I first met in 1991 when he invited me and Og Mandino to speak at a large conference in Atlanta, Georgia. Kyle then booked me and Jim Rohn to speak in multiple cities around the country. In 1996, Kyle booked me for a multi-city tour for a two-day event titled the *Success Mastery Academy*. In 2016, Kyle hosted the 20th anniversary of this epic event in Dallas, Texas, where I spoke for two days, plus we had special guest Darren Hardy and several more top business people in the audience.

Now, Kyle and I have traveled and worked together for more than 30 years. Not only was he the marketing genius behind Jim Rohn for 18 years, but Kyle also has a knack for attracting amazing people around him.

This new book Kyle has published, *The Transformational Journey*, is full of lessons, insights, and strategies from entrepreneurs and thought leaders you can use to take your life to a new level.

For years, I've spoken about the power of transformation—how, by changing our thoughts, we can change our attitudes, habits, and results.

I know it's possible because I've proved it in my own life.

In my seminars, I talk about *the superconscious mind* and about how you can activate the incredible mental powers you already have. You can turn on this switch and start to attract into your life everything you want—opportunities, ideas, people, resources, and more—simply by using the powers you already have within your mind.

Every great achievement in history has been a manifestation of superconscious thinking, a result of someone learning how to tap into this great power. And you can as well, just by deciding to do so.

Perhaps you say, "I want to be wealthy, successful, and highly respected. Maybe I don't have a university degree, and I don't have any money right now, but I do have my brain and my ability to work. And that's what I'm going to do."

If you do the work that others have done, as explained in *The Transformational Journey*, you set up a force field of energy in the universe that works 24 hours a day to get you what you want.

Happiness is the natural result of accepting total responsibility for every part of your life. We create happiness for ourselves when we make a habit of manufacturing positive expectations in advance of each event.

Never complain, never explain. Resist the temptation to defend yourself or make excuses. Repeat the magic words, "If it is to be, it's up to me."

Develop an attitude of gratitude and give thanks for everything that happens to you, knowing that every step forward is a step towards achieving something bigger and better than your current situation. The only limits are those you place on your own mind by the way you think.

In *The Transformational Journey*, you will learn more about how to get the most out of yourself than perhaps you had ever thought possible. Welcome to the great adventure!

Brian Tracy is chairman and CEO of Brian Tracy International, a company specializing in the training and development of individuals and organizations. Brian Tracy has consulted for more than 1,000 companies and addressed more than 5,000,000 people in 5,000 talks and seminars throughout the US, Canada, and 84 other countries worldwide. Brian is the author of over 90 books that have been translated into 54 languages, including *Eat That Frog!* and *Earn What You're Really Worth*. To learn more about Brian Tracy's book and audio programs, go to BrianTracy.com or visit Amazon.com.

"Yes, your transformation will be hard. Yes, you will feel frightened, messed up, and knocked down. Yes, you'll want to stop. Yes, it's the best work you'll ever do."

— Robin Sharma

KYLE WILSON

Our Greatest Teachers

Kyle Wilson is an entrepreneur, business and marketing strategist, publisher, seminar promoter, and speaker. He is the founder of KyleWilson.com, Jim Rohn International, and LessonsFromNetwork. com. Kyle hosts the Success Habits podcast and the Kyle Wilson Inner Circle Mastermind and has published dozens of #1 bestselling books.

Peeling the Onion

I recently hosted a two-day retreat with my long-time friend and mentor, the iconic Denis Waitley. I actually was Denis's agent back in the 2000s in addition to being Jim Rohn's agent for 18 years. Denis is now 90 years old. He has gone through three bouts of cancer, once during COVID lockdowns and in isolation for four months. He still isn't able to eat solid food due to throat cancer. And yet, at age 90, he was his all-time best at the retreat. In front of the group, I said, "Denis, I feel like you are your all-time best. It's not just the content, but your delivery, energy, passion, and insights."

In response, he said one word: "Pain!"

He said, "Kyle, I've been through a lot of pain, and I was forced to take the very advice I taught Olympians, POWs, astronauts, and millions of people in my audiences over the past 40-plus years."

I left the retreat thinking about that. None of us want pain, challenges, and difficult life circumstances. In fact, we as humans tend to gravitate towards our comfort zone and security.

But oftentimes, it's the things that push us out of our comfort zone that have a transformational impact on us.

I started thinking about this in my own life and the different experiences that have impacted me. Eight themes and catalysts come to mind in my own personal journey.

1. Pain

Jim Rohn, my 18-year mentor and business partner, would say we all change for one of two reasons: inspiration or desperation. I would have to say, the majority of the time, for me, it's been desperation. I grew up in a small town, never went to college, and had three older siblings who never got in trouble. I was always in trouble, including doing and selling drugs.

But after much pain and unhappiness, at age 19, I made a decision to stop the lifestyle I was in and take a different path. I got involved in a church, and the people and new environment really impacted my life for the better.

On one of my podcast episodes, I interviewed my friend Phil Collen, the lead guitarist of Def Leppard. He shared that he was 35 years sober and said it was 100 percent because of the pain drinking had caused him. Phil has also spent the day at my house with my Inner Circle Mastermind. As someone who has sold 100 million albums and lived the rockstar lifestyle, his message impacts many.

2. Life Events

Sometimes things happen we can't control. It could be something that happens to us individually, our family, our workplace, the economy, or even our nation. But things happen.

We've all heard the saying that change is inevitable. And when the winds of change come, they often push us to a fork in the road, and we get to decide what direction we're going to go.

That happened for me at age 26. After a series of events, I decided to sell my business and uproot myself from the town of about 12,000 people where I grew up, Vernon, Texas, and move to the big city of Dallas, where I knew less than five people and had no job lined up.

Within a few years, very serendipitously, that move led me into the seminar business, which forever changed my life and is where I went on to meet Jim Rohn.

3. Mentors

At 28, I had the incredible good fortune of going to work for Jerry Haines, who was a seminar promoter. Quickly, I became Jerry's top salesperson and eventually went out on my own to put on big events. That led to meeting and working with Jim Rohn as well as Brian Tracy, Les Brown, Mark Victor Hanson, Denis Waitley, Bob Burg, John Maxwell, and many others.

So many of the lessons I've shared on my podcast, in my blogs, and in previous books came from these mentors. I'm the guy who had done drugs and who never went to college, and now I was filling up huge seminar rooms and had access to these incredible mentors, not just while they were speaking at my events, but backstage, off stage, at their homes and my home, and for hours and hours of conversations. Truly, it's been beyond my wildest imagination.

4. Saying Yes

When I first went to work for Jerry Haines in the seminar business, he explained to me what would be involved. It was WAY outside of my comfort zone. But I was desperate. So, even though I was scared out of my mind, I said yes. First, I had to learn to make cold calls. Then I learned to present in front of a group, which totally scared me! Then I learned how to sell seminar tickets to that group and get referrals.

Later, after going out on my own, and recruiting my wife Heidi and another couple, we learned how to go into a new city every 90 days and put on our own events and would hire Jim Rohn, Brian Tracy, and Og Mandino.

Then, in 1993, I made Jim Rohn an offer for exclusivity. We became partners, and I launched Jim Rohn International. I had to then figure out how to take Jim from 20 speaking gigs a year to over 100 while tripling his fee. Then I learned how to create audio and video training programs and how to publish books, eventually creating and selling over 100 intellectual properties.

Then I learned to build a team! I had become a rainmaker but not yet a good leader. That was maybe one of the hardest things I did and also one of the most fulfilling.

In 1999, it was learning the internet, and I went on to build a million-plus email list. Then, in 2007, I had to learn how to sell a company and transition the team, vendors, and speakers I was representing. Then, after seven years of retirement, it was learning to reinvent myself and do what I do now.

All of these skills and experiences were ONLY because I said YES to Jerry in 1989 and kept saying yes to each new opportunity.

5. Opportunity

I've come to believe that opportunity precedes personal development. Sometimes we have to have something that gets us so excited that we decide to do all the things that will change our lives—that gets us up early, keeps us up late, motivates us to read the books, attend the seminars, have conversations, set goals, keep a journal, etc.

That's what happened to me when I found the seminar business. That's what happened to me when I first heard Jim Rohn. I was inspired to become better. If I didn't have those opportunities, I wouldn't have made the changes and begun the new habits that forever changed my life.

6. Associations and Environment

Jim Rohn said that we become like the people we spend the most time around. After selling Jim Rohn International and YourSuccessStore in 2007 and retiring for several years, I went on a ski trip with Darren Hardy, John Assaraf, Eric Berman, and Steven Cox in 2013. They were all part of a San Diego mastermind and, even though I was semi-retired, they encouraged me to start my own mastermind in Dallas.

When I launched the Kyle Wilson Inner Circle Mastermind, it was primarily so I could spend time with other amazing people, grow, learn, and get better. And today, eight years after launching it in 2015, it's still my favorite thing I do. It's the most important thing I do. Whether it's business and marketing, finances, relationships, health, spirituality, or investments, this is the environment where I grow the most, and these are the people who have the biggest impact in my life.

7. Testimonials and Examples

One of the things Jim Rohn would say is that through testimonials and examples, we know everything is possible. That means, if there is anything you want to do, if someone else has done it, it's possible. I think that's one of the things editor and writing coach Takara Sights and I so enjoy about the books we do. We have now gotten to read and publish over 400 powerful stories of people who have common threads of resilience, faith, commitment, ingenuity, service, and generosity.

When we get around or read about other people who have lived through nearly anything and everything we've been challenged with and gone on to have success, then we know that if it is possible for them, it is possible for us.

8. Service

When we are in service to others, bringing our gifts to the marketplace, the opportunity for transformation can happen. I always say the best marketing is a transformed life in the people we serve. In fact, we're best able to help the person we once were by bringing our gifts, experience, and care to other people.

We Are All on Our Own Journey

I subscribe to what my mentor Jim Rohn said: "Success is whatever you want it to be." I'm not here to sell anyone on anything. You have to find what works for you. What makes you happy? What inspires you?

I believe we are all wired differently and have our own unique path. What works for one may not work for another, or even be important to them for that matter.

Because of my extreme entrepreneurial wiring, I've discovered things about myself over the past several years. I could have transformational experiences in business and still lack in other areas. I'm still learning something new about myself every day. I feel like change and transformation is a never-ending journey.

To learn more about Kyle Wilson's Inner Circle Mastermind, the #1 Bestseller Book Program, and The Strategic Marketing Wheel and to access over 100 blog posts and podcast episodes, go to KyleWilson. com. To receive over a dozen interviews by Kyle with Darren Hardy, Les Brown, Brian Tracy, and more, email info@kylewilson.com with Interviews in the subject. Follow Kyle on IG @kylewilsonjimrohn.

Quotable: None of us want pain, challenges, and difficult life circumstances. In fact, we as humans tend to gravitate towards our comfort zone and security. But oftentimes, it's the things that push us out of our comfort zone that have a transformational impact on us.

CHAD ZDENEK

From Rocket Scientist to Multi-Million Dollar Business Owner to Real Estate Investor

Chad Zdenek started as a rocket scientist working on the Space Shuttle main engines before building a multi-million dollar business, finally settling into a real estate investing career managing a portfolio of $200M today. He and his wife are raising five children, and in his pursuit of financial freedom, he is bringing as many people with him as possible!

Getting Started

I thought I'd finally made it—I owned a multi-million dollar business with my brother. We had built the largest Christmas lighting business in Los Angeles with a world-renowned client list that included Universal Studios, the Los Angeles Zoo, the Forum, the City of Beverly Hills, and any celebrity's house you could think of.

But, after 15 years, I was still working 100 hours a week during the busy season. I had my fourth kid on the way, and with no end in sight to a work schedule that made me an absentee dad for six months of the year, how would I be able to spend more time with my family?

I have been an entrepreneur since as early as I can remember. When I was 10 years old, my dad offered to pay me $1 for every bucket of weeds I picked in our backyard. Ecstatic at my new prospect of making money, the first thing I did after he left for work was gather my four younger brothers and sisters and offer them $0.50 for each bucket of weeds they picked! Despite the help, I still picked weeds myself. This is one of the many life lessons I live by to this day—never ask someone else to do something I wouldn't do or haven't done. It ended up being a busy day in the backyard, and when my dad got home, I showed him the completed work, collected the money, and paid my "employees." Everyone was happy!

Ten years later, at the age of 21, I graduated from Loyola Marymount University with my degree in civil engineering and began working at Boeing/Rocketdyne. As a structural dynamics engineer, I was working on the Space

Shuttle's main engines. It was a fascinating place to work with incredibly bright engineers and scientists.

While working full-time, I wound up earning my master's degree in structural engineering from USC and my MBA from UCLA. This helped put me on the executive management track. But, something was still missing.

Taking the Leap

In my first year as an MBA student at UCLA, both my brothers were also there getting their undergraduate degrees and playing football. My younger brother, Jason, had started a Christmas lighting business in his last year of school, and I happened to be focusing on entrepreneurial studies. I was able to use his business as my project at UCLA and offered consulting to help grow the business. It was my brother, Jason, my sister, and a few workers that first year. Jason steadily grew the business, and he wanted me to come join him.

The only problem was, I had a great job at Boeing/Rocketdyne, presenting regularly to NASA and visiting various space flight centers. It was an amazing job!

But as anyone close with their siblings knows, it's very difficult to say no to them. Even before starting at Boeing/Rocketdyne, I had started three other companies, not including the weed-clearing business! My entrepreneurial spirit was yearning to be unleashed, even while working on systems as cutting edge as the Space Shuttle. To make matters more convincing, the bureaucracy of a Fortune 100 company was eating away at me. I was giving the company 100% effort while continually improving myself but I was only getting 4-5% annual raises. Additionally, as with most large organizations, people who contributed very little and hid in the shadows of the organization were still receiving 1% raises. In my mind, the difference in work output was much more than a few percentage points, yet the compensation wasn't commensurate.

In the end, I made a deal with my brother—I'd leave Boeing/Rocketdyne if he could get the business to grow to a certain size. Jason did it, and after seven years at Boeing/Rocketdyne, I decided to leave that career path behind and took a massive 50% pay cut. That risky, entrepreneurial move was equally met with Jason paying me more than he was paying himself. We agreed to split the business 50/50 and got to work!

My engineering colleagues, close friends, and even some family members were very perplexed by my career move, but within 15 years, we ended up growing the business by 2,000% and it became the largest Christmas lighting company in Los Angeles. During the peak part of the season, we would have 75 workers operating from three different warehouses and installing projects from San Diego to Santa Barbara.

Difficult Decisions

Over time, I realized I couldn't break through the ceiling created by a seasonal business. We had a year-round staff of 20 but needed to ramp up and ramp down for six months of the year. Everyone wanted to have their lights up the week before Thanksgiving and have them taken down the week after New Year's Day. We did hundreds of jobs, so this made it very difficult to scale. No matter how "smart" I tried to work, I was working 100+ hour weeks during the peak of the season.

It was very difficult to decide what to do about the conundrum I was in—I loved working with my brother and had helped build a good-size company. However, sacrificing family time was very challenging. Each year, I'd tell myself next year will be easier—we'll hire more people and institute more systems and processes. But in the end, I still was an absentee dad for too much time. I felt like no matter what I did, I was getting the same results—working too many hours and sacrificing too much.

As a way to process difficult decisions and attempt to think more clearly, I began working out. It seemed as though the challenges of being a dad and running a company were getting more difficult to process, so I would endure longer and longer workouts, in part so I could ponder on things more. At about the same time, I met David Richman, an endurance athlete who would end up becoming a great friend. He pushed me to channel these mind-clearing workouts into triathlon training and ultramarathons. I ended up doing five full-length Ironman races (2.4-mile swim, 112-mile bike, and 26.2-mile run), dozens of half-Ironman races, and several ultramarathon runs ranging from 50 miles to 65 miles. The workouts gave me an opportunity to think through issues without the barrage of employees, clients, or kids.

Around the same time, I also explored the career of hosting TV shows. I hosted several shows over a period of 10 years with the latest being called Inside Mighty Machines which aired on the Smithsonian Channel and

National Geographic. It was great work with incredible experiences in front of the camera, but the work was very sporadic and not something I could realistically do full-time.

Eventually, I realized that I had to pivot once again, and I decided to sell my half of the business to my brother and get back into real estate. I had worked for Swinerton Builders for two years prior to Boeing/Rocketdyne and worked in residential construction, eventually getting my general contractor's license. I also earned my professional engineer's license in civil and mechanical engineering. When the lighting business was slow in the off-season, I did structural engineering design for custom homes and small commercial buildings. This proved to be very helpful in real estate.

What really convinced me to get back into real estate was coming across several successful businessmen who, regardless of what their business was, had made a significant amount of their wealth in real estate. I had always heard of the advantages of real estate with respect to taxes and leverage (borrowing money). However, it's a lot like riding a bike—until you actually do it, it doesn't fully sink in.

In the first full year of my real estate career, I purchased two cash-producing buildings and I received a 50% refund on my taxes! At that point, I knew I had made the right decision.

Pursuit of Freedom

I've started or been a founder in eight different businesses in my career. In the five years since I started my latest venture, CSQ Properties, which stands for Challenge the Status Quo, I've grown my real estate portfolio to $200 million in assets under management. I own properties in California, Kansas, North Carolina, Alabama, Florida, and Texas.

I'm what is known as a real estate syndicator, essentially the quarterback that puts deals together for the mutual benefit of myself and outside investors. This includes finding the properties, securing the debt, raising the capital, managing the property managers, managing the general contractors for rehab, refinancing, and eventually selling the property. I was able to do this on my own when I was doing two- to three- million-dollar deals, but I've discovered on the larger, $20-$70 million deals I've done, it takes a team of general partners. Over the last several years, I've joined different mastermind groups, including the Entrepreneurs' Organization, to help with both my continuing educational development and networking with like-minded entrepreneurs. The partnerships I've developed through these groups have really allowed me to scale the business. I've definitely come to learn that syndication is a team sport!

The real attractiveness of real estate is passive income, which is the regular cash flow an investor can receive from commercial real estate. The goal of many real estate professionals and investors is to replace one's active income with passive income to provide financial freedom. If an investor can do this, they can decide to work because they want to work, not because they have to work. I prefer to take this a step further and pursue true freedom, not just financial freedom.

History is riddled with examples of very wealthy people losing their freedom. They were financially free but learned the tough lesson of how much more important true freedom is. We saw this most recently during the pandemic when many people lost their freedoms—freedom of speech, freedom to conduct business, or even their medical freedom, depending on where they lived. For me, it's important to stay focused on our freedom as a whole. If we lose sight of that and only focus on financial freedom, we may be unhappy when we reach the destination we're chasing without our other freedoms as well.

I have five kids now, and trying to be a good dad is more important than ever. Although I love what I do, I'm still working much more than I'd like to and I haven't achieved the level of financial freedom I aspire to yet. I do, however, see a clear path forward, and I'm aggressively pursuing it while bringing as many people along with me as possible. I've found that many people focus so much on their primary source of income, they have no capacity to create—or even fully contemplate—passive income opportunities for themselves.

Although it has taken three different career paths, I can see clearly now. When I was at Boeing/Rocketdyne, I was doing exciting work but was working from 7:00 a.m. to 4:00 p.m., five days a week and did not have much flexibility or hope for meaningful advancement. When I left Boeing/Rocketdyne to work for myself, I learned the real truth to the statement, "Why would you work 40 hours for someone else when you could work 80 hours for yourself?" I had day-to-day flexibility, but it required a ton of commitment and affected other important aspects of my life. I believe the "third act" will be the charm as I combine my work ethic, training, attention to detail, and my love for entrepreneurship with the endless opportunities that exist in real estate. By leveraging these qualities, combined with a fierce passion for creating freedom for myself and my family, I create more and more passive income with each deal I close for myself and my investors. The road ahead is an extremely exciting one, and I am eager to continue the journey toward an ever-growing reality of true freedom for me, my family, and my investors.

Chad Zdenek is a speaker, TV host, and real estate investor pursuing freedom in all aspects of his life. He puts together real estate syndications to bring institutional-quality assets to investors who wouldn't otherwise have the opportunity to own them. To learn how these opportunities can create freedom in your life, visit www.CSQproperties.com or social media @CSQproperties or email info@CSQproperties.com.

Quotable: Life is never a straight line, but with perseverance, continual improvement, and a lot of grit, you'll end up where you want to go. When you finally get there, be sure you've found your own sense of freedom!

 Scan to schedule a call with Chad.

CHRISTIE FRIEG

The Dream Becomes Reality

Christie Frieg is a visionary, speaker, and entrepreneur passionate about providing strategic, custom software and delivering results that exceed expectations. Her company primarily serves the defense and space community. Christie delights in her husband Alex and their three daughters. Through her expertise and business platform, Christie is exploring ways to elevate disadvantaged communities.

The Angel of Destiny

It's amazing how you can be going through life, minding your own business, and suddenly your destiny comes for you.

My destiny came for me in January 2020 with a crazy, lightning-fast series of events that forced me out of the status quo I had been comfortably riding through the previous few years.

The catalyst was an out-of-the-blue meeting request from my new boss. Blindsided and nervous, I made my way from my office to the conference room. I knew I had nothing to worry about from a performance standpoint. I had outstanding marks year after year on my work as a software engineer. But I still knew that whatever waited for me behind the door probably wasn't good.

I sat down and forced a smile. I listened as my boss told me that my partial work-from-home schedule would no longer be possible if I wanted to stay in my current position.

My heart sank. This schedule (two days in the office, three days at home) was enabling me to spend time with my new daughter, an ability I had dreamed about and planned for since my teen years. I chose computer science as a career precisely because of the flexibility it would afford when it came time for me to start building my family. I wanted to spend time with my daughter now, and I wanted to be able to spend time with the children my husband and I planned to have in the future.

I asked my boss if there was any way to make an accommodation or come up with an alternative, to no avail. He gave me six weeks. In that time, I could look elsewhere in the company for a position where I could continue my hybrid schedule. At the end of those six weeks, I would no longer retain my current role, unless I was willing to work in the office five days per week.

I walked back to my office reeling from shock. I had given my best work to the company as a software engineer for the past three years and had been recognized by both employees and clients. I'd received an award for accomplishment and accepted increased responsibility on one of my main projects. My career trajectory looked perfect; within a year or two, I expected a promotion. I loved the people I worked with and the company as a whole. And now, my comfortable little train lay on the side of the tracks, completely derailed.

After a couple of weeks of mulling things over, I knew I didn't want to adjust to the new schedule. I also knew I didn't have to. Software engineers were in high demand, and I had enough connections in my hometown to find another job where I could keep my family my focus. The way I saw it, I was not willing to sacrifice my family values and my dreams on the altar of a steady job.

However, this put me in a very challenging situation. Shortly after I came to this conclusion, we discovered that I was six weeks pregnant with our second child. The Family and Medical Leave Act requires a person to have worked at their current job for at least a year before becoming eligible for FMLA leave. How would I take care of my new child without maternity leave? I could find another position at my current company, but I would be a square peg in a round hole. This new boss oversaw all the opportunities within my expertise, and anything outside of that segment would not fit my career goals.

I was caught between a rock and a hard place. But in the back of my mind, a crazy possibility was forming... a small hope awakening... maybe there was a door number three.

Door Number Three

Two days before my boss had called our surprise meeting, my husband and I had dinner with Aaron, an old family friend whose kids I used to babysit. For the past decade, Aaron had worked as a software engineering consultant.

If you'd asked me in college what I wanted to do with my computer science degree, I would have said I either wanted to be a product manager or a consultant. Seeing what product managers do day-to-day had convinced me I didn't want anything to do with that line of work, but the consultant option still sounded intriguing.

I asked Aaron about his experience with consulting. He absolutely loved it, for all the same reasons I thought I would love it too.

The idea resonated strongly with me and planted a seed in my mind. I knew I wanted to take that path, but I thought it would come about much later.

Deciding to Leave the Comfort Zone

A few weeks after I was given the job ultimatum, I met with a group of wonderful ladies who volunteered their time to pray for people and share anything they felt God putting on their hearts to say. They had given me several words through the past few years that were spot on and that sustained me through some tough times. I loved that it was always three different women each time we met and that I didn't know them personally. I never disclosed any details about my life before going in. Thus, anytime they shared something, I knew it wasn't skewed by their knowledge of the circumstance.

During my time with them that day, one of the ladies said to me, "God showed me there is something you put on the shelf, a dream God put in your heart. He says it's time to take it off the shelf. But it comes with a word of caution—He wants to do all the work to make the way for you, so don't force it to happen by yourself."

I knew immediately this referred to my dream of becoming a consultant, and it made me wonder even more about the possibility. However, I was in the middle of applying for other jobs.

Five days later, I nailed an interview with another defense contractor in town. The hiring manager told me, "I don't know why we bothered with the second interview—I was sold from our first phone conversation!" He also told me the exact salary range for the position and advised me to ask for the very highest end of the spectrum. The level of favor I had with him blew me away. I thought this had to be God leading.

I practically jumped up and down as I showed my husband the job offer they sent me, a 50% raise from my current position! I asked him if he thought I should take it almost as a joke.

"I'm really happy for you babe," he said slowly, "but I just don't have a good feeling about it."

My jaw dropped and so did my spirits. "Wait… are you serious? But…" There was no point in arguing—my husband and I have a policy in decision-making. Both of us must feel a peace in our hearts about the decision or it's a no-go.

He continued, "I think taking this job would perpetuate the status quo we have going right now. I think there's something better for us, even better than that salary. What if we blew the whole thing up, and you pursued consulting instead?"

My jaw dropped again. My husband is not the risk-taking type. He had already exchanged his full-time job for self-employment three years back, and my job represented a stable paycheck, healthcare, PTO, a 401K, and job security for our family. For him to suggest that we "blow the whole thing up" while we were six weeks pregnant with our second child—well—I knew that had to be God working in his heart, because he wouldn't have felt comfortable with the idea otherwise.

I gave myself permission to start dreaming. *What if I succeeded as a consultant? What if I could create my own schedule, make all the decisions, work when I wanted to, and stop when I didn't?* The idea felt crazy, especially since I knew absolutely nothing about how to start a business, let alone run one!

I had a great rapport with the vice president and senior vice president of the company I worked for at the time, and I asked them if they would allow me to quit my formal employment and continue my current work with them as a consultant. To my surprise, they both wholeheartedly supported my suggestion, and we got the ball rolling immediately. I had a contract in hand within three weeks, and my company Alethia Software was born.

My Inner Dialog

Looking back at my journals during this whirlwind of events, I can't help but swell with pride at my inner journey. On January 28, 2020, I wrote, "I choose from the beginning of this to view the situation as if I already had hindsight to see that God was guiding me the entire time because I do believe that. I know that this has happened for a reason—I just don't know what the reason is yet."

Up until that point in my life, when a crisis came, I would panic. I would ride the roller coaster of circumstance and be up or down depending on the outlook at that moment. I remember that, at this crossroads, I wanted to handle it differently. I could look back at my life and see God's hand in every crisis I faced, even when it felt scary in the middle of it. So, I took that information and projected it forward from where I was. Instead of focusing on the injustice of it all, I chose to believe that God would use these circumstances for my good.

In my journal, I also wrote that I asked my husband, "What if we're on the brink of the best decision we've ever made?" It turns out I was right!

After celebrating our third year in business, Alethia has 10 employees, several active contracts, some big dreams, and an extremely bright future. I wake my kids up every day, make them breakfast, play with them, and head to work in my home office, where they get to pop in periodically throughout the day. I don't ever have to leave them unless I want to. My husband also works from home, and we get to spend 95% of our time in close proximity. We are enjoying financial freedom like we only dreamed of when we first got married, and we are able to overflow in generosity to organizations and causes we believe in to help others be successful as well.

Preparation Meets Opportunity

When I look back on what brought me to where I am today, I see the transformation that had to happen in my heart and mind long before the opportunity came to make it all possible.

First, and most importantly, I learned how to hear the voice of God in my life. I believe there is no more critical way to spend your time than learning to hear His voice in times of peace. He speaks to each of us uniquely, and it takes time to find that out. Once the crisis hits, it's often too late. If we don't know how to hear Him when the storm comes, we panic, second-guess, self-doubt, and risk missing the path he desires us to follow. However, if we have confidence in our ability to hear Him, when the train flies off the tracks, we can stand firm in our course of action as we navigate the path forward.

Second, years before the actual opportunity to start my company presented itself to me, I had begun a mindset-shifting journey. My husband and I began switching out our music for Brian Buffini podcasts during our workouts back in early 2019. We listened to at least one podcast every day, and between the interviews with Brian Tracy, Shad Helmstetter, Jon Gordon, and many other inspirational speakers, our thoughts about ourselves, our purpose and meaning in life, and our methodologies steadily changed.

I used to look at wealthy people with jealousy, thinking, *How many heads did you have to step on to get there?* That was a poverty mindset. I used to think my emotions were objective truth. I didn't realize I had to actively govern them or that my brain accepts as truth whatever thoughts I allow myself to think. I thought I had to have my ducks in a row before starting a business. But I learned that no one knows exactly what to do when they begin, and we all must discover the steps as we go. By the time my chance to step out came, I had built these beliefs into a foundation that could support the ups and downs, the risk, and the firehose of learning required.

Third, I made a promise to myself that I would keep the first things first in my life. This commitment was the driving force behind me turning down my boss's ultimatum in the face of uncertainty. I esteemed my family goals higher than the security of my familiar job. I carried this commitment forward into my business. I will not compromise, even under the inevitable pressures that come with owning my own business. Though there's always more money to be made, I draw a hard boundary between my business and my family, spiritual, and health goals. I'm running a marathon, and the distance spans my entire life. I can't afford to treat it like a sprint and sacrifice the real substance of life in the process.

Ultimately, I believe my decision to start my business and my journey to success were built by thousands of tiny choices along the way—choices that were either a little harder or a lot harder than the ones others were making. Listening to a podcast instead of music. Reading a personal growth book in the evening instead of vegging out on TV. Getting up earlier to pray and meditate. Heading to the gym and turning down dessert at parties. As I transformed because of those small decisions, new opportunities came my way that I wouldn't have been ready to take advantage of otherwise.

Looking to the Future

My dreams have only expanded since starting Alethia. I now spend a large portion of my mental and emotional energy strategizing business growth and community initiatives that I believe could change my city, my state, and eventually, my nation.

With each new victory of faith, my vision expands. Even though challenges still come frequently, and I must adapt and learn to overcome them, I couldn't imagine living a happier life than the one I'm privileged to live.

If your company could use custom software or a small business partner on government contracts, visit https://alethia.software to learn more about Alethia. If you'd like to discuss a partnership with Alethia or invite Christie Frieg to speak at one of your events, you can email Christie at christie@alethia.software or connect with her on LinkedIn: https://www.linkedin.com/in/christie-frieg/.

Quotable: There's always more money to be made, but we are running a marathon, and the distance spans our entire lives. We can't afford to treat it like a sprint and sacrifice the real substance of life in the process.

 Visit our website.

TYLER VINSON

Rebuilding from Scratch
Creating a Thriving Real Estate Portfolio
Outside the Box

Tyler Vinson is a professional real estate investor with 21 years of experience and a real estate tokenization expert, author, and speaker. He is the Extant Investment Company founder/CEO and the Retokens USA Inc. co-founder/CEO. He is an Eastern Washington University alum with degrees in marketing and international business.

The Day the Real Estate Market Stopped

In 2008, I was three years into building my real estate business while acquiring rental properties. In March of that year, at 28 years old, I had become the father of twin girls who joined my six-year-old son. Life with my new career and young children was challenging, or at least, I thought that it was at the time. I had no clue just how challenging life was about to get, bringing me to the edge of my real estate dreams and total financial disaster!

I remember that day in August 2008 like it was yesterday. I was walking out of a class at my local real estate association when I got a call from my mortgage broker. I will never forget his words: "Ty, none of your deals are going to close."

I said, "So, like, we need extensions?"

He said, "No. They are not going to close at all. There are no loans available anywhere. The secondary mortgage market is shut down, and banks can't make the loans."

I sat there in silence for what seemed like 10 minutes before the lender told me sorry and hung up the phone. I sat in my car running numbers in my head. I had just lost tens of thousands of dollars in commissions and the acquisitions I had under contract as well. All of it. The entire drive home, the only thing I could think about was how I was going to support my young family in a dead real estate market.

The Beginning

I got into investment real estate when my best friend Nick told me he had some friends at the University of Washington who bought an apartment building and were getting into the space full-time. I said, "That sounds super cool!"

About a week later, Nick and I attended a real estate investment seminar in town. It was just a rah-rah sales pitch, but we signed up for the three-day event, and I called in sick to my job to do it. That three-day course was a low-quality sales pitch to buy the next education package. When the third day was over, we looked at each other and agreed we didn't learn much. Then Nick said, "Well, let's just go buy some real estate," and we went out and bought two duplexes over the next few months. I fell in love with the sport of investment real estate so, in 2005, I got my real estate license, quit my job, and started working for a large real estate firm.

Selling millions of dollars of real estate as a rookie in 2005 was much more challenging than I thought because everyone and their mother-in-law was getting licensed in the soaring market. But, by early 2008, I had pretty good momentum and had managed to buy a handful of rental houses. I was also flying around the country on credit cards learning from the best real estate investment mentors I could find.

The problem was I didn't have a lot of experience or the proper financial reserves for what was about to happen. When the real estate market collapsed, I had no source of income, and nobody was really able to buy or sell. My financial situation quickly became month-to-month and then week-to-week! I fought to stay alive in the industry and support my family. Then, December 17, 2008, came.

Nightmare on Main Street

The second week in December, I started calling my tenants. Five out of nine hadn't paid rent, and I couldn't support the mortgages without that rent for more than a month or two. By December 17, the tenants in four of the five houses I had bought at the height of the market said, "The keys are on the counter," and were gone.

Back then, I did most of the work myself. I went to survey the vacant properties in hopes of turning them around quickly to re-rent them. Each of the four houses was destroyed. It would take $100,000 and four or five months to bring them back.

My home was in Spokane Valley, Washington, but most of my investment properties were in the city of Spokane, Washington, and North Idaho. My last stop was on the South Hill in Spokane, and as I drove home on I-90, thinking about how I could save myself and support my family, it started to snow, and snow hard. The freeway got icy, and traffic came to a quick halt. I almost hit the line of cars in front of me but stopped in time. I looked in my rearview. There was a large fruit truck headed my way, and it was not slowing down. Sure enough, it hit me hard. My Jeep Grand Cherokee was totaled.

I was alive but now injured, unable to work much on my properties or leave the house to acquire new income-producing properties, and without a car.

The Mirror

By Christmas in 2008, I couldn't make money as a Realtor due to no loans and "The Great Recession." My real estate was cash flowing negative $5,000 per month, and I was out of money. I couldn't fix the properties myself because I was injured and needed a car because I was fighting with the insurance company. I had three small children, and the two newborns needed special formula. I was feeling very much me against the world.

One afternoon, I sat talking to my wife at the time, trying to figure out how I was going to pay next month's mortgage payment. She was scared, so in no uncertain terms, she let me know she had zero faith in my ability to produce in real estate and that I needed to "get a real job!"

At that moment, I believed her. I locked myself in the bedroom and cried, my real estate dreams and self-confidence crushed. Eventually, I wiped away the tears and started to update my resume. It was a dark moment.

I printed out my resume, but I just couldn't do it. It was like I was physically incapable of sending it anywhere. I stared at it for a while and then put it in a drawer. I couldn't quit and give up on my dream.

I said to myself, *You are in this position, so you're obviously not that smart. But, you are educated enough to know that you cannot solve this problem from the mindset of "needing" money.*

I had read in the book *Think and Grow Rich*, a story of faith, belief, and burning desire. The short version of that story is that a character in the book needed one million dollars. He saw himself in possession of the money and gave a speech on what he would do with it. After the speech, someone approached him and gave him instructions on how to receive the million dollars the next day.

So, knowing I needed to approach things from an abundance mindset, I said to myself, *Pretend you have a million dollars in the bank right now. What would you do?* I immediately thought, *I would be buying up real estate!* I went to work writing out the business plan that eventually made me a multi-millionaire and that I still use today.

No Matter How Hard You Get Hit, Keep Moving Forward

Multi-millions did not happen right away. In fact, I would get knocked down to nothing again in 2013.

The last day of 2012, I closed on a 7,300-square-foot office building that was freeway frontage, and I felt like my dreams were coming true! It was a very exciting purchase, and right away, I was looking forward to moving in my investment real estate company and leasing the rest of the property to make it financially viable. I moved into my office, but then, I had a problem. The building had been vacant for over two years, and despite my best efforts, I was not able to lease the rest of the space. The economy had not recovered. I had staffed up my company for growth and had spent a lot of money to get the building and set it up for additional tenants that had not come.

In April of 2013, just 12 days after my wife at the time and I closed on our dream home, I was served divorce papers. I lost most of my net worth. I was broke again, mentally, spiritually, and financially.

At 3:30 a.m. on a Tuesday in May of 2013, I was at my desk in the office crunching numbers. My dad passed the office on his way to the airport for an early morning flight and saw my light on. He called me and said, "Damn, you do wake up early! What are you doing at the office now?"

I replied, "I'm trying to figure out how to make payroll today so I can stay in business." Faith is a powerful thing. Even given the circumstances that morning, I felt that I was in the right place and doing the right thing. I was about $600 short of making payroll. I had no answer or credit, so I prayed.

At 9:30 a.m. that same morning, the mail came. There was a check for $690. It was payment on debt a former business partner owed me. It was the only money he ever paid me on $16,690 owed from our failed partnership, and it was perfect.

Results Matter

Today, I am remarried and madly in love with my wife of almost a decade and have four thriving children! The results of this transformational journey so far include a new dream house on acreage, a lake house, and a large real estate portfolio. And I could retire if I wanted to.

Transformational success requires belief, faith, and hunger. It also requires massive action. I believe habits, routine, and behavior are the foundation. I developed strong discipline in my daily routines and self-development. I often get asked about my morning routine that I practice and have written on my vision board hanging on the wall of my home office. I wake up at 4:02 a.m. and have one cup of black coffee while I let my mind calm down and meditate in the dark. Then, the lights go on and I have hot lemon water while I study scripture, pray, and read books. At 5:45 a.m., I grab my pre-packed bags for the day, and head to the gym at 6:00 a.m.

In business and real estate, you gain a competitive advantage by constantly educating yourself. I crawled my way out of down times with none of my own money or credit. I had something far more valuable. I had the knowledge and ability to find great real estate deals and structure creative financing stacks where everybody wins.

The model I developed in my bedroom on that dark night around Christmas in 2008 which created my financial freedom is this:

I would drive around areas where I was interested in owning real estate. When I saw something interesting about a property, like a bunch of deferred maintenance, or simply a property I would like to own, I would dictate the address into my phone. Back at home, I would hop on the county tax assessor's site to see who owned the property and for how long. If they had owned the property for at least seven years, I would research the owner and write them a personal letter. If they didn't call me within a week, I would call them and ask if they received the letter. I picked seven years because I needed seller financing. If someone had owned the property for a long time, they likely had a lot of equity, or the property was paid off, making seller financing with them a possibility.

In 2010, I attended an event in Orlando where I trained on "the art" of seller notes and deal structure, also known as seller financing. In the years previous, I had trained with a financial and real estate mentor out of Phoenix. He had awesome private money training in his model. I was able to combine creative seller financing with private money to create a very profitable acquisition model. I also set up scores of appointments over the years with attorneys and accountants to become extremely well-versed in legal structure and tax strategy.

The art of my deals was finding properties with low or little debt and showing the sellers how they could defer a lot of tax and bring in a monthly income by selling their property to me on contract. I wrote a book on this called *Freedom Through Cash Flow*.

One of the top tips I give early-stage real estate investors is to give equal effort to raising private money as you do to procuring deals. Building great private investor relationships is extremely valuable when scaling your investment real estate portfolio.

For the acquisition, I would put a property under contract with seller financing and then work with private investors to fund the rest. I structured the deals so that the investor would bring in the money for the down payment, fix-up costs, closing costs, and cash reserve.

Real estate investment and wealth building is a long game. That is why, in my model, I structured each deal so I would get paid a real estate commission, between 3-6% of the price of acquisition and disposition, and monthly property management fees.

My investor would get paid their money as interest or equity, and I would get paid distributions and capital gain on my equity in the deal. My earliest deals were, and my multi-million-dollar deals are, structured with the investor or investors in an equity position. For deals under one million dollars, I have a "private money lending program" that pays the investor a very nice monthly return while I keep 100% ownership.

Most importantly, I always do what I say I will do. This has built strong trust with my investors and is why private equity and private investment is one of my superpowers today. Honesty, integrity, communication, and transparency make or break you when it comes to working with private money.

Today, my passion project is REtokens, a company I co-founded two years ago that tokenizes real estate and provides a capital platform to manage these investments. Before REtokens, tokenizing real estate was complicated and expensive. We have streamlined the process while making it safer and more user-friendly at a fraction of the cost.

Our goal is to get as many quality real estate assets on the blockchain as possible. The more quality tokenized real estate, the more robust the secondary market and liquidity options will be. We can start to meet small investors' demand for real estate. This will level the investment real estate playing field and help to narrow the socio-economic gap that inflation exacerbates.

Tyler Vinson specializes in private investment real estate assets and creative deal structures. He leverages this skill set and 20+ years of experience to help real estate owners and syndicators take advantage of blockchain technology to enhance their investment strategy. To learn more on private investment, visit www.ExtantInvestment.com | To learn more about real estate tokenization, visit www.REtokens.com | P: 509-414-5123

Quotable: Life Wisdom: Be who you are. This is not usually who you are today, but the person you visualize in your mind when you picture your best self. This is the person God intends you to be.

 Tyler Vinson

CHRIS GRONKOWSKI

From the NFL to *Shark Tank* as the Founder of Ice Shaker

Chris Gronkowski played four years in the NFL along with his three brothers, Rob, Dan, and Glenn. Chris graduated from the University of Arizona and, after leaving the NFL, appeared on Shark Tank in 2017. He left the Tank with a deal with Alex Rodriguez and Mark Cuban for his company Ice Shaker. Chris is from Buffalo, New York, and now lives in Southlake, Texas, with his wife, Brittany, and three kids.

Growing Up in Buffalo with Four Competitive Brothers

My parents raised five boys. Growing up, they said, "You're not gonna sit around playing video games and watching TV. Get outside and get rid of some energy." In Buffalo, New York, we lived in this awesome neighborhood. Every couple of houses there was another kid our age. We had that house where everyone comes over, and we would make up games in the backyard and play against each other. Every sport you can imagine, we competed in. I believe that bred competition among us brothers and the neighborhood kids.

As we got older, we started playing competitive sports in leagues, mostly hockey, baseball, and football.

My dad started a fitness equipment company from scratch and worked long hours. My mom was in charge of getting all five of us to school and sports events. Five boys. We all played multiple sports for multiple teams and were on travel teams. I still don't know how she got all of us to all our practices. She physically could not bring us all to every practice and game. Plus, we were going to church and other functions too. She had to bring in coaches, friends, and family from other neighborhoods. Thinking back on it, she did all that without a cell phone.

My mom cooked every meal and made all our school lunches. If we all behaved, she would reward us once a month with the $1.99 Out of Your Mind Grand Slam Breakfast at Denny's. There were multiple times when we were good for the whole month, and halfway to Denny's, we were all fighting in the back of the car, so she'd turn right back around and we'd have to eat at home!

I had my mom on my podcast for a Mother's Day episode, and I told her, "Wow, the more kids I have, the more impressed I am with you, Mom!"

Ivy League or Football Scholarship

My dad played college football, and at one point, he had a Bill's contract hanging on the wall at home. He was a good player but then got injured.

All five of us brothers grew up wanting to go to college and play pro sports, and all of us did.

I wanted to play college football but wanted to make sure I also got a good education so I could become a CPA and make good money if pro sports didn't work out.

I committed first to the University of Pennsylvania. My dad was excited. I would be the first Ivy League son in the family. We wouldn't just be the family of dumb jocks. And I was the one to prove it.

At the last minute, I ended up getting a full scholarship offer to play for the University of Maryland. I wanted to play at the highest level, but at the same time, I also didn't want to pay for college. At the University of Pennsylvania, I would probably graduate with $200,000 in debt. So, two weeks before the summer ended, I accepted a full D1 scholarship to Maryland.

That scholarship really came about because a bunch of their players were about to go on academic probation and some of the incoming players didn't make it because of grades. So, they gave it to the guy who had good grades that could come in and bump up the GPA for the football team a little bit. I tell people all the time, I got my first athletic college scholarship by having good academics.

I ended up transferring to the University of Arizona where my younger but much bigger brother Rob had also decided to go play. He was a coveted 4-star recruit. I was just hoping to make the team. Since I was a transfer, I had to sit out a year. So, that first year, I played baseball, and after two years, I went full-time in football.

I never thought I'd make it to the pro level, but I got my chance.

NFL for Four Years

I was undrafted. I was fortunate to have an agent believe in me and sponsor me to train for several months in Miami for the NFL Combine. That led to an opportunity to try out for the Dallas Cowboys. My wife is from Buffalo, but her dad got transferred to Dallas-Fort Worth six years before I went to the Cowboys, and everyone fell in love with the area.

I made the team. I hoped I would be playing for the Cowboys forever. It lasted a season before I started bouncing around to other teams.

I made it four seasons in the NFL, which locked in some nice benefits. After I retired, we came back to the Dallas area. We love it here. It's a great business environment and having family around is really important.

Life After the NFL That Led to *Shark Tank*

I wasn't rich by any stretch, but I had a pension and a nice 401K built up (the NFL offers a nice double match). Plus, you get severance pay and healthcare benefits. So, I had a good chunk of money without debt. I had gone to school and only had to pay for one semester. At age 26, I was leaving the NFL far ahead of everyone else my age.

I had this money that I could invest into whatever I wanted. I first went into business with my wife. She had started a business and Etsy shop while I was playing with Denver so she could work from home.

She did really well. I helped her, and we ended up making more money than when I was playing in the NFL. It was a good transition for me.

But having grown up in fitness and having played football my whole life, making wedding gifts wasn't really me. After five years, I thought of the idea for Ice Shaker. I could go to the gym, and I could call it work by making product videos at the gym. It was awesome. I thought, *Let's go all in and see where it goes. Let's start this as a side hustle. Let's see if it gets to a place where we can make this a full-time thing.*

Lessons from the Tank

I remembered getting an email in 2012 when I was with the Broncos that said ABC's *Shark Tank* was looking for current or former NFL players to pitch them. Four and a half years later, I emailed back. That was the spark that got me to pitch the Sharks.

Being on *Shark Tank* was huge for us. I first reached out to them about three months into the company's life. We only had $20,000 in sales, but at least I had proof of concept. They asked me to submit a video. They liked it and said I had three months before we would film and I should get ready. My focus became to get as much revenue as I could so I could get the best valuation possible.

When I went on the show, we had around $80,000 in sales, and I was asking for $100,000 for 10% of the company.

After I did the initial pitch, I had all my brothers come on. They brought a lot of energy, and we had fun with the Sharks.

One of the big lessons is to just show up with confidence, have fun, and know what you're talking about!

I watched every episode. I wrote down every question they ever asked. I felt like I was best friends with every single Shark. So, when I walked out there, instead of being nervous, I could say, "Hey, I feel like I know you guys."

I ended up getting a deal with Mark Cuban and Alex Rodriguez. Later, my brother Rob bought Alex's position.

Right away, with their help, I was able to get Ice Shaker into The Vitamin Shoppe, Lifetime Fitness, and GNC, as well as appear on QVC, *Good Morning America*, and many other outlets. Most recently, Ice Shaker went into 1,900 Walmarts.

Starting, Growing, and Scaling a Business

I love a shaker bottle. That was what I would use all day when I could. But it wasn't perfect. I started on the journey to create something that could blend powders and keep your drink cold. So, I took what I loved from shaker bottles and replaced what I didn't love. I added insulated, kitchen-grade premium stainless steel to keep drinks cold or hot. I loved the easy-open pop top. I wanted a handle on it as well so it was easy to carry. I took all my favorite things and put them into one cup.

Through my wife's business, I've been able to incorporate the ability to customize Ice Shakers and do bulk orders fast for customers.

I've had to learn that you cannot conquer the entire market overnight. You can't just throw money at it. Most of your success will come from relationships and figuring things out.

I have a family, a wife, and kids, so working a hundred hours a week doesn't work for me anymore. That forced me to put people and processes in place, which takes time!

Learning from My Dad

My dad has 32 years in the fitness industry, and over that time, he has built 17 retail stores. He wanted to be a mentor to me in sports and business. At first, I didn't listen. It took time for me to realize the value of his wisdom. When the pandemic hit, things slowed down. There were no processes in place. There was no budget. I could only come in the store when half of my employees were there because of the new COVID restrictions and my kids at home. With the way things were, I realized I had better figure things out pretty quick.

It was time to figure out how to do this the right way and to build the team. I went back to my dad and said, "How'd you build your business to

200 employees? That's insane." At the time, I was trying to manage eight employees. I asked, "How'd you get there?"

My dad said, "I asked you from day one. What's your game plan? What's your budget? What's your forecast? How are you incentivizing people? Tell me that first, and I'll tell you how to fix it."

That's exactly where I was going wrong. First, there was no team. It was me making every decision and me with all the responsibilities. I thought that was how it was supposed to be because it was my business. Finally, when it couldn't be like that anymore, I was forced to delegate, which was one of my dad's keys from day one.

When I started to share the responsibility, I realized that people responded well. They felt like they were part of a team. They could make their own decisions. They loved it and they wanted more.

Next was figuring out how everyone could win. I had to start figuring that out with the whole team. We had a fulfillment team that wasn't feeling like they were winning when we made sales. They didn't have a piece of that pie or input on the goals we had set. We had to realign all the goals, and rather than just certain individuals, we had to incentivize everyone as a team.

Once we did that, I would walk in with a big sale, and everyone in the entire company was pumped. That's when I knew we had figured this thing out.

You can follow Chris Gronkowski on Instagram @chrisgronkowski and go to Iceshaker.com to order your own Ice Shaker. You can also order in bulk and have your order customized with your logo. You can order from Chris's wife's company at EverythingDecorated.com.

Quotable: One of the big lessons is to show up with confidence, have fun, and know what you're talking about!

Snag the best, ditch the rest. Ice Shaker's 26oz Shaker bottle is third-party tested to hold ice for over 30 hours, and the patented twist-in agitator will help mix your favorite drinks and powders.

DEREK DOMBECK

Live Your Vision, Love Your Life

Derek Dombeck is a real estate investor who loves creative deal structuring, lending, and educating entrepreneurs through his masterminds, real estate conference, and speaking engagements. Through thousands of transactions, with his wife Tracy and three children by his side, Derek has set himself apart through his love for helping people achieve success.

What Is Success?

Why must I have to learn everything the hard way?

I used to say this to myself often.

Like many, I started as a real estate investor in 2003 while working a full-time job. For many years, my goal was to build up enough cash flow and assets to leave my full-time employment. Back then, all the education I received talked about owning 100 rental units that cash flowed $100 per door. The goal was to make $10,000 per month—that was what was considered successful—so we could live a good life.

The part of that "success" nobody tells you about is the brutal path that it often takes to get there. You see, while I was blinded by the illusion of making enough money to be financially free, I was looking past the beautiful life God had put right in front of me. I would work 40+ hours at my job and then every night and weekend at a project house somewhere. I missed the first three years of my daughter's life as I worked to build an empire.

I told myself I was doing everything for my family, when, in fact, I was harming my family.

As the years progressed, I realized that I was not enjoying being a landlord. I never understood why I was doing what I was doing. I realized that the goals I was working toward were goals that were told to me instead of goals that I had created. It wasn't until 14 years into my business that I came across this thing called vision.

Just Do It

I was skeptical and a bit reluctant to believe that writing out a vision for my life would change anything, but I figured it couldn't harm me to try.

Now, many would say, "I have a business plan," but that is not a vision. Your vision is how you live your personal life first, and then, after that is established, you build your business to fit within the allowed time and boundaries your personal vision puts into place.

Your vision can be written in any format that makes sense to you. It could be a story format, bullet points, or an outline. I wrote mine in story format. The focus is continuously asking yourself why. If you want to write in your vision "I want to make a million dollars a year," you want to write what that million dollars would do for you. For example, "I want to have a non-profit to help children," or "I want to have enough revenue to take mission trips to third-world countries." You want to write and understand what the money is for instead of writing a dollar amount.

When you are dreaming of what your personal life can be, it's very important to not engineer how it's going to happen. That comes later. Picture the Imagineer employees at Disney. Their sole job is to dream of new experiences and rides for Disney World. It's not their job to know how it's going to happen, it's their job to dream. It's one of the hardest things for people to do, not filter their dreams with money or time as a factor.

You want to write your vision as if it's already happening, without filtering it. An example would be, say you want to have a beach house in the Caribbean, but you have no idea how you'd afford a beach house in the Caribbean. Perhaps you rent a house for 30 days a year rather than owning it. You're still able to live your vision without spending hundreds of thousands of dollars to do it.

My mentor had taken a month-long RV trip, and I indicated to him how fantastic I thought that would be but that there was no way I could ever do it. He challenged me to write it into my vision. The following summer, I took a five-week RV trip with my family across the country. For the first two weeks of that trip, I was a nervous wreck. The third week, I finally started to realize that my staff was capable of handling our business without me being there every day. By the end of the trip, I came to the conclusion that about 50% of what I did in my businesses was not a goal of mine anymore. I continue to take long RV trips every summer as a result of this.

Tools to Use

The exercises I went through started with writing down what your perfect week would look like. Remember, you do this without considering time or money, meaning money is not a factor, which is hard to do for most people. Take a weeklong calendar and start filling in the time slots of each 24-hour day. Your perfect week may involve taking the kids to school, exercising, doing some reading, taking a walk, etc. It can be anything you can imagine doing on a day-to-day basis that you want to do.

When you fill in your week, often you realize that there are only two to four hours a day left for work. That's when you start to build your business to fit in the time that is left in your week. In contrast, what most business owners do incorrectly is work 40 – 70 hours a week on their business, hoping that someday they will be able to enjoy the fruits of their labor.

Another exercise my mentor gave me is called Burn It Down. I was running multiple businesses, and my mentor asked me, "What business are you really into? If it all burned to the ground and you had to start over, which business would you focus on?" Entrepreneurs are typically blinded by shiny objects and take on multiple businesses at the same time, which means not running any single business to the best of their ability. After this exercise, it became clear that our lending business would be our number one focus moving forward. We saw exponential growth, almost overnight.

The next exercise that was extremely helpful for me is called Your Unique Genius Zone. I sent an email to 16 of my peers, including some people that knew me really well and others that were just colleagues, and asked them, "Based on your perception, what am I really good at? What is my unique genius zone?" The feedback from that will often tell you or clarify what you're really good at and passionate about. If you can design your vision for your life so that the majority of your day is spent doing what you are very good at and what you enjoy, then it doesn't feel like work. This was a turning point for me, primarily because I finally understood that there was nothing wrong with outsourcing the parts of my business that I'm not good at or that I don't enjoy.

Secret to Life

The Japanese word *ikigai* describes the secret to a joyful life. Do what you love, what you are good at, what the world needs, and what you can be paid for.

When I wrote my vision, it included educating and teaching other real estate investors. I included that I wanted to lead high-end mastermind groups with real estate investors from all over the country and travel to fun places while doing that. I had no idea how that was going to come to fruition, but shortly after getting clear on our business vision, we were given an opportunity to take over a real estate conference that we call Generations of Wealth. In hosting Generations of Wealth, we started a couple real estate mastermind groups called the Circle Of Trust. And there's been plenty of travel involved, most of the time with my family by my side.

Also, in our vision, my business partner and I had written our goals of expanding our lending business, and within that same timeframe, our lending business grew by 300% in one year. It was all because, on a daily basis, we were reviewing our vision for our lives as well as our businesses.

I now look back on the day I embraced this process as the single best turning point in my life and business. It brings me great joy when I can help others realize their life dreams too.

Derek Dombeck co-owns a private lending company called Best REI Funding (BestREIFunding.com), a national mastermind group called REI Circle of Trust (REICOT.com), and an annual advanced strategies and networking conference for real estate investors called Generations of Wealth Voyage (GOWVOYAGE.com). To learn more about Derek, visit Derekdombeck.com. Contact him at Derek@BestREIFunding.com or on Facebook and LinkedIn.

Quotable: The part of that "success" nobody tells you about is the brutal path that it often takes to get there. I realized that the goals I was working toward were goals that were told to me instead of goals that I had created.

CINDY ARONSTAM

Journey of Resilience, Wealth Building, and Giving Back

Cindy Aronstam is a successful real estate advisor and investor, dog lover, and philanthropist. She helps people build fortunes through real estate, donates to animal rescue with every home sold, and is the founder of Winston Project, a 501(c)(3) non-profit organization dedicated to raising money to support dog rescue groups and shelters.

Roots of Resilience

I grew up on Long Island, New York, and when they say if you can make it there, you can make it anywhere, they aren't kidding. I had a pretty easygoing childhood, until I was about 10 years old. Then, the world as I knew it changed.

My dad had fallen ill. He did all he could to continue working to support our family, but ultimately, he became disabled. My mother went from stay-at-home mom to full-time retail worker so we'd have money coming in and medical insurance. They couldn't make ends meet, almost lost the house they built, and had to move us into a rental in another town.

At the grocery store, my mom would hand over our food stamps to the cashier, who took her time counting them while the people in line behind us looked on. My wardrobe consisted mostly of hand-me-downs from neighbors and friends. We put things on layaway when we needed to buy something. To take me out for an ice cream sundae, my mom would save up for an entire month. Our family of four had one car—a beat-up, very faded and rusted, mint green 1977 Chevy Nova, which my parents got for $500. As a teenager in the '90s, in a new town, I was mortified to be seen in it. Learning to drive it was no prize either. During one lesson, the transmission dropped, and quickly I had to learn how to "coast" without it.

I felt shame and embarrassment around our financial situation, and I lost my sense of my carefree upbringing. I was just trying to survive, and fit in, and as I got older, ensure I'd never be in this situation again.

These experiences gave me the drive and determination I have today to go after what I want, help people along the way, and never again feel the pain of that worry.

Finding Strength in the Midst of Adversity

My dad died in 1996. I was only 18 and in my first year of college. It hit hard and now, in addition to grieving, I also carried with me the financial worry of how our family was going to survive.

My parents had given up their life insurance policy years prior in order to put food on the table. I still had an entire college career to complete, and my mother, now a widow, didn't have the financial means to take care of herself, me, and my brother.

I made a conscious effort to put up a wall and sever ties with those closest to me. My thinking was, If I'm not close with anyone, then I never have to experience this type of pain again. Thankfully, a professional therapist helped me see that this was not the best approach to going through life. Letting people in, being vulnerable, and being open to new experiences has helped me during my most challenging days. After my dad died, the one thing that changed everything was experiencing the kindness of friends, and even strangers, who helped our family keep going.

I knew leaving college wasn't an option if I wanted a better life than I was used to, and without the financial backing of my parents, I had to get creative. I took out student loans, received financial aid, and worked three jobs each semester and over the summer. I was strategic about applying for a job selling advertising for the school newspaper because they paid me in class credits, which meant less money I'd have to borrow in student loans. I became an RA (resident assistant) because it covered my room cost. I stayed in when everyone else was partying. I was in survival mode.

Discovering My True North

After finishing college, I began working in my chosen career as an account executive at an advertising agency. At the time, ad agencies didn't pay very well because so many young college grads were vying for those positions. I wanted to buy myself a condo—to start building equity and own something to call mine. So, on my meager $28,000 salary, while paying back student loans and living on my own, I began saving for a down payment.

When I had finally saved up a modest down payment (truly, all I had!), I started where every person should begin when thinking of getting into the real estate market. I asked friends and family for recommendations for a good real estate agent.

To my surprise, NO ONE could say something nice about an agent they had worked with, let alone recommend them! I thought, How could this be? I was about to spend everything I had worked so hard for and couldn't risk it in the wrong hands.

I thought if I took a real estate class I'd learn "inside information." I'd still hire an agent, but at least I'd know if they were doing right by me. Boy, was I wrong! Sadly, when you take a real estate class, you're there to memorize material so you can pass a test. The true experience, skill, and knowledge comes from being in the field, working with buyers and sellers, and handling the day-to-day operations of the business.

But taking that class did do something for me. Twenty minutes into it, something sparked, and I said to myself, I'm going to be the real estate agent everybody recommends. I wanted to change the perception of real estate agents and make a difference to a buyer like me.

A Bumpy Beginning

After I passed the class, I was on my way. Seven months later, I quit my advertising job to focus on real estate full-time. Real estate has had plenty of ups and downs—especially when I got my license in 2006 right before the biggest market crash of our lifetime, now known as the Great Recession of 2007-2008.

During this time, I became a short sale expert. My clients were human beings going through a difficult financial situation, and they didn't need judgment. They needed reassurance that they'd be okay and that we'd get them through this so they could rebuild their finances and eventually realize the American dream of homeownership once again.

My compassion for people, and especially animals, soared. Unfortunately, this was a time when some people abandoned their pets, leaving them inside the home they fled. It still makes my stomach hurt to remember dogs left alone inside with a pile of food scattered across the floor (among other, far less pleasant piles). My job became one of not only helping people find new homes but finding homes for dogs as well.

In the years since the Great Recession, I've helped connect home buyers and sellers with real estate professionals across the US. Since 2010, I've been trained and coached by the top real estate coaching company in North America, and each year, I travel to four real estate training seminars throughout the country. This not only allows me to sharpen my skills and knowledge but also gives me a chance to network with the most elite real estate agents who are also upping their game to help their clients buy and sell the largest assets of their lifetimes.

From Adversity to Prosperity

Over the years, I've helped thousands of people reach their real estate goals and build generational wealth through investing in real estate. I've also been able to use my platform as a way to give back to the community. Through my real estate business, I've hosted and coordinated school supply drives and food drives (for people and dogs) and was named Leukemia & Lymphoma Society Woman of the Year in 2012 in recognition of raising the most money for the charity over 10 weeks. I'm now known as The Bulldog Realtor® because of my love for the breed, my unwavering commitment to getting the best deal for my clients, and the extreme love and connection of my soul bulldog, Winston, who very sadly, we lost in 2019 at nearly 14 years old.

And today, I'm the founder and president of Winston Project, a 501(c)(3) non-profit organization dedicated to raising funds to support dog rescues and shelters.

Winston the Wonder Dog

Our beloved English bulldog Winston is the driving force behind this passion project. In 2015, my significant other, Jim, and I relocated from New York to San Diego, California, for a better quality of life. Winston was 10 years old when we made the cross-country journey.

He loved being outside, and with weather that was consistently perfect in San Diego, he was loving a new life of going to the beach, making new friends at the dog park, and going for walks around the city. I started hosting Canines & Coffee events at the beach and dog parks and provided dog treats for the pups and free coffee for their humans. It was a great way to connect with the community and get to know other dog lovers.

When Winston was 12 years old, he suffered an injury to his spine. The vet determined that he likely had a slipped disc, but due to his age, surgery wasn't an option. So, we did acupuncture to ease his pain and took him for sessions on an underwater treadmill to help build up strength in his hind legs. He started off doing really well, and we saw great improvement for a couple of weeks.

Suddenly, we noticed that he was struggling in the water tank on the treadmill. For two weeks in a row, he was regressing. We had X-rays taken, and the vet noticed that his spleen looked oddly shaped. She encouraged us to have an ultrasound of his abdomen area, and while he was there and already shaved, we may as well have his chest looked at too.

After talking to the doctor, our entire world changed. Winston had arrhythmogenic right ventricular cardiomyopathy, a mass on his heart with fluid around it. We also learned he had kidney failure. We had to figure out what was next, how to keep him comfortable, how to reverse the heart failure he was in, and what all of this meant for his quality of life and however much longer he'd be with us.

Transforming Grief into a Lasting Legacy

I learned so much during that last year with Winston, and once he passed, the learning didn't stop. When he died, I was in a very dark and isolated place and consumed with grief. I was barely functioning each day. At night, in bed, I would just burst into tears whenever I closed my eyes. The gaping hole in my heart was massive and raw. I couldn't believe that this was hitting me harder than when I buried my dad at age 18. I was not okay.

After three months of being in this state, I met with a good friend who had a senior bulldog named Stella. He let me love on her while he basically yelled at me in a way only a true friend would. He knew that I had more to give and wasn't honoring Winston by staying in that state. That was the first night in three months I slept through the night.

From there, I was able to open my heart to a dog who needed a foster home. While I was in no way ready to have another dog, I couldn't let this dog live in a shelter. Before I knew it, a three-year-old English bulldog named St. Nick was dropped off at our home. I had every intention to foster him and get him ready for his forever home. The joke was on me because, within just two weeks of having him, he found his forever home with us. We now call him Harry Winston in honor of our first bulldog son.

Seven months later, we adopted a sister for Harry, an English bulldog named Olive. Our home was feeling whole again, and my heart started to heal.

I took all I learned about growing through grief and turning loss into legacy, and I founded Winston Project, Inc., a 501(c)(3) non-profit organization. Our mission is to raise money to give grants to other non-profit animal groups—who are in the field, pulling dogs from horrific conditions of abuse and neglect and providing life-saving, euthanasia-preventing, treatments for pets of families in financial need.

We are on track to save thousands of dogs who have been abused, abandoned, and neglected and ensuring they get to live their best lives. We do this through a variety of fundraising efforts, particularly our annual gala, where we have a fun, themed party with incredible raffle baskets. Our inaugural gala was in June 2023, and we raised over $28,000!

As we grow our community, we plan to build out additional programs, including pet therapy where we bring dogs into hospitals and care facilities, education where we teach school children how to treat and care for animals, and mobile spay/neuter clinics where veterinarians go into neighborhoods of those with low incomes and provide discounted or free spay/neuter surgeries.

Eventually, Winston Project will expand its reach to areas outside of San Diego and duplicate our foundation's model throughout the country. My ultimate vision is to put an end to animal abuse, backyard breeding, puppy mills, pet stores that sell dogs, and kill shelters. Animals are voiceless. They need us to speak on their behalf. Winston Project is their voice!

From the challenges I've experienced in this thing we call life, I have learned:

1. You already have everything within you that you need to succeed.
2. Be your authentic self.
3. Chase happiness, not money.
4. Listen to your gut! Your intuition is never wrong and always there to guide you. Don't ignore it.

I lead with gratitude. I am grateful for the simple things, which really are the big things—like waking up each morning, and the opportunities ahead. I am so grateful for the incredible people in my life who love, support, and challenge me. Every single setback and hardship I've faced has shaped who I am today.

I hope my journey of challenges and resilience can make a lasting impact in this world.

For complimentary access to Cindy Aronstam's professional network of top real estate professionals, email cindy@cindyaronstam.com or connect via thebulldogrealtor.com Instagram @thebulldogrealtor or Facebook: Cindy Aronstam. To support Winston Project through volunteering or donating, or to share your "growing through grief" story, email info@winstonproject.org or follow on Instagram @WinstonProject.

Quotable: Selling real estate allows me to help people build generational wealth and enjoy financial freedom. With every home sold, I donate to animal rescue and help to save dogs' lives.

 The Bulldog Realtor

MARK HASEBROOCK

Lessons From a Serial Entrepreneur

Mark Hasebroock is the founder of Dundee Venture Capital and has invested $100 million into 50+ early-stage startup companies across the USA. Mark also co-founded Giftcertificates.com and Hayneedle.com. He loves helping founders realize their dreams and has successfully helped hundreds of startups visualize and execute their plans.

The Moccasin Mishap

While I was in college at the University of Nebraska, I was just like any other student trying to make ends meet. I was always looking for ways to make extra cash. So, when spring break was around the corner, I knew I had to do something to fund my trip to Padre Island.

That's when I had the idea to sell colorful moccasins. The moccasins were affordable, fashionable, and perfect for the style of the day. My roommate and I went around to various sororities and pitched my product. To our delight, we were met with enthusiasm and sold out within a few days. And it was a unique way to meet girls! We sold enough to fund our trip to Padre Island.

When we returned, we saw a few girls waiting outside our fraternity house holding their moccasins. "We're going to be rich," I told my roommate.

Unfortunately, our customers weren't happy. The dye from the moccasins stained the girls' feet. I was devastated. I had to refund everyone's money.

This experience taught me a valuable lesson. Sometimes things don't work out the way you plan, and you have to be prepared to pivot and try again.

The Popcorn Business

After college, I was a banker for a short stint and realized it just was *not* for me.

I went into the popcorn business. I sold ready-to-eat popcorn in retail stores. It was a small business, it was profitable, and I enjoyed it. I also had a seasonal popcorn gift canister business that did well during the holidays. I enjoyed interacting with customers and the challenges of starting a brick and mortar store.

When competitors started selling directly to grocery stores, I knew I had to adapt. But I had no idea how to sell to grocers. It was tough, and I was often thrown out of stores by the snack food buyers, but I was determined.

So, I got busy learning. I followed the Frito Lay guys around and I learned the lingo, the pricing, and how to tailor my message to each store. And it worked. I was able to get my product on the shelves of major grocery chains, and my business thrived.

I sold this business and made approximately $11. I had selling skills. I had finance skills. I knew how to start and run a brick and mortar business. What was missing? The internet.

GiftCertificates.com

One day, I was in a shopping mall buying a mall gift certificate. It was a tedious process that involved filling out a paper form and waiting in line. It got me thinking there had to be a better way. That's when a friend and I had an idea: *Why can't we buy gift certificates online?* The internet was starting to become mainstream. We decided to make it easy to purchase gift cards for nearly any retailer you could think of, all from the comfort of your home.

GiftCertificates.com was born. It was the late '90s, the height of internet mania, and we were convinced we had stumbled upon a winning business idea.

Building a new business from scratch creates unique challenges. We had to raise money to grow and we couldn't do it locally.

We presented to a venture fund in Seattle, and the managing partner commented, "You don't need $500,000. You need $5 million. Then we will fund it."

While this was the trend of the day—raise way more than you need and spend it all quickly—it went against our Midwestern nature. But, we figured these folks were way smarter than us and followed their lead. Our portion of ownership in the company was diluted time and again as we raised more and more money.

And, we grew and grew. We had offices in the World Trade Center, Seattle, and Omaha, 400 employees, and Sophia Loren as our spokesperson.

It was lunacy. The bubble eventually burst, and we had a front row seat. We had grown the top line to nine figures but continually burned cash. As values were plummeting, it was clear, whoever put in the next few dollars would more than likely own a big chunk of the business.

My co-founder and I wrote a thesis on what was needed next. Shrink the business. Cut spending. Monitor cash flow. Focus on sustainable growth.

But, being in a minority position, we were ultimately ignored. The vision the investors had was to wait out the storm and continue to grow the top line. It was certainly one strategy but not one that made sense.

We co-founders decided to find something else and start over. I now had an excellent complement of skills and experiences under my belt. I had learned what to do, and more importantly, what not to do.

We had made some monumental mistakes. The dilution of ownership caused by raising so much money from investors led us to manage the company the way the investors wanted, not the way we wanted. We lost sight of our original vision and ended up focusing more on pleasing our investors than on building a sustainable business.

Despite the challenges, GiftCertificates.com was a success. It was exciting to be part of the startup scene in the late '90s. We were one of the pioneers of the online gift certificate market, and our platform was used by millions of people. It was a thrilling ride, and I learned so much from the experience.

Hayneedle

Starting over involves trusting fate. For me, it all started with a phone call.

I was cleaning out my desk at Giftcertificates.com one rainy, cold Friday night in early 2002. The phones were ringing. No one was around to answer, so I picked up. I had no idea that the conversation that followed would change the course of my entrepreneurial journey yet again.

"Giftcertificates.com, this is Mark...." The person on the other end of the line was a man named David, and he told me about his online store selling hammocks.

At first, I wasn't interested. He wanted to become an affiliate of our company, and this was the last thing I wanted to talk about. I was depressed. I was angry. I had a family, a wife of 18 years, and eight kids. I was wondering how I was going to pay our bills and go on with life.

But, the more he talked, the more interested I was in hearing his story. As he shared, I began to realize he didn't seem particularly passionate about his business. So, on a whim, I asked if he would be interested in selling. To my surprise, he said yes.

I wasn't sure what I was getting into. My background was in gift certificates, not hammocks. But it was an exciting new challenge, and I was ready for it. So, even though I didn't have any idea how I would fund this new business, I bought Hammocks.com.

I mortgaged our house—a second mortgage actually—and then went about figuring out the hammock business. I was starting over, this time out of panic and fear as well as intrigue. This HAD to work. I had no other choice.

My friends thought I had lost my mind. They couldn't understand why I would want to get into the hammock business. "Do you think Mark will get a job soon?" my wife's friends would ask. But I knew this was something special. It wasn't just about selling hammocks; it was a lifestyle brand around relaxation and enjoying the outdoors. These were products no one really knew how to find that needed photos and explanation.

Of course, there were challenges along the way. For one thing, I had to figure out how to run an e-commerce business that sold physical products. Gift certificates were easy to sell online, but hammocks were a different story. I had to learn about shipping, inventory management, and customer service. But the biggest challenge was probably starting over yet again. It was humbling, but it also gave me a sense of purpose. I was excited to build something new and see where this journey would take me.

My co-founder and I officed out of a Barnes & Noble cafe because we could not afford a space yet. We played around with the old website, built a new one, and then watched as the first day we had two sales. Then we had five. Then we had 20. This was starting to actually work!

One day, a customer called: "Hey, I got my hammock. Love it! Do you sell porch swings?"

I kicked my co-founder, and whispered, "Look up porchswings.com!" He quickly saw that the domain was available, and we bought it.

I asked this customer what he was looking for in a porch swing. "I don't know. Wood?"

I asked him what size. "Uh, six feet? I am not sure."

Frantically looking up manufacturers, I asked, "Would you want oak or cherry wood?"

He finally asked, "Are you in the porch swing business, or what?"

I told him of course we were. I just wanted him to get exactly what he wanted.

We processed that order, and then we had an "aha" moment. What if there were others looking for more, different kinds of products for the backyard?

We drove around Omaha and peered over fences looking for other ideas for products we could add to our now growing inventory. "Bird baths! Patio umbrellas! Wind chimes! Adirondack chairs!" With each idea, we procured the domain and then lined up suppliers. Suddenly, we had dozens of these "stores" open and selling backyard products.

We also stumbled on early data science techniques by actively mining our customers' buying habits and predicting who would buy what and when. We then would actively email those customers with offers. "How did you know I was looking for bird feeders?..." This allowed us to spend more on the front end to acquire a customer. We knew that later sales would be free if we simply emailed them with complementary, alternative products.

Seeking Funding

We needed to raise money to continue our expansion. We went around Omaha and pitched our idea. It was largely ignored. Again, we had to look outside our market to raise money and landed in Silicon Valley pitching to Sequoia Capital.

Part of starting over is taking the leap and not looking back. Perseverance and no fear give way to the realization that this HAS to work. Not being desperate but committed. Focus and hustle can win many battles. With Sequoia, we had to demonstrate our knowledge, the future, the opportunity, and overcome the objection that nothing interesting happens outside of Silicon Valley much less in Omaha, Nebraska. The team at Sequoia was incredibly well-prepared with insightful questions. We impressed them enough to receive a term sheet on my Blackberry by the time we arrived at the airport to return to Omaha.

The capital we raised from Sequoia as well as Insight Venture Partners allowed us to scale properly and aggressively in a short period of time. We ultimately built over 400 stores across one platform called Hayneedle.com. I remember thinking, *Someday I want to change the funding landscape out here in the hinterlands. There are some great founders with unique ideas. Why can't we be like Sequoia or Insight?*

We grew Hayneedle and ultimately sold it to Jet.com who sold it to Walmart. The exit was anticlimactic. It was an achievement, but it was also like letting air out of the balloon. *Is this it?* I think I lost some of my identity and wondered, *What now?*

The answer came pretty quickly when I sat in on a friend's startup pitch for his business. I thought, *No, no, no...this is all wrong. The message, the ask, the problem, the solution.... And the angels looking to invest are just not the right partners. I can do better for them.* So, I decided to start over.

Why not build a venture capital fund right here in the middle of the US and invest in founders like me?

Dundee VC

I kept wondering, *Why aren't there any venture capital funds in the Midwest?* The year was 2010, and the idea of a venture fund was mind-boggling to many. But I knew there was demand. I had lived and breathed it. And I knew there were certainly smart, creative people solving ideas locally. So, I started Dundee Venture Capital.

Starting a venture capital fund was the most challenging and exciting experience of my life. I had always been an entrepreneur, but a venture capital fund was a whole new ballgame. It was not just about creating a product or service and bringing it to the market. It was about identifying promising startups and investing in them to help them grow.

When I first started to explore the idea of starting a venture capital fund, I encountered a lot of resistance. Many conservative investors did not understand the concept of venture capital and saw it as too risky. They were comfortable with the traditional investment model of buying and holding stocks or real estate for the long term.

To overcome this, I spent a lot of time educating people about venture capital and why it's important to an ecosystem. I showed them how venture capital can help fund early-stage companies with innovative, potentially industry-disrupting technologies. I explained how venture capital can help bridge the funding gap between angel investors and public markets and generate outsized returns for investors.

I had to learn to be persistent and creative in my approach. I attended countless networking events, spoke at conferences, and made hundreds of presentations to potential investors. I even started to invest my own money to build a track record and demonstrate my commitment to the industry.

Over time, my persistence paid off. It was exciting to see the impact our investments had on the companies we supported. We were able to help entrepreneurs take their ideas to the next level, create jobs, and create value for their customers.

The Hardest Chapter Yet

Starting a venture capital fund taught me that starting over is not just about overcoming obstacles and challenges. It's also about embracing new opportunities and taking risks. It's about pushing yourself out of your comfort zone and daring to dream big. And it's about having the courage to pursue your passions and make a positive impact on the world.

It has allowed me to invest in dynamic young founders like Lori Coulter and Reshma Chamberlain. Lori and Reshma started Summersalt in St. Louis. Summersalt is solving the fit problem in women's swimwear. When I met Lori and Reshma I saw so many of my own qualities in them. I knew they would succeed. They are "glass chewers" and never satisfied. When we invested, they were doing $400,000 in annual sales. It was fun to help shape their plan and execution, especially in the early stages. Soon, they will exceed $100 million in revenue while establishing their brand as a one of a kind, consumer-focused, data-driven business.

I get energy from these founders and their ideas. In fact, I am convinced a unique renaissance of creativity is just beginning. I am fortunate to be on the front lines.

Looking back on my entrepreneurial journey, I can see that each time I've had to pivot to a new business or industry, I've been forced to learn new skills and overcome new challenges. And each time, I've come out stronger and more resilient.

As I approach my 64th birthday, I'm more excited than ever about what the future holds. I truly believe I'm just getting started, and I can't wait to see where my next adventure takes me. Whether it's building another business from scratch or finding new ways to enjoy life, I know that starting over will always be a part of my story.

To contact Mark Hasebroock about his story, leadership, speaking, mentoring, or coaching, please email Mark@dundeeVc.com or text him at 402-850-1802.

Quotable: Starting over involves trusting fate. Sometimes things don't work out the way you plan, and you have to be prepared to pivot and try again.

LYDIA R. ESSARY, MD

Pianist, Physician, Entrepreneur, Financial Wellness Advocate & Investor

Lydia R. Essary, MD, is a successful physician dermatopathologist, entrepreneur, as well as multifamily real estate syndicator and investor with over 4,300 apartment units. She co-founded Lift Equity, a private equity firm, to help busy professionals invest and create financial freedom.

Education, Priority of a South American Family

I remember waiting with other students in the hallway of our music school for my turn to see the piano teacher. It was a nice hall with marble floors in a colonial building in downtown Lima. We were all quiet and nervous, hoping to pass the test and the class. A missing note could evoke a shout and a hand slap from the teacher. It was a traumatic experience but thought to be normal in those days, and I was determined to pass those tests.

My parents were ambitious, and education was a priority for them. My two sisters and I were born and grew up in Lima, the capital of Peru. We enjoyed the warm climate and summer vacations along Lima's beaches. We enjoyed winters attending the theater on an almost daily basis. The ushers knew us and would walk us to our box. My dad loved zarzuelas, a Spanish operetta. We sisters enjoyed the show and especially enjoyed the chocolate bar we got at the end of the performance while my parents socialized with their friends. Dad was also a leader with our Peru national soccer and boxing teams, and during the season, you could find us at the stadiums.

Mom is more business-inclined. She owned a fashion design business. She leveraged her elite clientele and she closely followed what the clientele's children were doing.

One day, our parents surprised us when they brought home a piano. The three of us were soon enrolled in piano lessons. I was 10 years old then, but I had a three-year history of accordion training.

A year later, my audition earned me a piano scholarship at the National Conservatory of Music in Lima. A new journey started for me, and I fully enjoyed the classical music space. My classmates were very skillful in their respective instruments, and we started putting on and attending each other's recitals and concerts. These performances added a lot of work and practice hours. I felt sorry for my family having to put up with my piano practice late into the night.

I survived the hand slaps and scolding from my piano teacher. I was determined to work with her, as were the other students because she had national recognition and had formed excellent pianists. She gave us a great hand technique, and my appreciation for music soared. Music enriched my life, and I loved sharing music with my classmates and later with my students.

Turbulent Pivot

My professional journey in music was just taking shape when it came time for me to make a difficult decision.

I had been studying at the conservatory of music in parallel to my high school education. Soon, I had to think of picking a career, just like most parents guide their kids to do. My parents encouraged me to become a doctor. So, I prepared for the medical school admission test in my last high school year, and I was accepted to the top-rated medical school in Peru.

When I was in my second pre-med year, I had to pick: music or medicine. I struggled so hard with the decision. I loved music so very much, but my mentors and family advised me that medicine offered a greater range of career opportunities. I chose medicine.

I was very sad and frustrated. My young and inexperienced mind did not understand very well the benefits of my decision. Time was a healing factor. With time, I started enjoying my new ambiance as a pre-med student, the group activities, and the new friends I made. The power of teamwork, purpose, and friendship helped me during this turbulent time.

Life as a White Coat Student

Medical school was unbelievably busy, and I was fortunate to have good health in coping with the long days and commute. Being a medical student was a team sport, and I don't think we could have passed those tough tests if not for the power of group study. We managed to enjoy each other's company during our rotations and build solid friendships. Our greatest reward was seeing patients getting better and celebrating with their families.

My musical abilities made me popular with my peers in med school, and some of my friends joined me in going to concerts. My father's position gave us free access to an assigned box at the theater where the national symphony orchestra performed. We had six box seats, and one of my classmates coordinated who would go each week. It was charming to see my friends list themselves to attend the concerts on Sundays. We shared time together thanks to our love of music.

In the last years of med school, many of my classmates were preparing to continue their education with specialty training in the US. I was very curious about doing research and pursuing my specialty abroad and the United States appealed to me.

My family was not happy with this idea. "Why do you want to leave if you have everything here?" my mother would say. I didn't have contacts in the US like many of my peers did, which would make my journey more difficult, but I couldn't get the thought of training abroad out of my mind.

Trying the Odds Abroad

Having graduated with my medical doctorate in Lima, I was looking forward to continuing my studies abroad. I came to the US with the interest of finding a medical research position. I didn't have a lot of savings, but I had optimism and the support of a few good friends. During this period, I met Frank, a nice fellow, who became my closest friend and my husband.

After guidance from classmates, I accepted a research position at a renowned university. My work there resulted in several publications and invitations to residency positions at strong programs. I was overjoyed to join excellent residency and fellowship programs, and the years of training were moments to learn, share, and contribute to the field.

Following my training in dermatopathology in Dallas, Texas, I was offered the opportunity to stay at the training institution and join my mentor on the clinical dermatology faculty at the local medical school. Dermatopathology focuses on diagnosing skin diseases through a microscope. Our final goal is to provide an accurate diagnosis that helps our colleagues, dermatologists, and other specialists provide the best care for their patients.

Some family members and friends thought I was working too much. I was aware of my long hours, but amazingly, I was very happy and enjoyed my work and teaching. Teaching makes you better at your skill, and the constant questions from students challenge your knowledge. It is very gratifying to help and to see your trainees graduate and practice on their own. They become like your own family.

Music Memories Re-Emerging

My dad used to play his tango record collection on Saturdays. We sisters did not like it. I'm ashamed to say, we were sick of it. It sounded like music for old people. I couldn't understand how it could be a favorite musical genre for anyone. But, somehow, the memories of my dad's love of tango haunted me.

Amid a busy life as a mom and pathologist, I signed up for a weekend Argentine Tango workshop in Houston. I don't know what got me to do this, but tango grabbed me. The music was so beautiful and so familiar. The steps were beautifully complex and required careful training and practice. And there was something about tango music from the golden age, how the instrumentation was skillfully arranged and required musicianship to bring it to life while keeping it danceable.

I would get so involved in listening to the arrangements that there were times when my dance partner would ask me, "What are they saying?" I am Spanish-speaking, so he would think I knew what the song was about. But, ashamed of myself, I would reply, "I don't know. Let me see...." Even today, I listen so closely to the music that I almost never bother to listen to the lyrics. They are said to be beautiful and romantic.

Tango is a culture, and it can be viral and addicting. When you are listening to tango while driving, daydreaming about tango at work, and shopping for tango and tango only, you know you've become part of the club.

My tango journey lasted quite a few years. I had the honor of training with seasoned tango masters across the US and in Buenos Aires, Argentina. I taught tango at local dance studios and performed at different venues. Despite my busy schedule, I found a balance between traveling for tango and medical conferences, being a mom and wife, and working as a dermatopathologist and dermatopathology instructor. I am very grateful that, during that period, my husband took care of the finances and investments.

The Call to Investing

I was exposed to real estate investing through my husband. He kept a portfolio of single-family homes. But, for many years, I didn't give much thought to the value of passive income, until I read *Rich Dad Poor Dad* by Robert Kiyosaki. Soon, instead of a tango workshop, I was looking for a real estate investing workshop.

My husband was excited to see me finally interested in investing. We soon discovered apartment investing through a local group. We joined them and worked with coaches to sharpen our skills in market evaluation and underwriting. We learned many lessons, most importantly, the value of having a reliable property management company and leveraging good advice from mentors and experienced fellow investors.

Looking back at my journey, I can see that physicians need to learn finance early in their career. Doctors need to make their money work for them and start building financial freedom along with building their career. The sooner physicians act, the better. Financial stability will allow physicians to practice on their terms.

A few years down the road, my husband and I started investing passively in multifamily syndications. In doing so, we joined a nurturing community of investors, and that inspired our interest in having a more active role in syndications as general partners. We quickly learned the power of teamwork and started leveraging other people's skills. We joined other teams as general partners. As general partners, we can provide good asset management, protect the interests of the investors, and give back to our community of residents by providing improvements to properties and better places to live.

Creating passive income through apartment investing was a new concept to me, but I quickly learned and put it into practice. In previous years, I believed the indoctrination that stocks and other paper assets were the only way to save for retirement, and that had held me back. We grow up hearing about investing in stocks and even learn from our family to set money aside in our 401K. The truth of the matter is that real estate investments are long-term but offer superb returns and are safer and more stable than stock market investments. Financial education is key to financial freedom.

We learned the benefit of investing in cash-flowing real estate assets that increase in value. Real estate investing, although less liquid than stock, offers many advantages, including leverage, meaning using borrowed money to acquire a larger property that yields larger returns than it would if it were paid for in cash, and ample tax advantages.

The Mission to Educate

All along my investing journey, my medical colleagues watched me, and several of them asked me about the investment process and the returns. Some of my colleagues seemed curious but were not quite ready to invest; the concept of apartment "syndication" sounded too foreign. A few of my colleagues knew a little about real estate syndication or had been reading about it.

I soon developed a mission to educate my colleagues, so they could enjoy the benefits of real estate investing too. Being focused is important. However,

I believe in learning about the different asset classes and investment options. I put together an informative newsletter to introduce my colleagues to basic investment terms and concepts, which would help them prepare to evaluate an investment deal when an opportunity came their way.

Medical doctors don't receive financial training in their core curriculum nor are they trained to face the constant changes in regulations that occur in the practice of medicine. As a result, many physicians burn out before they have started outlining their personal and financial goals.

Mindset is important. Always be open to learning and fostering successful habits. Some people are too fast in responding, "I don't have time for more education." There is always time. Like Jim Rohn said, "If you really want to do something, you'll find a way. If you don't, you'll find an excuse."

I realize that my skills and habits as a disciplined pianist and organized doctor helped my growth as an investor and educator. "Discipline is the bridge between goals and accomplishment," Jim Rohn famously quoted. Discipline is a key factor to success and to building financial freedom. Having experienced the benefits of real estate investing, my goal is to share the information I've come to understand with my medical colleagues and investors and positively impact others' lives. Financial wellness is a path to live a life on your terms.

Lydia R. Essary, MD, enjoys educating physicians and investors on apartment investing and helping them build passive income and reduce taxes. To start building your financial freedom, or to book her to speak or to be a podcast guest, email invest@liftequityinvest.com or visit www.liftequityinvest.com.

Quotable: Determination, discipline, and taking action are keys to success. During your journey, be of service.

Dr. Lydia Essary LIFT EQUITY Website

DOMINIC LAGRANGE

Win Against the Shame of Your Past to Become a Visionary Leader

Dominic Lagrange is an expert advisor for inspiring business leaders who wish to reach their full potential and influence their business and community in a culture of excellence and self-realization. He began his career 25 years ago as a sports performance coach and draws on his experience and achievements as an amateur bodybuilding champion.

From Pain to Success

With great satisfaction and a sense of accomplishment, I concluded my meeting with one of my clients, an associate of a major wealth management firm here in Canada. We discussed his 100-year vision (his multi-generational purpose), the impact of his actions, and most importantly, how he could inspire his team and associates. We talked about how, throughout his journey, he could position himself benevolently and gradually move towards fulfilling his purpose and role as a visionary leader. We had been working together for four years to achieve a common goal, an idea that consumed us day and night: to create a world of visionary leaders, each of us leveraging our unique strengths and abilities in our own way.

I walked out to my car. Sitting in the driver's seat, I couldn't help but smile. I was living my purpose. It was so wonderful! I started thinking back on the vast expanse of memories: where I came from, what I had experienced, and what my family had experienced.

I turned on the radio and heard the voice of Jim Rohn, one of my favorite mentors. It was one of his best sermons on personal development: "Living Your Best Year Ever." And at that moment, he repeated the phrase that had once shaken my life: "If you want more, you have to become more."

A tear rolled down my cheek. I thought back to what I had put my family, especially Sylvie, the love of my life, through as I walked the path to define myself as an inspiring leader, an expert advisor for visionary leaders. I particularly recalled the winter day when I discovered a powerful concept, one that allowed me to rise up and become the man, the father, and the leader I had always wanted to be.

The Breaking Point

At the end of 2016, I was feeling ashamed of myself, and experiencing failure, both professionally and personally. Deep down, I knew that I was hiding behind a packed schedule and excessive workouts to avoid facing the fact that I was on the edge of a precipice. Financially, even though I worked triple the hours, a student earned more than me. At home, with my son, Robin, it was challenging. As a newborn, he would wake up every hour and a half every night, and at seven years old, he was still waking up once or twice a night. Since we had Mélodie, five years old then, both children were waking up repeatedly throughout the night. We hadn't had a restful night's sleep in years. Our life was miserable, and I was largely to blame for it. I was absent, broke, and desperate. Yes, I had been practicing gratitude for a year now, but it didn't help.

Even though I tried to stay positive, I was internally destroyed. I had no one to talk to. As a coach, I was there to listen to everyone else and to help others grow. But could anyone listen to ME when I needed to talk?

Despite the fact that I was surrounded by loving friends and family, I pretended nothing was wrong. My parents were very receptive, but I did not want to alarm them with this. As if I could hide something from my parents. As if my mother couldn't sense when her child was not well. My friends were there too, but I felt like I was in a different dimension. And, the false notion that, fundamentally, men have no feelings and are incapable of speaking honestly helped keep me isolated. Sylvie, well, how could I talk to her about how I was feeling without causing discomfort? How could I reopen a still-bleeding wound? And my leaders, they didn't pay me to constantly talk about me. Despite being very close to them, I felt obligated to keep my distance. Honestly, I was probably ashamed. How could a leader's coach be so mentally unwell? So, I was alone in my head.

This day in the winter of 2016 began just like the others. From 6:00 to 7:30 a.m., our home was an asylum. Sylvie and I barely looked at each other while we were dealing with the children's crises. Robin didn't want to get dressed because we were transitioning to a new season. He is on the autism spectrum, and for him, understanding the switch from long sleeves to short sleeves was a real challenge. We might as well have been cutting off his arms! Mélodie demanded attention too, as we needed both of us to dress Robin and get him out of the house. Poor sweetheart, it's no wonder you're so strong and independent today. I'm proud of you.

This morning, I was in a hurry. Sylvie and I had argued during breakfast. We were exhausted from our sleepless night. I was irritated, angry, impatient, and running late! Once Robin was dressed, he was still crying and wailing. He couldn't speak at that time; only sounds came out of his mouth. Mélodie was crying too. And this was when my patience dropped off a cliff.

I opened the front door, grabbed Robin's bag, and threw it down the stairs. Then I closed the door, only to open it again, pick up Robin and Mélodie, put them on the front porch, and slam the door, leaving the kids screaming outside. There, problem solved!

My wife looked at me in shock. I was as red as a lobster. That's when we noticed that two little girls from the neighborhood had witnessed the entire scene from the school bus stop in front of our house. Imagine being those two little girls. What a scene.… My heart is still disturbed thinking about it.

Inside the house, the atmosphere was incredibly heavy. We didn't know where to turn. The kids stopped crying after a while as Sylvie and I had a serious discussion about what had just happened. I was frustrated and Sylvie was ashamed of my gesture. It was a terrible way to start the day, and it was time for the kids to go to school and for me to get on the road to Montreal.

The Awakening Moment

I was speechless on my way to Montreal, unable to get that scene out of my head, unable to shake off the image of Sylvie looking at me with despair, unable to turn off the image of the children taking the bus, their faces darkened with confusion and their eyes swollen with tears. I could still feel the contempt in Sylvie's gaze.

Driving, I was listening to a podcast by Brian Tracy, but in reality, I was much more lost in my thoughts than I was focused on listening. But then, something in the program caught my attention. It was the concept of "I like myself."

Brian Tracy asserted that a leader must constantly repeat to themselves that they appreciate themselves. If they took the time to say it several times a day, it would completely change their perception of themselves and reality.

At that moment, I realized that I was 100% responsible for how I felt about life. I realized that I could define and build my self-confidence. I discovered that I didn't have to wait for others or depend on them to feel good. I didn't have to delegate that responsibility to others. I was responsible! I was responsible for loving myself and feeling strong and confident.

Just like gratitude, which I had learned from Jim Rohn's speeches, I understood that my brain, through repetition of the mantra "I love myself, I appreciate myself, thank you life," would eventually believe it and give me a whole new feeling. I understood that my brain doesn't differentiate between receiving that compliment from someone else and me repeating it to myself.

So, driven by wanting to act and not knowing what else to do, I started practicing it. What did I have to lose? Repeating this phrase, simple to say, yet so easy to procrastinate, became a practice that completely changed my life. The change was slow at first, but the more I repeated it, and the more I dared to say the mantra in difficult moments as well as in happy moments, the more I felt a difference.

At first, it was a feeling of lightness. The anxiety attacks I had been experiencing became less intense, and I bounced back into a positive state more quickly. I became increasingly proud of myself and my journey. I started seeing my journey more as destiny rather than fate.

I noticed the impact I had in meetings became much more powerful. I was solid, reassuring, and calm. I presented myself to others with serenity. I no longer felt the need for approval from others to feel good. I no longer craved appreciation or love to be happy. I was now capable of giving without expectation. I could tell my wife that I loved her because I wanted to, without needing anything in return. I could compliment or help someone, expecting nothing back, and be perfectly fine with that. I could do these things for myself, to do good. My ego occupied less and less space within me.

So, like any good super achiever, I started saying "I love myself, I appreciate myself, thank you life" 10, 20, even 100 times a day, both in the morning and before bed. And, the effect completely transformed my life.

Be No More a Slave of Your Past

Today, I still realize the impact of this process. This process has made me the leader I am. It's what enables me to engage in meaningful discussions with my leaders. It has made me a person who knows how to listen, unaffected and unattacked by comments and remarks. I accept them with gratitude. Today, I realize that all those years of repeating this mantra are what enable me to publicly share my story.

What's wonderful about this idea is that you don't even need to believe in it initially. You only need to start saying it. Make a decision that, from now on, every morning and evening, you will say to yourself, "I love myself, I appreciate myself, thank you life." If you're not comfortable, dare to do it. For me, it was a game changer.

So, yes, I'm smiling, as a super achiever, a husband in love with the same wife for 20 years now, and a loving father. Today, thanks to gratitude and self-appreciation, I am able to embrace every event, live my relationships with others in kindness, and see them as opportunities to fully realize myself in my 100-year vision. I am myself, capable of loving and appreciating without expecting anything in return. I'm action-oriented and no more a slave of my past.

Super achiever leaders contact Dominic Lagrange to define their purpose for existing and to become an example of healthy success for their family and community. Dominic coaches entrepreneurs to lead their businesses in excellence and to build legacies of knowledge sharing, recognition, and self-fulfillment. To join the 100-year vision group and impact society as a visionary leader, contact Dominic at: www.dominiclagrange.com or info@dominiclagrange.com.

Quotable: We are 100% responsible for our self-confidence. No matter your past, be resilient and be in action for yourself every day.

 Be part of my list, in the mind of a super achiever.

JIN WANG

Within's Force Created an External Course

Formerly a CPA and auditor, Jin Wang is now owner of a real estate investing firm focused on acquiring and operating large multifamily properties in the Sun Belt states. She is passionate about helping others build generational wealth, without a tremendous sacrifice of their time, through real estate investing.

Starting Out in Opportunity

Seven was an age to remember. The year was 1990, and my family and I embarked on my first journey, from China to the USA, a land full of promises and opportunities.

Upon arriving in Washington, DC, we moved in temporarily with my aunt. Soon, my dad found a job washing dishes at a Chinese restaurant and my mom found work sewing clothes. I started second grade and struggled through most of it not knowing how to speak, read, or write English. I remember getting a spelling test back and getting zero of the 10 words right! I was mortified. Attempting homework brought tears of frustration on many evenings.

Once my English started improving, I became obsessed with learning, and the library became one of my favorite places. Starting in fourth grade, things clicked, and I figured out how to study and how to excel academically. This love for learning combined with my keen sense of logic and practicality; life was relatively easy to figure out. As the oldest of four children, I learned how to be resourceful so I could fill out paperwork and help my family of six get what we needed. Despite the many responsibilities I had as the oldest child, cooking, cleaning, helping my siblings with homework, and so forth, I had a great childhood surrounded by family.

At school, I did well enough to get into all the colleges I applied to. I selected the University of Southern California to study business and accounting because those were practical majors to ensure a good, stable career. I also had in the back of my mind in high school that one day I would like to be a business owner, and I thought mastering accounting would be critical to being successful.

The goal for most accounting students was to work for a Big Four accounting firm. I secured an internship by the end of my sophomore year at KPMG's Washington, DC, location. One internship led to another and eventually to a full-time offer. Working as an external auditor put my work ethic to the test. I met some of the best people, and because of how many hours we spent together, we were like family. Actually, I saw my colleagues more than my family at this point in my life.

Eventually, I transitioned and worked for the next 12 years at two highly-regarded nonprofit organizations in DC for a better-balanced lifestyle.

Tugged Toward a New Path

Externally, it seemed like I had it all together. Life up to this point had been masterfully orchestrated, and I was happy. I was where I was supposed to be; a CPA working at a great organization that offered the work-life balance I was looking for, married to the love of my life, raising a healthy beautiful boy with a second baby on the way, and a homeowner; I was living the American dream.

At the start of my second pregnancy, something in my brain stirred, *Life can't be that simple, can it?* I was constantly busy, keeping this lifestyle going, working my W-2 job, helping my family, trying to be the ideal wife, mother, and friend; and while I was content giving my time and energy to make other people happy, I started to wonder, *Is this really who and all that I am? What do I really want?* It didn't feel like the track I was on was helping me answer any of these questions.

As the most time-consuming activity in my life, work became more of a chore than a joy. I started to resent making the long trek to work. Daily, we commuters were packed like sardines on crowded metro cars. I felt like I had shackles around my ankles as I walked up the long escalator from the metro station each morning. Where I used to enjoy problem solving, I felt annoyed that I was constantly fixing problems other people created, and it was never-ending. My brain couldn't help but focus on all the negatives.

Sometimes, I would read a motivational book and I would snap out of it, feeling guilty for feeling this way about what, in actuality, was a great job with a great team. Inevitably, I would fall right back into the valley of despair after a few days. While I didn't understand why I was feeling such negativity then, I realize today the source of my unhappiness with my job was not the job itself, but the fact of the matter was that I was giving away what I realized at this point, was my most precious commodity, my TIME. I was giving up the majority of my day to someone else when I needed it most for myself.

For once in my life, I was facing questions that I couldn't easily find the answers to. *How do I get my time back so I can focus on me? What can I do to replace my income so I don't have to exchange my limited resource of time for a paycheck?*

The Spark That Ignited the Fire

Two years earlier, in 2013, I had picked up the book *Rich Dad Poor Dad* by Robert Kiyosaki. After reading the book, my best friend and I attended a two-day Rich Dad education seminar. The message introduced in the book was amplified: We must take control of our financial literacy and our family's financial future, and we can no longer rely on the social security system to take care of us in retirement. After my many years in this country, the land of opportunities was starting to shift in meaning for me.

For the next several years, tapping into my inner child's love for learning, I dedicated time on my long metro rides to and from work in DC to reading books and listening to real estate and investing podcasts. Creating passive income through real estate seemed to be the obvious answer to take back my time.

However, I was stuck asking, *HOW do we find the money to buy our first real estate investment, and would it be justifiable given the cash flow in our area may be closer to zero?* The numbers didn't quite add up. Even if we could buy our first property, it would take a while to save up another down payment for the second property. *How long would it take to achieve financial freedom at this pace?*

These were the burning questions running through my head as I tried to figure out how to make real estate the answer to getting my time back. Unbeknownst to me, I had a case of a scarcity mindset, limiting beliefs, and was asking the wrong questions.

An Encounter That Changed Everything

In late 2017, on the last night of the New Orleans Investment Conference, I saw the man who had planted a very important seed in my head in 2013, Robert Kiyosaki. Near the end of the conference's celebration party, something pushed me to ask him politely for a few moments of his time. He graciously agreed, and we sat down to talk.

What do you say to a legend? I started by telling him about my family, particularly my parents, and how they came to the US with very little. Their mindset was similar to his poor dad—study hard, get a good job, save your money, buy a house, and work until you retire. Well, I was doing quite well on that track, but I wanted to do what my parents weren't able to. They did their best with what they knew and what resources they had. They made sacrifices and worked long, hard hours so their children would have the opportunity to be anything they want to be. I wanted to build on that foundation. I was trying, but I didn't see a way. I didn't know HOW.

Mr. Kiyosaki said, not in these exact words, that everything we could ever want in the external world has to start within.

It would take me several years of being on a constant self-discovery journey for me to understand, and to be frank, I continue to learn what *going within* really means because there's always a deeper level. That night, I also heard Mr. Kiyosaki say self-development, which I have always been obsessed with, but this time, I knew I had to do things differently. I needed to not just read a good self-help, finance, or business book, but to identify, internalize, and execute on the parts that would help me reach my next level from where I was when I picked up that book.

The price tag for the self-development company Kiyosaki recommended was not in my budget at that time, but a book called *The Miracle Morning* by Hal Elrod was. For the next few years, I dedicated my mornings to practicing the seven methods under the acronym SAVERS laid out in the book: silence, affirmations, visualization, exercise, reading, and scribing. Spending the time on these exercises daily changed my habits, my mindset, and my thoughts, and more importantly, made me realize the incredible power of spirituality.

Although I was skeptical at first, I found peace and comfort in turning inwards during those early morning hours, and over time, I gained greater clarity on my life and my next steps and I started asking better questions. With a shift in mindset, I realized the power to change my circumstances lay in my own hands.

This shift unlocked resources I never knew I had. I recognized opportunities instead of doubting myself and letting them pass. Rather than dwelling on scarcity, I asked myself, *What do I have? Who do I know or who can I get to know? And how can I leverage that to take me closer to where and what I want to be?*

Putting the Wheels in Motion

All the pieces of the puzzle that I saw scattered around me in 2015 were starting to fit together.

With my new perspective, I soon discovered the latent potential in our home's equity, leading my husband and I to cash-out refinance to purchase our first rental property together in 2018, a turnkey duplex.

The following year, we did something similar with another property I co-owned with my mom and purchased another duplex. This duplex was not turnkey, and we took control over the entire renovation of the two units, along with tenant placements.

Although closing on the properties was exhilarating, the process of renovating them, managing the contractors, and finding quality tenants was very time-consuming. We quickly realized that this was a process we'd need to repeat multiple times to build a portfolio capable of generating significant cash flow. I started asking myself, *Who can help me accelerate this process and make it more efficient?*

As we were building our portfolio one duplex at a time, we were also exploring commercial real estate options. In 2018, we decided to pour our focus and resources into apartment investing. I was attracted to the economy of scale—the opportunity to leverage an experienced team, nonrecourse debt, and other people's money. This was in addition to the massive tax advantages, controllable valuation through value-add strategies, the potential for cash flow, and owning real assets that provide a basic human need, shelter. As a woman of practicality, this made sense to me.

Getting into the Game

To play at this higher level, I knew I needed to set lofty goals and invest in furthering myself. I immersed myself in an environment with real estate investors who were more experienced than I was, which kickstarted forming my company dedicated to real estate investing. I learned how to access and assess multifamily deals and I co-sponsored over 1,000 units with other operators between 2019 and 2020.

Through my observation as a co-sponsor, it became apparent to me that to go far in this business, I needed a team. I was blessed to find two incredible women in late 2019 through my network who were also CPAs and who also started their auditing careers at a Big Four accounting firm. As numbers-driven, risk-averse, analytical women, who understand hard work and the value of money, and whose professional work revolved around identifying and mitigating risks for public and private businesses, I knew we could do more to help both ourselves and others through our deals by working together. The Sage Investing Group was founded in September 2020, and with the grace of God, I got what I wanted most, control over my TIME. I left my W-2 job in November of 2020.

We co-sponsored another 1,000 units together from late 2020 through 2022 while sourcing our own deals. The years I started in apartment investing, 2019 leading up to mid-2022, were very exciting times in the multifamily industry. High occupancy, compressing capitalization rates, and rising rents across the country post-COVID created high transaction volumes and fantastic returns for investors. However, the unprecedented rise in interest rates from 2022-2023, inflation, and a rocky economy tampered with property performances and investor returns.

As Warren Buffet said, "Be fearful when others are greedy and be greedy when others are fearful." Despite the market optimism, we erred on the conservative and cautionary side at all times. Sticking to our guns brought great frustration as we were beat out on numerous deals during this time. If the numbers don't make sense, we don't push it. The deals have to work on our terms. Ultimately, we sourced and acquired two deals totaling 388 units during 2021 and 2022 in a tertiary market in Alabama that, through thorough research, demonstrated strong market fundamentals.

Today, we are proud of our existing assets under management and the team we've built. We have since then refinanced on the first property that we acquired in 2021 and outperformed the initial investor return projections in half the time projected. We are diligently working through the value-add business plan on our second acquisition, a portfolio of five properties. Despite some market challenges, as long as we buy right and operate right, we still strongly believe in our ability to generate cash flow and increase our properties' valuation. I am grateful for my partners' abilities to recognize the need to stay conservative despite so much market optimism a few years ago, and we will continue to apply these same principles moving forward. As Zig Ziglar said, we can only "hope for the best, prepare for the worst."

Good Things Take Time

While I dream of building a real estate empire to create generational wealth for our investors' families, my partners' families, and my family, I have learned everything fundamentally sound takes time to build, whether it's our portfolio as we're starting out or our company that's running the business and managing the portfolio. We've been thoughtful and meticulous about how we approach our acquisition and asset management process and in what direction we want to take our company from day one. We've sought out others for guidance and support, knowing we can't always find the answers between ourselves. The team has encountered many thorns through the process of building our company, but when we took the time to take care of them, those thorns gave way to buds, which blossomed into roses. I am proud of ourselves as we've learned through our trials and tribulations to operate our business and work with one another with grit, grace, and gratitude.

Convergence of Two Paths

In one respect, I am grateful for the journey that has taken me from a small village in China to where I am today, this land of opportunity where I can create my reality and serve others by offering them opportunities to honor their families and build generational wealth along with us.

In another respect, through the challenges and successes of building a business, the journey has led me closer to *home* than I have ever felt in my entire life.

While this is still an ongoing journey, this is what I have learned so far. Whereas I was so accustomed to surviving and thriving by being logical and practical, using my head to figure things out my entire life, I now realize that I have neglected to listen, to see, and to speak to others with my heart. My unhappiness when life seemed so perfect was my wake-up call to seek this truth.

I am grateful to my business partners and my husband for being a part of my journey and for bringing to light what I was unable to recognize on my own. To think, how much of myself I would've never known if I had not set out to seek a way to find the truth, is unfathomable to me today.

Many of the questions I've asked have been answered, and they have led me down many unexpected paths; yet ultimately, I am arriving precisely at my target destination *for now.*

Life has a funny way of telling us that there is more to you than meets the eye. Listen, ask questions, and take action. May you find your truth with the power of grit, grace, and gratitude.

To get in touch with Jin Wang and start building generational wealth through the power of commercial real estate investing, send an email to jin@sageinvestinggroup.com. To learn more about her business, visit her company website at www.sageinvestinggroup.com.

Quotable: Life has a funny way of telling us that there is more of you than meets the eye. Listen, ask questions, and take action.

Create generational wealth with the Sage Investing Group.

BEN BUZEK

From Troubled Youth to Military Special Operations

Ben Buzek is a family-centric Special Operations veteran and real estate investor. He's earned everything he has, coming from very little. Ben has survived bull riding, 27 combat deployments, three motor vehicle accidents, and a parachuting accident. He thrives on living life to the fullest and creating opportunities for others to learn and grow.

Life Is Fragile

I am a lucky dude. After all I've been through, I should be dead. Seneca, a Roman philosopher, is credited with saying, "Luck is where opportunity meets preparation." I've prepared myself my entire life, even when I didn't quite know it.

Life is fragile, and most importantly, it is worthwhile. This lesson I've continually learned over the years.

I've always believed that "people don't change; situations change people." Many people perceive that we have no say in our lives. This mindset couldn't be farther from the truth! It may not appear as such, but we have choices that can change our lives.

The Angry Teen

Luck came to me early. As a confused and furious adolescent, I sought adulthood too young when I left my parent's house at 15. We couldn't find common ground, and I made a lot of poor choices. I was hanging out with the wrong crowds and seeking acceptance from people going nowhere. Over the next year, I bounced around state-run institutions before getting kicked out of the group home I was living in.

At the culmination of my rebellious actions, I vividly remember sitting at a large, boardroom-style table with my parents, state employees, the group home's foster parents, and others I didn't recognize all staring at me.

The group was gathered to remove me from state care, and the alternatives were for me to move back to my parents or to go to a wilderness camp, secluded from the outside world, for three months. The picture they painted of wilderness camp wasn't glamorous: hard work, labor without pay, and a rigorous schedule. I felt trapped. I knew I needed to change my life, but I couldn't return to my parent's house.

Given my options, the wilderness camp actually sounded enticing until the state representatives told me I wouldn't have a place to live afterward. When I asked if I would move back into the group home after completion of the camp, the state representative seemed caught off-guard. They said I'd have to find new housing, despite months without earning income for living expenses, or move in with my parents.

At 16 years old, I refused both options and made my choice; I would move on alone.

Stumbling Upon a Mentor

I attribute luck to one of the most pivotal decisions of my life. I made my way to the local university and searched through pages of roommate offers. Thinking I was clever, I saw an ad from a Cary looking for a roommate nearby. I thought having a female college roommate sounded phenomenal, so I called the number using the payphone.

"Hello?" said a deep, scratchy voice.

"Hi, this is Ben, and I'm calling to talk to Cary about a room."

"Yea, this is him." My fantasy world crumbled as I learned that Cary was a male, but the rent and deposit were what I had saved up. So, I met Cary and the roommates.

Cary was older than me, and so were the other college roommates. I didn't know it, but meeting Cary was the right opportunity at the right time. I grew up a lot over the next year under his mentorship and working four jobs while attending high school.

A New and Radical Opportunity

Luck has a way of finding me. It could have been anyone in the high school hallway, but the US Army recruiter chose me as his target. I knew I needed a drastic change and yearned for a disciplined lifestyle.

I agreed to meet with him and take a prerequisite test for military service called the ASVAB (Armed Services Vocational Aptitude Battery). To my surprise, I did well enough to qualify for Army Aviation.

After much persuasion, my parents signed the paperwork allowing me to enlist at 17, and I entered the Army in November of 1999. Provided I graduated high school and didn't get into any trouble, I would start basic training in June 2000.

And then, I got into trouble. While skipping school with classmates, we got caught doing the wrong things in the wrong place. The police dropped us off at the school, where we awaited law enforcement and the school's administration. Due to the severity of our actions, my friends received expulsion or transfer to other schools. Luck had a different fate for me.

The vice principal was in the Army National Guard. As a Captain, he decided to take me on as his pet project. He must have seen the impact that service in the Army could have on my life trajectory.

The administration pursued my satisfactory completion of every past-due assignment. This would allow me to pass and graduate to attend Basic Training. The hole I had dug myself seemed insurmountable. The Captain had me report to him daily and show my completed classwork. I persisted and barely graduated with a 1.8 GPA. Three weeks later, I was heading for Army boot camp.

Defiance Can Be a Strength

I found out very quickly that the military, mass punishments, and micromanaging were not my style. I believed I had made a colossal mistake.

Once again, I saw an opportunity. A Special Operations recruiter was to present to the Army's aviation school, and I attended with curiosity.

What the special operations forces (SOF) recruiter shared and how he presented himself massively resonated with me. I fell in love that day. Challenging myself to test my grit through physical, mental, and psychological evaluations seemed fascinating. Putting yourself through these challenges was the opportunity for "big boy rules." In special operations, you would earn trust by your merits and be responsible for your actions.

I connected serving in special operations with leaving that boardroom just a few years prior. Staying in the conventional Army for me was like allowing life to be on autopilot, as would have been going to wilderness camp or returning to my parent's house.

When the recruiter asked, "Who's interested in applying?" I shot my hand up. I was the only one in a room of 50 to volunteer.

After the briefing, I received a packet and instructions to return it before the recruiter left the next day. After mandatory lights out that night, I feverishly wrote my answers under the covert illumination of the red lens on my Army-issued green elbow flashlight. It had to be perfect.

The next morning, I persistently sought out the recruiter before his departure and handed over my packet. A week later, I received a call on the barracks phone. My heart fell out of my chest as the SOF recruiter declined me. That's how I learned the Army had already created orders for me to go to South Korea for a year.

"Can't you get me out of going?"

The recruiter laughed and said, "Nope, have fun in Korea! If you still want to come, fill out another packet halfway through your year, and we'll see if you're qualified then."

Six months and one day into my rotation in South Korea, I faxed a new packet to the recruiter. At the end of my tour, I was finally placed on orders to go to special operations aviation assessment, and I reported in March of 2002.

An Incredible Transformation

I succeeded in tryouts and excelled in the climate of special operations forces (SOF). SOF moves at the speed of trust, built or degraded with individual and team decisions, mission completion, and interactions inside and outside the organization. SOF are critical of each other and, more importantly, ourselves. It causes one to strive harder, remain disciplined, and work at being the best version of themselves. A friend of mine said it best: "I have never worked so hard to be so average." The caliber of people around you is that high. Challenging myself and remaining persistent has created a journey I am eternally grateful for.

I would average five to eight months away from family yearly for the next two decades, filled with deployments, military schooling, and training trips. I began to take positions of greater responsibility, and becoming a leader of highly functioning teams became my career's most challenging and rewarding experience. The team flourished, although the increased time devoted to work created strains in my personal life. Nonetheless, my family became resilient and adaptable. Despite my absence, I'm proud of how well my family has endured and thrived.

Although the COVID-19 pandemic was a tremendously difficult time for some, the mandatory lockdowns created a massive opportunity for me and my family. Our state's lockdown was approximately three months. We couldn't travel or train, allowing more time at home and togetherness as a family. It's hard to believe, but I never spent 90 consecutive days with my family until the lockdowns. This reality changed our perception of what we wanted out of life, and I was grateful for the time.

Luck and Near-Death Experience

In September 2022, my wife and I kissed our family goodbye as we flew across the country to attend a SOF marriage retreat. An incredible organization named Operation Healing Forces hosted. It was an opportunity of a lifetime, and we were so excited to enjoy eight days together without any responsibilities or stress.

The Lodge at Trout Creek in Montana was picturesque, and the hosts, Randy and Julie, welcomed us to their lovely bed and breakfast with tremendous warmth and gratitude. The events during the week engaged the couples and encouraged togetherness. It was a first-class event, and our retreat guide, Chris, was the perfect fit. One of the last events was an ATV ride to the top of a mountain for a scenic lunch.

Aimee and I were on the last ATV in the convoy as we went up the mountain. Our vehicle hit a rut that launched us off the road. By some stroke of luck, at the exact time our ATV went flying off the side of the cliff, Randy and Chris joined the convoy in time to watch us disappear.

When I awoke, I was in intense pain and couldn't move. I didn't know where I was or what happened. I gathered as much strength as possible to move my eyes so I could look for my wife. We had landed down the mountain, where small trees and shrubs stopped us. We were both gasping for air, couldn't move, and couldn't communicate. We thought we were alone. For the first time in my life, I was utterly helpless.

It wasn't long before we heard Randy and Chris calling for us. They couldn't see us because of the steepness of the cliff and the dense foliage. Neither Aimee nor I could make any noise.

Eventually, they made it down to us. Once aware of what happened, the entire group joined the rescue efforts. Cell phones did not work in this remote area. The only way to request medical help was via satellite phone. Thankfully, one of the hosts had one, and they immediately phoned for help, although support was far away.

There was incredible heroism that day. Aimee and I lay upon the jagged rocky surface for nearly two hours before help arrived. Thank goodness we were with special operations folks. They figured out how to hoist us to the road by combining winches and sheer human strength. Aimee and I knew we had become the mission, and the team would not let the mission fail. We are eternally grateful to these heroes, wonderful people who were strangers just a few days prior, for their selfless work performed at great personal risk.

The aircraft flew us to the hospital for analysis. Aimee had broken 13 ribs, lacerated her kidney and liver, and shattered her left hand. I had 14 broken ribs, a lacerated kidney and spleen, and the entire left side of my body was as purple as Barney the dinosaur. Thankfully, my neck and back suffered minimal damage despite the initial assessment. It is incredibly humbling to lay in a hospital bed, unable to move or use the bathroom without assistance. I felt immense guilt for what I perceived as my fault in causing this damage to my wife. I had a lot of time to think and continually concluded that life is fragile. This event made me appreciate life and Aimee so much more.

People in our life stepped up. Aimee and I have always helped those in need. We never expected to have to rely on others to help us. We didn't realize how much people loved us. Our beloved friends and neighbors, extensions of our family, created a two-month meal train. The roster, providing meals for our kids and their caregivers, was filled in 12 hours. My Army family, our daughter's team 757 Swim, and various other friends in our network tirelessly cared for our family. Family members took turns living at our house to support our children. My mother-in-law was incredible throughout, and we are so grateful for her.

After a week in the hospital, Aimee and I were on the mend and able to move around somewhat independently when, suddenly, things went downhill. I had a lung collapse and a chest tube inserted. The next day, we nearly lost Aimee. For the second time, I felt utterly helpless. Without quick intervention from the nurses and doctors, the artery that burst in Aimee's lungs would have killed her. After a few surgeries and two chest tubes of her own, Aimee came back to us.

One month after leaving for the retreat in Montana, Aimee and I were delivered back home to be with our family and continue healing. It was weeks before we could walk up our stairs (a chair lift was donated and installed) or do normal activities independently. Months of physical and mental therapy followed. Aimee and I are incredibly fortunate. The persistence of the remarkable people around us helped to transform this challenging journey into one of positivity and gratitude.

This chapter of our lives highlights the idea that life is fragile. We can encounter a situation that will significantly impact our future at any given time. This is one reason I always tell those I care about that I love them, regardless of any disagreements or extenuating circumstances. Far too many times, I have been in harm's way, wondering if that phone call was my last opportunity to tell someone how much they meant to me.

Despite my luck, I have realized I do not have 100% control over situations and their outcomes. We can be prepared for those moments and persist through the resistance of life to become transformed on the other end. Then, we must reflect with a critical eye to determine who that transformation makes us.

Opportunity Is Luck Meets Preparation

Life is a collection of transformations. As my father would say, "Enjoy the journey." Life is fragile and beautiful, and it can be one incredible journey if you take ownership of growing yourself and those around you!

In the words of my assistant dean at the William & Mary Business School on the first day of class, "You belong here." I needed to hear those precise words when I realized I was way over my head and full of self-doubt. I was amongst brilliant people in a respected master's degree program. This was my first time entering a college classroom since I earned my online bachelor's between combat deployments. For a moment, my perception was that I wasn't lucky or didn't deserve this opportunity. I was distorting the facts. The truth is, luck brought me to business school because I was open to the opportunity and prepared to challenge myself.

My advice is to know your worth and trust yourself because YOU belong. Prevent the negative perception and enjoy life by transforming. Taking a chapter from the Army Leadership manual and the Be, Know, Do leadership style, **Be** persistent, **Know** there are opportunities out there, and **Do** stay prepared when luck comes knocking!

Ben Buzek has always sought a path different from the status quo. In every decision, he considers the values his parents provided: courage, humility, integrity, and curiosity. Ben thrives on creating opportunities for himself and a blueprint for others to follow. That is his gift to the world, a non-standard approach to growth. To hear more stories or to connect with Ben, check out www.benbuzek.com.

Quotable: Luck and persistence have grown my character. Applying action to character ensures success is inevitable. Be the 1% that challenges the status quo and grow!

JACKIE MARUSHKA

From Bullied and Broken to
the Oscars Red Carpet

A 30-year public relations veteran, Jackie Marushka founded Marushka Media, Nashville's first Latina-owned PR agency, growing her entertainment clients' brands through curated media coverage. Formerly with Sony Music, Jackie loves yoga, hiking, writing, and her dogs and serves on multiple boards in the Nashville area.

Bullied

Running. Hiding. Negotiating. Praying.

I was a tiny kid. Almost daily at school, the bigger girls, and some boys, would push me into lockers, knock me down, and tear at my clothes. It started in elementary school, and as I got older, my frame wasn't catching up to those of the other kids. I know now, I was an easy target for bullies. Back then, all I knew was I had to find a way to work around them.

I adjusted my routes to take me down random hallways and through classrooms with second doors. I even ducked behind blackboards. But it didn't always work.

When they did catch me, the pushing, spitting, tripping, pulling at my clothes, or knocking my books out of my arms came with a colorful lexicon, especially as I got to middle school. The words the kids used—sometimes in Spanish and sometimes in English or Tewa, the language the kids from the local pueblos spoke—were the words you'd hear on TV shows you weren't supposed to be watching or when an uncle would slam his thumb with a hammer while working on something for Grandma.

While mom was a teacher and I could very well have ratted out these kids, even then, I knew there'd be severe social consequences. So I developed a balance of running, hiding, negotiating, and praying.

Isn't God Supposed to Protect Me?

Most of the kids were just out to prove a point to the other kids by picking on the small kid with the funny last name. Beyond a shadow of a doubt, something inside me knew that it was all done for love. They were doing it for love.

Not my love. The love of people who mattered to them most. Their parents. Siblings. Friends.

Negative attention is still attention. And this—this broke my heart.

As I worked a wad of chewing gum out of my hair using a little lump of lard I begged from the cafeteria lady, I heard that still small voice say, *Pray for them. They hurt you because they're hurting.*

It didn't make sense. My family went to church. There were statues of Mary, St. Jude, and Jesus all around the house, and I prayed all the prayers I'd learned in Catechism. I thought God was supposed to protect me.

In that moment, I began what would become a life-long conversation with God.

Deep Roots Support Growth

My mom is a beautiful, olive-skinned woman with cheekbones so high any supermodel would turn green with envy. Her family blends bloodlines of Spanish, French, and Apache, all of whom made the Sangre de Cristo Mountains their homes beginning in the early 1600s.

My maternal Grandma Sylvia's family traces back to a Spaniard named Sebastian de Martin who was sent by the king of Spain in the 1600s to homestead the new territory that would eventually become New Mexico. The Spanish, "Martin," is where the surname "Martinez" came from. "Es de Martin" literally translates to "is of Martin."

While Grandma Sylvia's family is mostly Spanish, her mother, Abelina, was half Spanish and half French. Her husband Grandpa Mike's family is Spanish and Apache.

Our roots run deep in heritage and colorful traditions.

My family worked the rich land for generations, mostly as farmhands for wealthy landowners in New Mexico and Southern Colorado. But Grandpa Mike, the second youngest of seven children born to Ruperta and Pablo, had other plans. A farmer by tradition with an entrepreneurial spirit, he learned carpentry and worked tirelessly to build a life on his terms. He and my Grandma started the only fueling station and general store in 100 miles at the time. They called it "Mike's Cash Store and Texaco Station" and the brightly lit round Texaco Star sign mounted on a 25' tall pole, drew patrons from around the world who were driving through on Highway 68.

Velarde and that Texaco station is where I watched the "sunrise to sunset" work ethic of my grandparents, their attention to detail, and their love-in-action of people and their animals.

Like generations before me, this drive is in my blood. It's what helped me put my pride aside and hustle when I first moved to Nashville where one of my first jobs was for a local YMCA as a janitor.

I wasn't embarrassed picking up the snotty towels, cleaning toilets, and folding towels. I was grateful to get to do it because it afforded me a gym membership, extra income, and even CPR training.

My mom, Evelyn, the olive-skinned classic beauty, is Grandma Sylvia and Grandpa Mike's only daughter and was raised in Velarde. She became an elementary school teacher and retired as superintendent of her school district. My dad, Jack, worked for the state of New Mexico's Parks and Recreation division. On weekdays, Dad left the house early and came home late but found weekend peace from the rat race on the 18-acre farm he and mom had purchased piece by piece. Not one of my childhood memories is without my dad on his 1976 orange Kubota tractor with the mini front-end loader, which made a great spot during hide and seek when cousins came to visit.

The roots my parents and grandparents demonstrated are what made me believe I could not just chase, but actually catch my dreams. There were scary days on my journey, but I knew anything was possible, and I pressed into every challenge and made the most of every opportunity to grow.

Let Go. Let God.

As it turns out, God was teaching me lesson after lesson in a "wax-on, wax-off" kind of way. I understand why now; through my experiences as a kid, I had to learn the basics before seeing the bigger picture.

Through the kids who treated me so poorly, He was teaching me how to navigate personalities I'd run across later in life. He prepared me by leading me to read, run (which came in very handy), negotiate, and most important—trust in Him.

I have always heard His voice. Many would call it a gut instinct or intuition. I've always called it God. My faith was underscored by Grandpa Mike, who would pray, then cross his forehead, mouth, and heart before every meal.

"Why do you do that, Grandpa?" I asked once.

"Because I am asking God to bless my thoughts, my words, and my intentions. Think good. Say good. Do good, mijita," he said. "You can never go wrong if you're in the center of God's will."

I never forgot that. I still remember his emerald green eyes looking directly into mine as he said those words.

All of this, from work ethic to kindness to generosity, I learned under the light of that Texaco star. All of this I learned from the stars who lit up my life.

My family. My roots.

Think Good. Say Good. Do Good.

With each year that passed, I learned to negotiate my way around the group of "mean girls" like a champ. I wasn't a friend, but at least I wasn't being chased down like in years prior.

Each pack of mean girls seems to have a ring leader. Mine was "Rayna," which is not her real name. She was small but tough. Like a badger. You just didn't mess with her. School legend says she beat up a senior when she was in seventh grade—AND she had three older sisters who were just as mean as she was.

I stayed away from Rayna at all costs.

One day in ninth grade, I was walking through an empty school hallway, a bit late to my English class from PE across campus, and I saw Rayna go into the bathroom.

She was crying.

That still small voice I knew was God, nudged me to check on her.

But this was Rayna....

God...are you SURE you want me to go in there? His nudging continued, so I took a deep breath, mustered all the courage I had in me, and walked into the bathroom.

Rayna was sitting on the floor in tears. Her head was down and she had her arms around her knees in a sort of seated fetal position.

"Hi, Rayna? Are you okay?" She looked up but didn't make eye contact. It was then I saw bruises and fresh scratches on her face.

Every bit of the tough, strong, and scary bully I had known her to be was streaming away with the tears running down her cheeks.

I approached her slowly. Without words, I wet a brown paper towel, knelt down, and helped clean her scratches. She was wearing yesterday's clothes and when she raised her arm to take the wet paper towel, I saw what looked like cigarette burns that hadn't yet scabbed over. I gave her the light jacket I had. She put it on and put the hood over her head to hide her face a little.

She looked at me and said things weren't good at home. She looked terrified and exhausted. "Please don't tell anyone," she whispered.

I helped fix her hair, and we walked together to the nurse's office, the only place she felt safe going, where she stayed most of the day.

It turns out, she had been beaten by her mother and her mother's new boyfriend the night before.

My heart fell. This tiny-framed girl of 15 was full of potential. She was a natural-born leader, who had built a shell around her to remain safe from the predators she had been fielding at home. Home. A place that should be safe for a kid.

That day I began praying for her safety, her family, and her future. I also felt something new…an overwhelming flood of gratitude for the family I was blessed to have.

The days that followed were interesting. Though I never shared that I'd spent that time with her, Rayna's friends stopped picking on me. But I didn't see her around anymore.

Years later, I ran into her at a Walgreens. She told me she got help through the school nurse and her mom had gone to jail for helping her boyfriend commit a crime. She went to live with her aunt, changed schools, and got what she called "a new lease on life."

She studied because she didn't want to turn out like her mom or her older sisters who had all eventually gone to prison.

Now, Rayna was a social worker. She told me that she spent her days providing resources and support to kids going through situations similar to what she did.

I did all I could to keep it together. I hugged her right there in the Walgreens line holding my toothpaste. We looked at each other and cried.

God had intervened.

That moment brought back Grandpa Mike's words, "Think good. Say good. Do good," and his daily example of laying his steps before God.

It also gave me three big lessons that transformed my life:

1. Do not judge anyone—ever. We can't know everyone's backstories. The janitor you snub today may be the executive you want to impress tomorrow.
2. Words matter and can heal. Proverbs 25:11 says, "Like golden apples set in silver is a word spoken at the right time." If you can offer a good word, it could change the course of someone's day or maybe even their life.
3. Even the smallest kindness can make a positive impact.

In this case, the small kindness I found within me helped change Rayna's life. I thought I was helping a bully get to the nurse's office. But God had bigger plans for her and the youth she now cares for.

I was just a small bullied kid. Even if you're small, God CAN change any circumstance for you or the Rayna in your life.

My Future on the Red Carpet

I remember, like it was yesterday, stepping onto the lush, 800-foot red carpet for the first time. I'd been in the entertainment business for over 20 years and I'd walked celebrity clients down some of the most prestigious red carpets in the world, including the Cannes Film Festival, the Grammy Awards, The Billboard Music Awards, Clive Davis's exclusive pre-Grammy party, plus countless film premieres, but this—this was the Academy Awards. The Oscars. And there I was. The grown-up version of an always-tinier-than-the-other-kids, Hispanic/Hungarian girl who never knew such a life existed while picking fruit in my grandparents' orchard or while checking oil, pumping gas, or tending the store counter at Grandpa Mike's Texaco station.

A little girl whose upbringing was as blessed as it was rough, had broken into the entertainment business and become the first Christian music publicist to work the Grammy Awards red carpet, even creating what is now known as a "tip sheet" out of branding necessity (because no one knew who my artists were). I have been honored to work with teams representing artists like Bruce Springsteen and Brian Littrell of the Backstreet Boys, to help rebrand the Americana Music Association, and to help launch a trendsetting Christian film company.

This once-broken kid had made it through layers of challenge working early days and late nights, sacrificing traveling home to see family, and not going out because I was so focused on catching my dream. That kid was now on the Oscars Red Carpet.

I look back now and realize I never doubted myself. Call it innocence or even naivete, but I knew my life would be different than anything I'd grown up with.

I always felt different. Not so much special, but the odd-duck in the room. I never quite fit in, and while it was lonely and I was bullied for being different, I don't regret staying on my path.

I now run my own business. I'm the first Latina to own a PR and film agency serving the entertainment industry in Nashville and what I love most is helping clients realize their dreams.

To contact Jackie Marushka for speaking, writing, and PR—or to request her as a panelist or moderator for your next conference—please email jackie@marushkamedia.com or visit marushkamedia.com

Quotable: Think Good. Say Good. Do Good.

Scan for more about Jackie Marushka.

SETH MOSLEY

How a Three-Time Grammy Winner Lives Full Circle

Seth Mosley is a three-time Grammy winner and one of the most awarded songwriters and producers in Christian and country music. He has been named Songwriter and Producer of the Year, has written/produced 33 Billboard #1 songs, and has songwriting credit on over 1,500 songs. He is the founder of Full Circle Music and creator of the Song Chasers Songwriting Community.

Full Circle

Our company is called Full Circle Music for a reason. When I was a kid, my first CD was *Take Me to Your Leader* from the band Newsboys. In 2009, the first label record I got to work on as a producer and co-writer in Nashville was Newsboys' *Born Again.*

My whole life has been this big series of full circle moments, working with people that I grew up listening to and loving. I have now worked and collaborated with incredible Christian artists including TobyMac, Michael W. Smith, KING & COUNTRY, Unspoken, Jeremy Camp, Jon Foreman, Christine D'Clario, Matt Kearney, MercyMe, Hillsong Worship, Bethel Music, Elevation Worship, Skillet, Casting Crowns, and many more. I've also had the pleasure of working with incredible country acts including High Valley, Rodney Atkins, Tim McGraw, Blake Shelton, Gabby Barrett, Luke Combs, and James TW.

That's one of the big reasons I wanted to start the Full Circle Music Academy and the Song Chasers Songwriting Community. I want to help other musicians along their journey.

My 10,000 Hours and World Tour

I've been a music fan as far back as I can remember. When I got home from school every day, I would go down to the basement, turn up records, and jam on a plastic hockey stick. Music was the thing I always wanted to do. I had no plan B. I had to make it work.

Thankfully, I've had great mentors that have helped me on my way. One thing leads to the next, and I've built my career a little bit at a time.

I started out as an artist—most people do when they're passionate about music. I taught myself piano and guitar. When I got into my teenage years, I started leading on stage at church.

Eventually, I figured out a way to record some of my songs on my parents' computer. When you're from a small town, there are no recording studios. You've just got to figure it out. I saved money from mowing grass and teaching guitar lessons to buy basic gear and start a recording studio in our basement. I would only come up for air, food, and water. I released some things on my own in high school, and then some friends asked me to record them too. That was where I found my calling as a music producer and songwriter. I learned the art of the creative process by doing it over and over again.

After I graduated high school, I was hired straight into a little recording studio in Columbus, Ohio. I was being paid full-time to do something I had planned to go to college to learn! That is where I got my 10,000 hours.

Wanting to start my own thing, I then toured around the world with my band Me In Motion for more than five years.

Initially, we would make a list of cities we wanted to tour, and since we were a Christian band, we would look up local churches and cold call 40 or 50 of them a day. If we got one or two to say yes, that was a big win for us. When we were starting out, we would book the whole tour just by getting on the phone and building relationships with promoters and local pastors. I believe you need to start doing it on your own before you bring in a booking agent or manager. You've got to learn how it works, and you've got to have something worth booking first.

From our very first tour, we brought opening bands with us, bands that I had worked with as a producer. We always felt like everything was a lot more fun as a team, even as we were piled in a van together, driving around through the middle of the night all across the country, setting up our own PA system, and doing it all. It was definitely a learning experience.

We ended up touring 10 different countries and played one thousand shows.

Taking the Leap and Moving to Nashville

Eventually, I decided to move to the center of country and Christian music—Nashville, Tennessee. If you want to be a part of country or Christian music, Nashville is the place to be.

I was young, and I wanted to go all in. I had no reason not to. I thought of it as an experiment. I figured even though I might fail, I could always move back to Ohio, go to college, and get what I considered a "regular" job if I needed to.

Get Ahead with a Servant's Heart

I've always maintained the habit of looking for ways to serve people. That's how I look at everything in business. It's always give first, not ask, not take. As Zig Ziglar said, "You can have everything in life you want if you will just help other people get what they want."

For me, much more important than being the guy on stage is helping other dreamers get there. That realization launched me into my incredibly successful role behind the scenes as a songwriter and Grammy-winning producer, which in turn, has given me the platform to mentor up-and-coming musicians on their journeys. The irony is that serving led me to success.

Full Circle Music Academy

After writing 29 Billboard #1 songs, I created the Song Chasers Songwriting Course and Community to share all I know about songwriting. I always tell people, songwriting is 90% perspiration and 10% inspiration. But you've got to do the 90% to be there for that 10% when it happens. Those are the moments songwriters live for. The songs are out there, and I believe they come from a place outside of us. It's our job to show up to grab them and steward them well.

We developed something that has not existed until now: a baby-step plan for the music industry. We take you step by step from the groundwork of deciding what you want to do, setting goals, creating a personal budget, and building your network, all the way through developing your skills and knowledge, to eventually, charging a premium for your services.

Most people aren't working a job where they can see the direct fruit of their labor. But when you write a song, you have it right there. That's an amazing thing. I can't really describe it any other way than as a God thing. God is a creator, and we get to co-create with him. I think when people realize the power of that, they're hooked.

We also added Song Chasers, which is an ongoing membership community where people get access to live and pre-recorded trainings on everything you can imagine related to songwriting, music, production, and promoting yourself. And an artist can implement this training in the context of a community, which is so valuable.

Many of our Song Chasers come to our yearly boot camp, which has grown a lot since our first 30-person meet-up in 2016. Our most recent boot camp had 300 people. It's become a family reunion of sorts for many members who have been collaborating, co-writing, and becoming friends virtually.

The testimonials of life experiences and transformational success have exceeded our wildest hopes. I still get goosebumps just thinking about some of them. Those are the kind of wins that are big to me, even bigger than the Grammys.

Mentors Along the Way

I have many mentors to thank who showed me the way. The guy that first hired me when I graduated from high school in 2005 used to run a studio, and he mentored me by showing me how to work in a room with other artists.

Ian Eskelin was the first producer that brought me to town in Nashville. I sent him a demo when I was 19. I still see him at the gym, and we have a good relationship.

Outside of music, Kyle Wilson is a mentor from whom I've learned so much about marketing and doing it in a way that's authentic, real, and from the heart. I don't know if we'd have our podcast, *Made It in Music*, if it weren't for Kyle Wilson's encouragement.

I also have to give a shout out to Craig Ballantyne, a great author, speaker, and high-performance coach.

There are many more mentors, some who probably don't even know they're my mentors. But I am grateful for every one of them.

Take action. If you learn about something that you believe will positively impact your business or personal life, implement it. Until you put the philosophies you read about into practice, they will do you no good. Only through taking steps forward will you see massive shifts in your life and success.

To connect with Seth Mosley about the Full Circle Music Academy or the Song Chasers Songwriting Community, visit fullcirclemusic.com or follow him on Youtube @OfficialFCMusic and Instagram @thesethmosley. Check out the podcast *Made It in Music* at madeitinmusic.com.

Quotable: Most people aren't able to see the direct fruit of their labor at work. But when you write a song, you have it right there. That's an amazing thing. I can't really describe it any other way than as a God thing.

PETE SCHNEPP

Anyone Can Be Anything in
Five to Ten Years

Pete Schnepp encourages what's possible, celebrates what's good, and positively impacts others by purposefully pursuing his best life. He is a world-traveling family man, investor, and entrepreneur. His businesses have been featured in the Inc 5000 and on ABC Spotlight, won the Gilbert Mid-Sized Business of the Year Award, and more. Pete lives in Gilbert, Arizona, with his amazing wife, son, and daughter.

My Transformational Journey

At work, I was the king of my domain. My clients respected me, and my staff did as I asked. But when I got home, I was told what to do and my kids did not do as I asked. Being a father was a complete role reversal from being a business owner or manager, and I had a lot of trouble with that. It was much easier for me to spend my time working than with my family, which meant I worked non-stop. This dynamic was a recipe for disaster.

My life was heading quickly in the wrong direction, without intention or purpose. I became roommates with my wife. We were passing each other in the house without love or affection and even resenting each other. I became obese, eating fast food daily and drinking every night. I was addicted to chewing tobacco. I was not present when I was home. Worst of all, I didn't realize I had any problems, or that life could, and should, be better.

There were several things that were critical in my transformation from living a life in a downward spiral to creating the life of my dreams with intention and purpose:

C-PAP

As my poor health choices led to weight gain, it also led to snoring, which led to lack of sleep for my wife, which led to more relationship struggles.

I didn't think much of it until I went to a bachelor party, slept in a room with a bunch of other guys, and got called out for snoring there too!

One of the guys happened to be in medical school and told me that I seriously needed to get it checked out. So, I found a sleep doctor, and he told me I had sleep apnea. My brain was waking up every 20 or 30 minutes, so I never got any good sleep, and neither did my wife! He said that using this machine, a C-PAP, would change my life. He said my energy would go through the roof, I would lose a lot of weight, my business would thrive, and my wife would be exhausted because my sex drive would go through the roof. He was right!

The C-PAP turned out to be the first major catalyst in a complete personal transformation over the next few years.

Relationship Counseling

At some point, we decided to try going to church together. We enjoyed the positive message each week, and from it came an opportunity to go through a relationship class called Re-Engage.

This was a turning point in our marriage because it gave us a program, an outlet, and a way to communicate what we weren't communicating. We re-committed to each other and our marriage and slowly got back on a good path.

The Miracle Morning

I listened to a book, *The Miracle Morning* by Hal Elrod, and committed to doing the miracle morning as the book described for 90 days. I started waking up at 4:45 a.m., five days per week, which created dedicated time to work on myself each morning.

I started making sense of what was going through my head and finding clarity on what I wanted. This was the kickstarter for a morning success routine that drastically changed my life and created many positive habits I still practice daily.

What Do You Want?

A business coach I had started working with kept pushing me to answer the question for my small painting business: What do you want? How big do you want the business to grow?

It was hard for me to answer, and scary, because I knew that growing my painting business would require MORE work, and there was no guarantee of additional profits! There were plenty of other, similar companies that forced revenue growth only to make the same profit, or less.

So, I came up with my answer: I want to Earn More and Work Less. This became a driving theme for the next several years of my life. The question "What do I want?" continued to re-surface.

I also started asking myself questions: *What would life be like as a divorced dad? A lot of people are divorced nowadays. It's not necessarily a bad thing. But is that what I want?* I decided that it was not what I wanted or who I wanted to be.

What kind of dad do I want to be? Do I want to be this overweight dad that works all the time, gets rich, and one day looks back and says, "I wish I would have spent more time with my kids?"

The answer was no, and this helped guide my decisions for the coming years. During my soul-searching to find out what I really wanted and how to define it, three words kept coming up: health, wealth, and happiness. From then on, it became a matter of defining what this looked like for me, what the optimal blend was, and how I defined my goals in each of these categories.

Copycat

Why reinvent the wheel? I continually researched successful, wealthy, and high-achieving people. What are their behaviors, beliefs, and characteristics? After all, my entire life I've done pretty well at being a copycat—copying systems and processes that others have perfected and learning from their mistakes. *I simply needed to find the right people to copy.*

Health

"Put *your* oxygen mask on first so *that* you can help your kids with their masks." Maybe it was a matter of timing, but when I heard this on a podcast, it really resonated with me.

I realized that I needed to become selfish to be selfless. If I wanted to be the best dad and husband I could be, live a long life, be a good role model, and pursue my full potential, I needed to take care of myself.

I made a commitment to a healthy lifestyle, and I now had a compelling reason, and permission, to be selfish in taking time for myself. I used lunchtime as workout time and started a replacement habit of packing healthy snacks and lunches. By having a lunch bag next to me at all times filled with healthy snacks, I had no excuse. Slowly but surely, it worked. I lost over 60 pounds and completely transformed my body and overall health level.

Meditation

Another common thing I saw successful people do was meditate. It was part of *The Miracle Morning* too. I started with a free app called Headspace. It was challenging and boring, but I kept with it and tried several different types of meditation. I was committed. I found one that I really liked, a Wayne Dyer

"Ah" meditation, which incorporates manifestation through visualization and sound, and it's become an integral part of my life. Another meditation tool I continue to use is called Brain Tap. I truly believe meditation is one of the single most important habits I've incorporated into my life.

Vision Boards

I built a large vision board on my wall. I look at it regularly—all the things I want to do, accomplish, and be. And I do this with emotion. It triggers something in the brain. In fact, there are certain pictures on my vision board that I have come to experience in real life. It didn't cost much money, it just took a bit of time, dedication, and intention.

Journaling Is for Nerds!

That's what I used to think. I now have a book filled with five years of my hopes, dreams, fears, victories, failures, ideas, plans, and much more. There is something special about putting pen to paper every morning with no distractions. Over a five-year span, I got off the wagon several times—there are big lapses in my journal, and I regret not keeping it a priority. I love the idea of having the deepest part of my life documented so my kids or grandkids can one day know me on that level. For the last six months of these five years, I've been journaling more than ever before because I now understand the power of it.

Although it's not a regular habit, I also create lists: How would I describe the best version of Pete? How do I act? What is my relationship with money? What's my relationship with food? What's my relationship look like with my kids? What does being a role model husband and dad mean? What does health, wealth, and happiness look like in my best life? Where do I want my life to be in 10 years?

Affirmations

Have you ever told yourself how amazing you are? I think very highly of daily affirmations. I was very intentional about creating the list of the things I want to tell myself every day, and it is part of my morning routine. I've changed the affirmations up a few times over the last several years because several of them have come true and I am now affirming bigger and better things for myself! I fully believe what you say to yourself and what you think has a big impact on the quality of your life and who you become.

"You Are the Average of the Five People You Spend the Most Time With."

You may have heard this before, and I took it to heart. I made a commitment to surround myself with people who were excelling in health, wealth, and happiness. This led me to join a group called EO, the Entrepreneurs Organization, a global organization with local chapters of business owners who help each other lead amazing lives and businesses. EO pushed me to aim higher, expect more, and be better.

In addition to EO, I've engaged mentors and coaches for myself and my businesses. Coaches provide a different level of advice than mentors or peers. The combination of peers, mentors, and coaches will raise your standard and help you get what you want faster. This was also a common trait of many of the most successful people in the world—they have coaches that push them, perfect their craft, and help navigate their journey.

Breathwork

I was at an EO event, and a facilitator did a breathwork session. I had no idea what to expect, but it was transformational. By breathing, I had an out of body experience. It felt like I was floating and vibrating. I connected with the Universe, with my Creator. I came out with a whole different perspective on my purpose in life and why I wake up every day. There are many types of breathwork; what I experienced was a form of holotropic breathwork.

I try to do this at least a few times per year and each time I have a powerful, yet different, experience. Let's say you got to meet your Creator and your Creator introduced you to the person that you are supposed to be. Then, you returned to your life as you know it…. Is there anything you would change?

Cold Plunges

I've done some cold plunging over the last several years. By doing things that are hard, you train your brain to believe in yourself. An easier way to do this is called "acute cold exposure."

When I shower in the morning, I start with cold water…for 30 seconds to a minute…sometimes I'll do the entire shower cold. Telling yourself you are going to take a cold shower, turning the dial on cold, and forcing yourself to get the cold exposure does something to your brain that is hard to describe. It makes you start to feel invincible, confident, and powerful. One minute of cold water in the shower over time can completely transform how you think, act, and feel about yourself.

To Laugh or to Learn

Before my transformation began, I listened to a lot of Howard Stern while on the road. It was the most entertaining show on the radio, and I couldn't get enough.

As I began my transformation, I knew that my drive time was valuable learning and personal development time, so I committed to replacing Stern with audiobooks and podcasts. For the next several years, my vehicle was a mobile university where I got a business degree, personal development degree, and real estate degree. This switch was a game-changer.

Givers Gain

In my study of high achievers and wealthy people, a common trait was giving. I read somewhere, "If you won't give a dollar when you have $100, why would you think you'd give $1,000 when you have one million dollars?" The philosophy of givers gain is that by giving, you will actually receive. I had never thought about philanthropy in this way, but it works on all levels.

I've used givers gain in several ways in my life, first in my relationship with my wife. When we were at an all-time low, I committed to giving over and over with no expectations. I went out of my way to please her, and I did not expect to get favors back, which was a big change for me. Eventually, I started getting everything I wanted in return and MORE!

I knew someone locally who ran a small non-profit helping homeless children in Phoenix. I had never donated money before—we were always so concerned with our own finances and well-being—but I committed to a small monthly contribution. Not only did it make me feel good about myself, it also led to introductions which led to increased business.

I also challenged myself to come up with ways to incorporate givers gain into my business, so we developed a Fresh Start Program, where we provide free services to people in need. Eventually, we started getting press releases and publicity for our acts of service, which led to more exposure and new paid work.

The Compound Effect

I had read *The Compound Effect* a long time ago. I read it again while starting my transformational journey, and another two times after that.

Everything in life compounds. You are the compound effect of what you think and what you do. If you eat fast food every day or an organic salad every day, what do you think the compound effect on your body will be in 10 or 20 years?

Once you gain clarity on WHO you want to be and what you want YOUR life to be like, you can use the compound effect to your advantage to help get there by instilling habits, behaviors, and repetitive actions that will lead you to become the next best version of yourself.

The magic of compounding is the exponential growth and change that happens over time, which most people never experience because they give up too soon. Do the things that others won't, so you can live a life that others can't. There are a million excuses for people to not take control of their lives. If you want something you've never had, you have to do something you've never done. It's not easy, but it's worth it.

Clear, Deliberate, Purposeful

These three words spoken at a business conference were so powerful for me that I came home and wrote them at the top of my whiteboard. They've been there ever since. It's a reminder that I have the choice, opportunity, and power to live an intentional life. So many people are living like a leaf in the wind that's blowing them somewhere they don't want to go yet are doing nothing about it. Life is an opportunity. These three words remind me to be clear on what I want, deliberate with my time, and purposeful with my actions.

BHAG: A Big, Hairy, Audacious Goal

Over the years, I've struggled with goal setting. I've gone from being a die-hard goal setter, to not wanting to set goals and disappoint myself, not knowing what I wanted, to being a die-hard believer in goals again.

A few years after I married my wife, I found a sheet with some goals I had jotted down, and one was to settle down with an amazing woman. We had a nice laugh about that. The reality is, I've come to realize that most of the goals I've previously written down have come to fruition.

At the beginning of my transformative journey, with my new thinking time in the mornings and newfound clarity on what I wanted, I came up with a BHAG: Five Years to Freedom. I wanted financial freedom and time freedom, to have the time to enjoy my family, and to travel. So, I wrote it down and posted it on my vision board, along with many images and quotes that portray a life of freedom. This became the driving force in all of my decisions for the next five years.

For me, real estate rental income was the easiest and best way to achieve the freedom and lifestyle I was seeking. After four years of living clearly, deliberately, and purposefully, I realized that I had indeed achieved financial freedom and time freedom. It didn't happen exactly how I planned, but it did happen. The life that I am living now is exactly the life I dreamed of, wrote down in detail, meditated about, put pictures of on my vision board, and described in my daily affirmations. It's truly amazing, and it can happen to anyone.

The Pursuit

Although I've written a lot about being clear on the end result you want, the reality is that true happiness and transformation are in the journey.

By chasing your dreams, you are forced to become a better person by overcoming obstacles, including your own head trash and self-doubts. It's through all of the ups and downs along this pursuit of your best self and your best life that you will find transformation and happiness, not upon the completion of a specific goal.

The Decision

Many little things have made big impacts in my life, and it all started with the decision that I wanted, *and deserved*, a better life for myself and my family. Today, I can honestly say that I am living the life I dreamed of and wrote about for several years, and am now creating the life of my new dreams!

Contact Pete Schnepp if you're interested in discussing your personal development journey or are looking for a no sweat way to build your financial and time freedom through real estate. Go to www.prs.properties, www.peteschnepp.com, or email him at pete@prs.properties.

Quotable: It all started with the decision that I wanted, **and deserved**, a better life for myself and my family.

Check out my No Sweat Real Estate Investing Program.

JOELL MOWER

How Tragedy Led to Grace and Forgiveness

Joell Mower is CEO of DomiNic's Place and leader of The Mower Group real estate team. As a youth advocate, Joell worked with Life Teen and spoke in high schools about forgiveness as a member of The Peace Warriors. This inspired her to build an organization to support hope in our most vulnerable youth. After the death of Joell's son in 2012, this goal was achieved through DomiNic's Place.

A Phone Call

It was a few minutes before 3:00 a.m., on July 25, 2012, and I had just awakened from a sound sleep when the phone rang.

Ken, my husband of 35 years, answered the call and was on for a few minutes with his back to me before hanging up. As he turned around, I caught a glimpse of his face in the shadows and knew the news was not good.

We had experienced troubling calls before, as our son Dominic suffered from the disease of addiction and had been known to reach out to us at all hours. I felt my chest tighten. We thought he was doing well, so hearing the phone ring now, at that hour, was especially worrisome.

The caller was a neighbor of Dominic's. She told us there were police cars, fire trucks, and ambulances at the shop where he lived and worked. She had heard there was a shooting. Even with our past experiences, we were not prepared to receive a message like this one. Dominic was not a violent person and, as far as we knew, did not own a gun. I still wonder at a strange thought I had at that moment: *What would be worse? Knowing our son had been shot or knowing he had shot someone else?*

Ken and I decided not to make the 20-minute drive to the shop and wait to hear more. Looking back, I think we were afraid of what we might discover.

I do not remember what Ken was doing as we waited for the next call. My world and focus had narrowed, and I was restless, unable to take a deep breath or stay in one place. I said a chaplet, a prayer, as I paced. The Chaplet of Divine Mercy had been given to me just a few months before, and I did not yet know how powerful God's mercy is, what His promises would mean to me, or why He wanted me to have them.

The Miracle

I answered the phone when it rang the second time. I will never forget. I heard the detective say, "There is no easy way to tell you this…your son has passed." Dominic had been shot and killed.

Time stood still. I could not breathe or feel.

Then, almost immediately, a miracle happened. As I closed my eyes, I saw the words, *Pray for the person who did this*. Without thinking, I followed the instructions that would change my life and the murderer's as well.

In that moment of prayer, I was able to forgive and feel compassion for the person who murdered our son.

Mercy

How I wished my act of forgiveness had the power to alleviate the excruciating pain that engulfed me. I would soon learn on a very deep level what Dominic used to call the "two-foot drop." It is the process of our consciousness transcending the "thoughts in our minds" to the "feelings, trust, and knowing in our hearts." I would come to experience and comprehend how merciful God is and how He always gives us exactly what we need, when we need it, if we pay attention and are open to His help.

I do not remember telling Ken the news of Dom's death or what his reaction was. Even so, there are some details forever etched in my memory of that day: watching our daughter vomit in anguish when she heard her brother was dead, the 90-minute drive to my hometown to tell my mother what happened, and holding her up as she collapsed while hearing my brothers cry out in shock and pain.

During our visit to the police department later that same day, we learned about a young woman who was shot along with Dominic. She had survived major injuries and was in the hospital. She insisted on speaking with us to let us know Dominic had attempted to save her life and that she would ensure the murderer would be apprehended and brought to justice.

Survival

After finally arriving home late that evening and needing some sort of normalcy, Ken and I decided to take our dog for a walk. I was struck by the first of many new truths as we moved through the quiet, deserted streets under the stars. I turned to Ken and said, "We've experienced our worst nightmare as parents today, and we are still standing."

The "two-foot drop" from my head to my heart became a part of my daily reality as we moved through the next days, weeks, and months. I was reminded repeatedly of how God's love and care are manifested through the presence of revelations, experiences, and people in my life. I learned men grieve differently than women, and each person has their own grief timeline. The successful navigation of my relationships with Ken, our daughter, extended family, and friends were not to be expected or taken for granted. Even getting out of bed each day was a major decision. God did not promise to remove the always present, numbing pain and the daily challenge of missing Dominic. He did, however, provide a roadmap to healing and hope. The gift of forgiveness was to play a very big part in that journey.

I was told 600 people attended Dominic's funeral Mass to show their love for us and for Dominic. I heard there were undercover police officers in attendance hoping to see people of interest in the investigation. I remember removing my sunglasses. I wanted to look into each person's eyes and be as fully present as possible.

After Mass, there was a long line of people of all ages who waited to tell me how much Dom's friendship had helped them and what a positive difference he had made in their lives. I missed most of the reception, as I listened to each heart-healing testimonial.

Along with his death, the news reports concentrated on Dominic's past transgressions. As Ken wrote in his impact statement, "It would be superficial for someone who did not know Dominic personally to look at the facts of this case and his history and draw conclusions. We have learned a person's life is so much more than what may be depicted in a newspaper or contained in a crime report."

We also recognized there would be no winners in our situation. As the mother of the person who took our son's life sat alone on the courthouse bench, we reached out to let her know we understood that there were two mothers who lost their son that day.

Help and Support

I am a Realtor by profession, and Ken and I have attended a personal growth conference, Mastermind, almost every August for the past 20 years. It had only been three weeks since Dominic was killed, but his funeral had taken place, and we decided to attend that year, knowing the message would be uplifting and we would be surrounded by people who cared about us.

It seemed like a good idea until we were standing outside the convention center. I froze for a few moments as I looked up at the huge building and all the people. Taking a deep breath, I held Ken's hand, and we went inside together. I do not recall exactly how we shared the traumatic experience of Dom's death with our friends there, but I do remember being enveloped with love and compassion. Looking back, I believe my years of attending Mastermind and other conferences and the lessons I learned as a result, were preparatory tools for navigating the tragedy that had been awaiting me.

As suggested by several people at home, we also attended GriefShare. I was angered by what they termed "new normal" because I knew nothing would ever be normal again. Right after Dom died, I felt isolated as it was hard for me to imagine that anyone else had ever suffered or felt the excruciating pain I was experiencing. I did not consider taking my own life to end the torment, but I was ambivalent about living. I could not come out of myself to realize Ken, our daughter, and other family members were also in agony and needed me to be there for them. The seven other couples who had lost children in our GriefShare group helped me to realize everything was not about me as they shared their heartaches. Through them, I was challenged to comfort and be present for others while my own heart was breaking.

Attending the Mastermind conference and the eight weeks of GriefShare helped us prepare for the preliminary hearing, which would determine if there was enough evidence to take the man accused of Dominic's murder, who I will call MM, to a full jury trial.

The preliminary hearing ended with the judge ordering MM to stand trial. Some of the testimony was graphic and extremely painful to hear. The young woman who was shot with Dominic was able to identify MM, and her courageous documentation was directly responsible for his conviction. There was also a recorded phone conversation where MM admitted to killing Dom and trying to kill her.

Conquering a Heart

In August of the next year, Ken and I were in San Diego attending the same Mastermind conference. The jury trial was scheduled to begin the day after we returned home.

We received a phone call from the prosecuting attorney. MM had decided not to go to trial, had agreed to a plea bargain of 64 years to life, and had pled guilty to first-degree murder, attempted murder, and special allegations of using a gun during the commission of the offenses.

Even though it was not a requirement, we were relieved our daughter and the young woman MM had attempted to kill both agreed with the plea bargain. Neither one wanted him to be free in their lifetimes, but the preliminary trial had been arduous, both physically and emotionally, and none of us were prepared to relive everything again in the public eye.

At a sentencing, the family can read impact statements to the person who committed the crime against them. I prayed the night before, asking God what He wanted MM to know and to help me to communicate it. I knew the Holy Spirit was guiding me as I wrote my statement.

The next morning, MM stood emotionless in the courtroom as Ken and I described how our lives had changed and what our family had endured as a result of his actions. As I read my statement, it was as if MM and I were the only two people in the room. Nothing I read seemed to affect him, until I said, "I believe God is using me to tell you how much He loves you."

It was then that tears began to run down his cheeks. I told him I had been praying for him, even before I knew who he was, and had forgiven him, not through my strength, but through God's grace. I said that I was forgiving him for me. He had already taken our son, and I would not allow him to take the rest of my life too by drinking the poison of unforgiveness and expecting him to die. I said it would never be too late for him to choose to change his life for the better and help others, even in prison.

My forgiveness does not mean I will ever forget what MM has done, believe what he did is okay, or hide or deny my feelings about what happened. It is something I did in my heart and is not dependent on him being sorry. It is leaving judgment to God, reinforcing my personal power, caring for my physical, mental, and spiritual health, and surrendering anger and blame. I received an incredible gift by choosing to pray for MM on the morning of Dominic's death. Forgiving has brought me peace, joy, and hope amid the sorrow, grief, and pain.

I have come to believe that mercy and forgiveness, while often thought to be weaknesses, are the most powerful "weapons" in the world, because they can conquer otherwise untouchable hearts.

New Normal

MM and I now write letters to each other and I have continued to pray for him. While he did not initially believe I had really forgiven him, he has now accepted it. He has written to me about how he has remained clean and sober to honor me and my family. He is taking classes to become a counselor to help others like him in prison and is training service dogs, something at which he has become quite accomplished. He seldom complains about his circumstances and always tries to be upbeat.

I cannot help but think how different the outcome of this story might have been for MM and for me, if I had not chosen to forgive him. The greatest gift for me was the ability to pray the Divine Mercy Chaplet at the hour of Dominic's death, allowing MM and Dominic to experience the unfathomable Mercy of Jesus.

After all these years, I have a glimpse of what my "new normal" is. I know I will always be sad on some level and the gift of tears is never far from the surface. Holidays, Dom's birthday, and the anniversary of his death are always challenging. I have a difficult time with small talk and tend to go deep very quickly. I have chosen to celebrate and even search for joyful moments and not feel guilty, as if I am somehow dishonoring Dominic by being happy. I know he would want that for me. Choosing to feel happiness helps me to heal. I wake up most mornings with gratitude for what I have, rather than hopelessness for what I am missing. Most of all, instead of wanting to die, I've asked God for at least 10 more years so I can see our grandchildren grow up, witness our daughter who is also a Realtor thrive and heal, and celebrate a 50th wedding anniversary with Ken. I love to talk about Dominic to whoever will listen. Bringing him up in conversation does not make me more sad, as there will always be sadness on some level, nor remind me of his death, something I will never forget. I am humbled to know my wounds cannot develop scars without the love and help of others and the sharing of our stories.

I have founded DomiNic's Place, a non-profit to honor Dom and to prevent other parents from experiencing the loss of a child. Our mission is to create a community where young people can feel safe, find hope, and receive healing for wounded hearts and where their unique gifts are recognized and encouraged. The vision is to enable young people to contribute positively to their communities by providing tools, resources, and mentors that build their self-worth and purpose in an environment of forgiveness, encouragement, and acceptance. We are currently collaborating with another non-profit, Youth Recovery Connection, to save lives through prevention and recovery services.

At DomiNic's Place, there is a "Forgiveness Wall" in the entry with a picture of MM and the word Forgiven. The young people we serve will be encouraged to post the names of people they want to forgive or from whom they would like to receive forgiveness. Like MM, they will be asked to leave any harmful deeds behind them and to choose a new life, making a positive difference for others and themselves.

I am also a member of Sacred Sorrows, an incredible resource for mothers and grandmothers whose children have died. *"Where deep grief meets the mystery of Grace."* The retreats they offer, both virtual and in person, are a safe and sacred place of healing in a shared community like no other I have experienced since Dominic's death.

Hope

I am working to create HOPE for myself and my family without Dom's physical presence in our lives. His love and spirit will always be alive in our hearts, minds, and souls until we meet in Heaven. Sometimes I ask God to give him a hug for me, even though I know he does not need it, because of how much I miss being able to hug him myself.

If you have lost a child or loved one, I am hoping this story will bring you hope and will allow me to somehow walk by your side. I am wishing you a good life where you embrace relationships with people who are still with you and share stories of loved ones who have passed. Where you experience joy along with sorrow, as they are both true, and where, rather than allowing the toxicity of unforgiveness to hold you hostage, you embrace the healing powers of mercy and forgiveness.

To have a conversation about the loss of a child or the power of forgiveness, reach Joell Mower at 831-818-3878 or by email at joelldfmower@gmail.com. Joell offers a connection to powerful resources, including her organization DomiNic's Place, as well as The Divine Mercy Chaplet, Mastermind, GriefShare, and Sacred Sorrows.

Quotable: I have come to believe that mercy and forgiveness, while often thought to be weaknesses, are the most powerful "weapons" in the world because they can conquer otherwise untouchable hearts.

STEVE TRENT

From Big Law to Building a Family Legacy with Real Estate

Steve Trent is president of Trent Property Company and Preferred Choice Homes. After a successful and entrepreneurial legal career, he is working with investors and families to help more people attain the benefits of home ownership.

A Simple Meeting

It was my banker who first gave me permission to think the unthinkable. He did it very simply and smoothly.

Bill was, and remains, the CEO of a thriving community bank in my area. We were meeting about my relatively detailed real estate business plan, which included both single-family rental properties and flips. After reading everything and listening to my verbal input, he looked at his chief credit officer and said, "It appears to me that Steve intends to be working on real estate full-time in a few years."

That comment was made in 2011, and it really grabbed my attention. I had been approaching real estate as a way to invest the financial rewards of a successful legal career. At least, that is what I had been telling myself. But I was actually acting like someone who wanted to make a career change.

Here was this very successful banker calmly evaluating the signals I was sending. He was not being negative or sarcastic. On the contrary, I was pretty sure I heard a hint of encouragement in his voice. After that meeting, I began to allow myself to at least consider the possibility of refocusing all of my professional time and energy on real estate or other entrepreneurial activities.

Legal Career

When I started practicing law, I enjoyed the work of a litigator so much that for years I would say to myself that I would do it for far less than I was paid. The work was challenging and the hours were long, but as a young lawyer, I took pride in consistently working 80-hour weeks. It was fun!

All those hours doing work I loved led to a lot of success. I had never been a natural public speaker. In college, I remember how incredibly unpleasant

I found speech class to be. I muddled through the moot court classes and other public speaking opportunities in law school. But in private law practice, I discovered something almost magical when I realized that deep preparation and command of a topic dramatically enhances one's ability to speak persuasively on that topic. This was liberating and opened many doors. I began to actually look forward to trials and other contested hearings!

Leadership

I was very fortunate to work at Baker Donelson—a law firm that provided outstanding opportunities for growth. Some law firms have a culture where the younger attorneys are expected to "stay in their lane." Baker Donelson was growing rapidly and promoted a much more entrepreneurial culture than did most other firms. I saw the opportunity to develop a strong practice focused on employment law, an increasingly important area of specialization in the 1990s. No other firm in my geographic area had made a meaningful effort to specialize on a large scale, so the door was wide open.

With the help of Jennifer Keller (who has since risen to the level of president and COO of Baker Donelson) and many other great attorneys and staff members, we carved out a substantial piece of the employment law market in our region. Eventually, we were by far the leading employment law practice in our market.

The leaders at Baker Donelson saw our success and encouraged us to keep going. I was able to build a book of clients that enabled me to easily become a partner. Then, to my surprise, I was offered leadership of the entire Labor & Employment Practice Group. Within weeks of becoming a partner in the firm, I was leading a practice group of attorneys across the entirety of our multi-state footprint. I was 33 years old.

Breakthroughs

I wanted to pursue big goals. I believed that our firm could establish one of the leading employment law practices in the country. With the support of Baker Donelson's leadership, we focused on building out a very strong employment law litigation practice. The firm was growing into other states and markets, and we played a major role in that.

Our successes and growth began to be acknowledged in very objective ways. One milestone I will never forget arrived when we appeared on the Top 10 list of *Employment Law 360*, a national publication. They compiled the data on the number of employment lawsuits involving every law firm in the United States. And Baker Donelson was in the Top 10 nationwide! I had expected success, but even I was a little shocked by this accomplishment.

I lived and practiced in Johnson City, Tennessee, and still live there today, which is a relatively small market in the context of a law firm like Baker Donelson. Nevertheless, I was elected to a seat on the firm's board of directors before my 40th birthday. That is an honor I will never forget.

I like to think I played a role in the firm's continued growth in the six years I served on the board. One thing I know for sure—I learned a staggering amount about business and success by spending time with the amazing people who served with me. Those experiences and discussions were incredible preparation for running my real estate businesses years later.

Changes

Life had given me tremendous professional opportunities. I had been able to enjoy the adrenaline rush of competitive litigation many times over. I had also enjoyed wonderful relationships with so many colleagues and clients over the years. And, to top it all off, I had played a large role in the growth of my practice area and my entire law firm. I enjoyed it all to the highest degree. Nothing was missing.

But, eventually, I began to realize that what I wanted was changing. In particular, I was losing my zeal for litigation. I think the constant adversarial nature was beginning to wear on me. I no longer eagerly anticipated the thrill of competition at a trial. Maybe it was my role in growing the business of the law firm. Or maybe it was just me. But my mind began to seek success in roles that were less adversarial and more "win-win."

After years of ownership in a large law firm, by 2010, I had benefited financially. I started thinking more and more about how to utilize some of those resources to diversify my financial future. I began to think about financial independence—maybe even not needing to work at all. (Spoiler: It turns out, not working at something I enjoy is not really an option for me. My idea of fun is too tied into improving my life and the lives of others for me to sit on the sidelines.)

I spent most of 2010 reading about ways to invest on the side. I was prepared to take some risks—I always have been. I think you are basically dying if you are constantly avoiding risk. In fact, I often think about the Peter Drucker quote about people who take risks making two big mistakes a year, while people who never take risks also make two big mistakes a year. I really believe in that statement, or at least the principle behind it. Being willing to seek life and business improvements through well-calculated risk-taking keeps us sharp and ultimately enhances our chances of wildly successful outcomes.

As I considered my options, I started thinking about my family and how they might be affected by my decision. As of 2010, Carol and I had been married for 21 years. Our sons, Andrew and John, were 13 and 10. Could I find something in which Carol could be active with me? Beyond that, was it possible to build something that could be a success vehicle for all four of us? Those questions became part of my criteria.

I settled on rental properties. I knew my legal background would be useful in that arena. Carol has a degree in accounting and had worked in that field for over a decade. That would be very helpful. We could take on a few rentals and see how it went. The boys were too young to help us, but we could show them the numbers along the way and see if we could spark an interest. In the meantime, I could continue my full-time legal career.

The first year exceeded our expectations. Real estate values in my area had dropped a lot during the Great Recession, but rental rates had barely dropped at all. The result was a wide selection of available rental properties that performed extremely well. Better still, we discovered that many of the available properties could be rehabbed and sold at a nice profit.

I started working harder to find more and better properties. We were seeing great results, so seeking more deals was the obvious next step. I remember taking Andrew and John with me for early morning property viewings and then going on to work later. I was starting to burn the candle at both ends. But, at 43, with a great family and a demanding career, I started to worry about where that road ended.

Growth

I knew we had a scalable business opportunity. But I had obligations to my family and to my law firm. I was far from ready to abandon a great legal career for anything, including a great business opportunity. Then, in a span of less than 24 hours, I had an idea that developed into a feeling of certainty. I knew I needed to add someone to our team and keep growing.

Someone who could focus 100% on the still very plentiful opportunities available in our market.

I had known Cliff since we were five years old and in kindergarten together. We had remained very close friends across all those years. He was at a place in his career where a change could make sense. We met for dinner and discussed the opportunity. It was crystal clear to both of us that we needed to take on this challenge.

Cliff came on board and brought tremendous energy to the business. No longer were we constrained by the demands of my legal career. I was able to refocus on my legal career and enjoy several more strong years, secure in the knowledge that we were growing a business that could be an outlet for my time and energy if I ever decided to take things in that direction.

Our real estate business grew rapidly. Within a few years, with Cliff handling acquisitions and overseeing the projects, we were flipping 50 single-family properties each year and we had compiled over 150 doors of rental units.

It was during those years that my banker gave me "permission" to think the unthinkable. We were discussing my business plan and arranging some financing when he made the comment about me planning to work full-time in real estate. It took me quite a long time after that day to actually make the transition, but from that day forward, I began to admit to myself that I at least wanted to eventually build a real estate business and not just a retirement plan.

A Family Business

My wife Carol was our real estate CFO from the very beginning. In 2011, she spent a few hours a week keeping track of things and writing a few checks. We talked about every deal and planned together. Carol's work grew more demanding with each passing year. Somewhere along the way, it became a full-time job for her.

I always enjoyed taking the boys around to view properties. Even after Cliff joined us, I would occasionally spend all or most of a day driving around East Tennessee with Andrew, John, or both. On the drive between properties, we would talk about things like cap rates, lending terms, and cash flow.

Andrew graduated from Lipscomb University with a finance degree in 2019 and joined us to manage vacation rentals. We started buying vacation rentals and have owned seven beach properties in South Carolina that Andrew has managed. In 2020, we began adding luxury cabins in the Smoky Mountains of Tennessee, and Andrew has managed those as well. More recently, he has added other projects.

In 2022, John also graduated from Lipscomb with a finance degree. He joined our business that summer. We have acquired seven beach properties in Florida, and John manages those along with other projects.

"Retirement" Is Not the Word

By 2022, it was clear that I needed to focus my energy on real estate. My legal career had been a tremendous blessing on every level. But, my passion was clearly with real estate. I made arrangements with Baker Donelson to begin phasing out of my practice. In a step that I would have viewed as inconceivable back in 2010, I "retired" from the firm effective February 1, 2023.

Retired. Ha! That is definitely not the word for what I have done. I am fully engaged in our business. And I have never had more fun. We continue to do the same things we have done since 2010, and we have grown into other niche areas of real estate. We flip homes and acquire rental properties. We also continue to run a thriving vacation rental business in multiple states. And more recently, we have added the next logical step in our progression—manufactured homes.

Vision for the Future

We have been buying and selling separate manufactured homes on land for a decade as part of our flip and rental businesses. A few years ago, I noticed that manufactured homes can be a very reliable and cost-effective housing solution. At first, this was a bit of a surprise. However, I came to realize that the federally regulated manufactured home industry—where homes are efficiently constructed indoors in a controlled environment—has a lot to offer in a country with a tremendous housing shortage.

Given the dramatic increases in real estate values in recent years, not to mention the increases in interest rates, the affordability of manufactured housing is now more important than ever. For many in the United States, it is the only practical option for purchasing a new home.

We have opened one retail location for manufactured homes, Preferred Choice Homes, and intend to open another very soon. With our investors, we are developing entire subdivisions for placement of manufactured homes.

I have been blessed beyond my capacity to comprehend. We built a family business that offers tremendous opportunities to help others in scenarios where everyone wins. When we rehab a home that was struggling, the list of winners goes on and on—the buyers, the contractors who did the work, the agents in the transaction, the neighbors who are delighted to see a better home, our investors, our lenders, and even the local government. The same is true when we sell a manufactured home. The goal is always for everyone to win.

I loved practicing law—but now I love every day of working with Carol and our sons to provide attainable housing options to people who need them.

Steve Trent has successfully purchased, operated, and sold hundreds of investment properties in the United States. To learn more about investment in attainable housing, contact him at Steve@Trentpropertycompany.com or 423-202-6076.

Quotable: America is headed toward a golden age of industrial redevelopment. Tremendous opportunity lies within the need to provide high-quality housing that is affordable for those in the workforce.

GREG ZLEVOR

Breaking Emotion's Chains
Embracing Emotion's Wisdom

Greg Zlevor, president of Westwood International and HopeMakers founder, has worked with Johnson & Johnson, The Singapore Police Force, Volvo, General Electric, and many other high-profile companies, co-authored eight #1 bestselling books, and shared the stage with greats including Jim Rohn, George Land, and M. Scott Peck.

The Chains of Emotions

I was born in Milwaukee, Wisconsin, and I grew up in Racine, just a short distance south, near Lake Michigan.

I went to grade school and high school in Racine. I enrolled at Lawrence University in Appleton, Wisconsin, for college. My first job was teaching science and coaching football in Appleton at Xavier High School.

I'm a cheesehead, a Packer fan, through and through. My whole family religiously cheers the Pack. They all stayed in Wisconsin.

I moved to Boston for graduate school. Out there, I completed my degree, got a job at the university, got married, had children, and unfortunately, also got divorced.

That catches you up on my first 45 years.

Since I moved away from my family when I left for Boston, those weekends after the divorce were quite long and lonely. Consequently, time with my kids was precious.

One Friday night, I took my son Daniel into Boston. We decided to visit Newbury Street, which if you're familiar with Boston, is very fancy—full of upscale stores, restaurants, and our favorite—ice cream.

The problem was, it was tough as hell to park. I drove around and around. NO luck.

"Daniel, let's double park right here at the end of the street and wait until someone moves. Then we'll be in position to pull up and take the spot as the person is pulling out."

We waited. And we waited.

Then, I finally saw brake lights come on: a car in the middle of a block. I zipped up. I gotta get this spot. At that moment, I also noticed this new car, backing up toward the spot from the opposite direction.

I thought, *No way, I'm getting this spot!* As soon as the car pulled out, I pulled into the left curb of the one-way street, getting in position and blocking the way.

The other car kept coming. The driver pulled right up next to our car, rolled down his window, and started yelling, "Hey, that's our spot!"

I angrily reached over Daniel and rolled down the passenger window to yell back. I said, "What? I've been waiting. It's my spot."

He said, "No, it's not. Move out. We were waiting at the end of the block!"

"I'm not moving anywhere!"

"Yeah, well, you wait and see what that car looks like when you get back. And when we see you, you'll look different too!"

"You're not doing nothing. I ain't movin'. This is MY SPOT." I rolled up Daniel's window, turned, and muttered some frustration.

Then my son caught my eye. "Daniel?" He was nine years old. Tears were running down his cheeks.

His voice quivered as he spoke. Shaking, he asked me.

"Dad, are they going to beat us up? Are they going to wreck the car?"

The incident and emotion had carried me away. I can't stand obnoxious drivers. I got triggered.

During the confrontation, Daniel "disappeared." I forgot what mattered.

Nothing replenishes me more than moments of fun and connection, especially with my son.

Realizing how shaken he felt, I quickly said, "Daniel, I'm sorry. Let's move the car and park where they won't find us."

Staying Connected to What Matters

A desire and goal for community, depth, acceptance, and conversation started for me back in college.

I spent a semester studying overseas in London. After that semester, I went backpacking for several weeks through Europe. I had so much fun. Every day, a new train, a new city, and new people.

One weekend, I was with two guys from San Francisco. We pulled into Innsbruck, Austria, on a Friday afternoon. As soon as we got to the hostel, we dropped our bags, ran to the bar, and sat down to enjoy the evening.

Lo and behold, two pretty girls sat next to us: Robin and Martha.

I took a fancy to Martha. She had black hair, blue eyes, and a radiant smile. I got so fancy I bought a round of drinks.

I started talking to Martha: "You enjoy reading? What's your favorite book? ... *The Road Less Traveled*, the book on personal and spiritual growth?! Me too. Best opening line ever: 'Life is difficult.'"

Enamored, I bought another round of drinks.

"How about movies? ... *Star Wars*? ... Me too! May the force be with you."

A beautiful woman. Fun, smart, open, and interesting to talk to. She was everything. Suddenly, they stood up. "Sorry, we gotta catch our train. Nice meeting you. Bye."

What!? No number or address. Gone! Poof! Lost forever. OUCH!

I continued my travels. Two weeks later, it was another day, a new train, a new city, and a new group of guys.

Ever travel with a friend who has an annoying habit? I'm that friend. I linger. It annoyed my friends. They saw me as slow. I saw it as being busy enjoying the awesomeness. Taking pictures with just the right frame and angle intrigued me. We were in the Salzburg Cathedral, and I was practicing my annoying habit, taking my time as the new guys hustled out.

I walked out of the Salzburg Cathedral, down the stairs, and scanned the square for my buddies. I spotted them talking to two girls.

"About time you met. What took you soooo long?"

"Greg!"

Miraculously, my buddies were talking to Robin and Martha! The girls gave me a big hug. I gave a big hug back. I didn't let go for seven days.

It was one week of bliss. More fun, laughter, deep conversation, and connection. With Martha, life was not difficult. It was exhilarating. It was everything that juiced me. She gave me life.

We parted ways, but this time I got her number.

She went back to University in Michigan. I went back to college in Wisconsin. We committed to staying in touch. In touch I stayed.

There were no cell phones. AOL was not invented. The internet didn't exist. We used hall phones and letters, with pens and paper. We communicated back and forth as much as we could.

And the relationship grew. During the Thanksgiving holiday, she came to spend time with my family. Over the Christmas holiday, I spent time with her family. It was getting so good that at spring break, I skipped going away with my college buddies and joined Martha on a trip to Florida.

That sealed the deal for me. I thought, *This is the one.*

When I got back to Wisconsin, I was excited to get that next letter. I checked my mailbox every day.

Finally, the letter arrived. I opened it up, and the first line crushed me. She wrote, "I can no longer go on being measly friends."

WHAT? You come to my family, I go to your family, I give up my buddies for spring break, and it's measly? MEASLY?

I was HURT. Scribble, scribble, scribble...scratch, scratch, scratch.... I don't recall what I wrote, but I was angry. I sent the letter, and it was over.

I finished college. I took my first job in Wisconsin. Four years later, I decided to go to graduate school in Boston.

To go from Wisconsin to Boston, one must drive through Michigan. Enough time had passed to quell the pain, but I still wondered about Martha.

I timed my trip for a possible lunch in East Lansing, Michigan. I called ahead. Martha would meet me.

So, I got there. Almost five years later, we sat down and did a little awkward small talk.

After small talk, she said to me, "What ever happened to our relationship?"

Ever have an "I told you so" moment gift-wrapped? This one was five years in the making. I said, "You wrote a letter that called our relationship measly."

Martha said, "I never said our relationship was measly."

I said, "Yes, you did. In your first letter after Florida, you called our relationship measly."

"I never said that."

I reached into my pocket. I still had the letter.

"Here it is." I pointed to the first line: "I can no longer go on being measly friends."

She looked at me. "You think that says measly? That's not *measly*, Greg. It's *merely*." Ironically, the letter had said exactly what I wanted to hear. I read and heard the opposite. I forgot what mattered.

I read measly, and I got angry and I held onto it. I didn't let go of measly. It cost me an important relationship.

Take a test with me. Put your fist in the air.

Now, every time you can think of when you've gotten angry, upset, hurt, frustrated, or anxious, about something that didn't matter to you at all, put up a finger. Try creating a list of those moments.

Why is this so hard? Because we don't have emotions unless it matters. This led me to an insight.

All my "ouch" times I made worse when I held onto the emotion and the story that fueled it.

What if there is something else that matters more than the emotion? What if emotions are simply messengers? What if the main role of emotions is to bring a message?

What if, when a difficult emotion shows up, I ask, *What is important to me? What really matters?*

Often, my emotions are like bottles in the ocean, they pop up and bob around on my surface until I notice them.

Anger? Anxiousness? Overwhelm? Resentment? If I hold onto the emotion, I bob and bounce around too.

What if I treat the emotion as a messenger, embrace it, and ask, *What is the message? What is important to me?*

I can notice the emotion, then I can ask, *Emotion, what is the message you bring me that matters even more?*

Thank you for bringing that message to me, Emotion. You have done your job. You can go now.

I can pause, let the emotion go, and ask, *If this is what matters, what is my next best step?*

Living Wisely by Breaking the Emotional Chain

As a consultant and speaker, I travel a lot for work. After one particularly long week on the road, I hustled to the airport, excited to get home for my son Daniel's birthday party.

As I was sitting at the gate for my connecting flight, I heard the announcement, "I'm sorry ladies and gentlemen, we are slightly delayed. The crew isn't ready yet."

Ready yet? You've had all week to get a crew ready.

Nervous, I looked at my watch and started calculating. I had a tight connection for my next flight. *I better make my next flight.* Time ticked by.

"Sorry about the delay. We are ready to board."

I calculated again. *Uh oh, I might not make my connecting flight home.*

I was sweating the whole flight. We landed. I only had nine minutes to make my connection.

Frantic, hoping my connecting flight was delayed too, I rushed out of the jetway and asked the attendant, "Where is the gate for the flight to Boston?

"Right there," he said, pointing to the next gate. *OMG!* The door was open and the plane was still at the gate. *I just made it!*

I ran over. "This is my flight, I can't believe I made it!" I panted to the gate agent.

"Sir, I'm sorry. The flight is closed."

"No, the flight's not closed. I see the plane right there. The door is still open. The flight's not closed."

"Sir, you don't need to raise your voice. Calm down."

Now, just a little note, in the history of calm down. No one's ever calmed down by someone saying calm down.

"That door's open. The plane is here. The flight isn't closed!" I gestured angrily toward the jetway. I leaned toward the door.

"Sir, if you go to get on that flight, I will call security."

"Your company is the one who made the mistake and didn't have the crew ready. I'm getting on this flight!"

She reached for the phone.

Arrghhhh!!!! I turned and stomped two big steps away.

Suddenly, I realized, I teach this stuff. *Hello, Anger, what's the message? It's been a long week and you really want to be home and celebrate Daniel's birthday.*

I don't want to argue or fight; I just want to get home.

I turned back to the agent. "Ma'am, I'm really sorry that I raised my voice. I know you're just trying to do your job. My apologies. It's been a long week. If I can get on that flight, I can make my son's birthday. Can you help me get on that flight?"

She paused, "Let me check with the pilot." She disappeared down the jetway to the plane.

When she returned a moment later, she said, "I talked to the pilot. He said you can board."

I learned again—don't get caught up in the emotion. Don't hold onto the messenger. Get the message, pause, and intelligently pursue what matters.

Embrace the Wisdom and Let the Messenger Go

If I embrace the wisdom of the messenger and get the message, I can save myself from ruining a night with my child, or losing a relationship, or missing a flight.

It's not the emotion that matters. It's the message. The wisdom is in the message.

Emotion. Pause. *Hello, Emotion. What message do you carry? What's important to me now?*

Get the message and let the emotion go. That's the wise move.

The true measure of a person's maturity and wisdom is determined by their ability to handle difficult emotions in trying times.

That's how the wise live wisely.

Contact Greg Zlevor about his books, coaching, leadership development programs, and speaking at gzlevor@westwoodintl.com, or look for Greg Zlevor on LinkedIn. To learn more about HopeMakers go to www.hopemakerscollective.com.

Quotable: The true measure of a person's maturity and wisdom is determined by their ability to handle difficult emotions in trying times.

Learn more about Greg Zlevor, Westwood International, and HopeMakers.

ROBIN BINKLEY

Breakthroughs and the Beautiful Other Side

Robin Binkley is a wife, mother, former long-term care administrator, podcaster, real estate investor, and entrepreneur. She is passionate about sharing what she has learned in investing and helping others reach their potential. She can help you take the next step in your journey to financial freedom.

What We Think and Plan Does Not Always Happen

In December 2022, I was anticipating the holidays. It was supposed to be the first Christmas season for Brett and me as new grandparents, and we were looking forward to spending time with our three-week-old twin grandbabies, Layne and Reese, and the rest of the family. I could not have expected the sudden turn of events.

At the beginning of the month, my daughter Kirsten and her husband Josh let us know that both babies had slight cold symptoms. That quickly turned into severe RSV, a respiratory virus, for both. Baby Layne was sent to the hospital and admitted to the intensive care unit (ICU) while Baby Reese stayed with Brett and me at our house. For one week, we cared for and loved this baby, working diligently to keep her well and out of the hospital.

But, as Baby Layne was healing and moving to a regular room at Texas Children's Hospital because of her improvements, Baby Reese took a turn for the worse. We took her to the doctor, and she was admitted to the hospital as well. Within 24 hours, Reese was in the ICU and on a ventilator.

The parents had both their newborns in the hospital. A complete and utter nightmare.

Kirsten and Josh lived at Texas Children's Hospital for another three weeks with Reese. It was touch and go on the ventilator for a total of eight days. Baby Layne was downstairs in pediatric in-patient care. Brett and I lived in the hospital with her for the remainder of her stay. My amazing daughter Ashton and her wife Rio rotated spending nights in the hospital to help care for Baby Layne too.

Layne was discharged nine days later, and we took her home to our house where she lived with us for two more weeks. We experienced Christmas with my daughter, her husband, and Baby Reese in the hospital. With Baby Layne at home with us and our other adult children, we washed clothes daily and brought water, drinks, snacks, and meals to the hospital for Kirsten and Josh. I would drive Layne to the hospital daily so Kirsten could hold and nurse her while the other baby was hooked up to every device to keep her alive.

This was the interim life we were all living. It was painful and exhausting.

The People in Your Life Are What Matter Most

I felt desperate and didn't know what to do or who to turn to. I began to realize that no amount of money or connection I had could solve this family health crisis. That was a startling realization to have.

That's when I turned to God and the people in my life. It is incredible to have a network of people who, when you need prayer, will do just that—they pray.

I was beside myself with grief and fear, hurting so deeply for my daughter and her family...not sure if her babies would live or die...or what physical or mental impairments the twins might face.

I had to be brave. I was the shoulder that could be cried on, the person to uplift, and the person who radiated, proclaimed, and declared hope for Kirsten and Josh in person. Visitation was limited to just a couple of people throughout the girls' stay at Texas Children's Hospital due to the severity of their conditions.

I would like to thank all the individuals who were there for me when I could not speak above my tears, when I was pleading for prayers and healing. They were available all hours of the day and night. I am overwhelmed by the memory of powerhouses who took the time to make me, my family, and these two beautiful twins a priority and who shared our need for prayer with the world.

I simply cannot explain the global prayer network that surrounded us. It was power outside of yourself. It was supernatural. I will be forever grateful for those who encouraged me and uplifted us all, for the messages that showed up at just the right moment to declare health, wellness, and God's promises.

God is clearly in the miracle business. Layne was discharged home first with Reese following two weeks later once she was able to wean off of the ventilator. The next two weeks proved to be tough, but daily, the twins regained their health.

After the ventilator, Reese had to relearn how to swallow. Both mom and baby worked with the speech therapist in the hospital, and slowly but surely, Reese was able to swallow again. Additionally, she had to detox from the heavy narcotics and paralytics her medical team gave her to keep her immobile while on the ventilator. It is amazing how the medications intended to help you also cause a lot of side effects. In Reese's case, she was unable to sleep. She would cry inconsolably. Noise and some textures, like some clothing or blankets, that touched her would set her off. You would also have to be extremely quiet. Through the coming months, this would resolve itself.

I am happy to say, if you were to look at these girls today at six months old, you would have no idea how sick they had been. They are miracles, and every time I look at them, I am grateful for another day, another moment, with them.

Grateful Beyond Measure

Success is the result of preparation and opportunity. I look back and see that my preparation and good fortune allowed me to put my business and life on hold during December 2022.

I look through the lens of success and great opportunity. During the previous year, I had worked tirelessly building the infrastructure of our real estate investing business with my husband Brett. Having navigated the waters of two syndications, involvement in several mastermind groups, starting a podcast, and attending a lot of conferences, my life and business were swirling. Having the ability to say "I'm out for a while" and just go dark to be there with my family was invaluable. I had no reservations about this decision and I have no regrets. In fact, I am grateful every day for gentle reminders of this experience.

My business has allowed me to have passive income through my investments. It is a business built on walking alongside and helping others. In some cases, this has meant aiding in developing a plan for success, and in others, it has included realizing wealth goals and creating a path for achieving them. Each person who has been placed in our path over the last two years has been powerful!

Creating a business that can run while your life is on hold takes a lot of preparation. It is the behind-the-scenes work of building the infrastructure and systems. This strong foundation has allowed me to operate from a laptop office when needed. In the virtual world we live in, laptop lifestyles are more of a normality. In this era of possibilities, it is imperative to have an automated process for your daily, weekly, and beyond business operations.

My team spent the better part of 2022 working on that very process, never realizing how quickly we would be relying fully on what we were putting in place. I am grateful beyond words for how what we worked hard to create has benefitted me and how those benefits have allowed me to look at opportunities through a different lens.

Like a Phoenix Out of the Ashes...I Have Found Strength

The Ancient Greeks and Egyptians described a mythical bird that is reborn from its ashes called the phoenix, a magnificent creature and a symbol of renewal and rebirth. Like the fabled phoenix, out of the ashes of this challenging time, a renewed being full of life and strength emerged in me. I have learned to embrace who and what I have been and, even more so, who I am becoming.

There are seasons in life that will propel you and moments where you must seize what's in front of you. I needed to incorporate saying "no" into my daily vocabulary to support my newfound strength. I would ask myself, *Did this scheduled meeting, conference, or connection serve me and my focus?* Most of the time, I discovered the answer was "no." Since I had been saying "yes" to everything, this was perplexing.

I found I wanted to say "yes" to the things that brought me joy, which was usually helping someone else discover the next step in their wealth journey and connecting people. I discovered I wanted to create educational content and use social media as a meeting room while leveraging the relationships I had been making.

Saying "no" this year has been freeing. In fact, I find myself saying "no" more than "yes." "No" has freed time to be creative, collaborate on passion projects, and explore other lines of business.

I've discovered that you're never too old to pivot. It's just, "Are you fearless enough to do so?" Life is too short to never try. The worst thing that can happen is I will fail forward, get back up, and try again. I don't want to get down the road and "wish" for something. I want to turn my thoughts and aspirations into a reality and go for it.

Pivot, Passion, and Intention

Had we not had this health crisis with our twin grandbabies in December of 2022, I don't think I would be as passionate about my time and intentions. I want to do the things that have been on my goal list. I want to be fulfilled and help others find this in themselves. I love to bring educational content to others that will help them create their roadmap for financial success and passive income. I want to be a conduit for helping others achieve wealth that goes beyond their bottom line. This brings me incredible joy.

My twin grandbabies Reese and Layne are living, breathing miracles. They are full of life and fully healthy in every way. I had the privilege to walk alongside my daughter and her husband during this heart-wrenching experience, never seeing how in the near future this would be the catalyst for me to pivot in my real estate business. You never know how God uses these hardships in our lives to propel us, inspire our passions, and move the needle on our intentions. Be open to the God Whisper and fear not where it will take you.

Robin Binkley is a wife, mother, podcaster, real estate investor, and entrepreneur. To connect and learn more about real estate investing, passive income, and generational wealth, email Robin at team@realequityip.com or visit Realequityip.com, Ladieskickinassets.com, or RobinBinkley.com

Quotable: Make every moment count, give more than you receive, love hard, and live fearlessly. The power of unlocking dreams and taking action is transformational in life, happiness, and business.

DAN FAULKNER

From the Ashes

Dan Faulkner is a Realtor, real estate investor, and youth advocate, in Seattle, WA. A University of Washington alum with honors, he's sold 750+ homes in his career. With a client-centered philosophy based on relationships, he's consistently been in the Top 1% of Realtors nationwide. Dan lives with his wife, Mallory, and two children in the Seattle suburbs.

It Isn't Safe Here

"It's time to go to bed," Mom said.

"But I don't want to go to bed." I was three years old, and I wasn't ready for my afternoon nap. And if I was going down for that nap, I wanted my toy gun. Back in the '80s, toy guns were common.

"I don't know where your gun is, you're just going to have to go to bed."

"But I want my gun!"

"Just go to bed!"

Absent my gun, I started to throw a real tantrum. With my mom bordering on a meltdown, I marched to my bedroom and tucked myself in.

A few minutes later, the door opened. My mother was in a rage.

"Here's your f@#$%^& gun!" she said as she threw the gun into my room. It bounced off the floor several times, hit me in the chin, and broke into pieces. I still remember what the springs inside the toy looked like, what the plastic pieces felt like.

Mom proceeded to scream at me, something I would get very used to in the coming years. As the pain and shock of being hit in the face set in, I started to cry. And then, as I would also get used to in the coming years, I slowly cried myself to sleep.

Best that I can remember, this is my first memory of being on planet Earth.

Perfection Is Necessary

Growing up, I was labeled a sensitive kid. I excelled in school, and most of the time my nose was buried in a book. My room was probably the safest spot in the house, and I could easily get wrapped up in a Hardy Boys adventure. That world was better than my own.

The "sensitivity" was a result of having to anticipate my mother's moods. *Avoid the landmines. Sense when she was about to spin out and try to change the subject or right the ship. Do anything to avoid an explosion.* I didn't know any of this at the time, and nobody taught me. I just learned it. It was survival.

When I was about eight years old, I started getting debilitating migraines. They would come on suddenly—crushing pain in my head. I'd get nauseous, throw up, and pass out sometimes for up to 12 hours.

The migraines started happening more and more often, at their peak, about once a week. It disturbed school and sports. My dad took me to countless neurology appointments, and eventually, biofeedback, which turned out to be a huge blessing. It's a skill I use to this day. In about fifth grade, the migraines went away, and we never found the cause. My suspicion is that it was at least in part a stress response.

There was high pressure to get good grades, to attain perfection. God forbid I brought home a B- on my report card. In hindsight, I think this was because my mom really wanted to go to college and wasn't able to because of her situation at home with her mother, who by all accounts was extremely difficult and volatile. It makes me sad to think about how my mom's life may have been different if her mom were different. Trauma is generational, and it's up to us who are affected to stop it.

On one occasion, despite having a tutor, I got a C+ in Spanish. My dad intercepted the report card in the mail, whited out the grade, and made a photocopy. Then he made a fake letter from the school saying the report card looked so goofy because they had a printer problem. My mom bought it, and we were all relieved. At least for that day, we were safe.

The First Time

When I was 14, my grades started to slip. I wasn't fitting in at school, and I was looking for a way to feel better. People without trauma probably won't really understand this, but I never really felt at ease. I was always subconsciously looking for the next threat. Constantly amped up, a little anxious, many times without even realizing it. I learned to function the best I could. But I did not feel great, physically or emotionally.

Some kids I was hanging out with asked if I wanted to smoke some weed. I thought to myself, *Anything is better than how I feel now. Plus, I get to hang out with the cool kids.*

So, I smoked. In my parents' backyard while they were gone. There were about 10 of us. After about 30 minutes, it hit me as I was taking a drink of Gatorade. I began accidentally pouring the Gatorade down the front of my shirt. Confused, I made eye contact with this kid named Derek, who was sitting across from me. He said, "He's stoned. I can see it in his eyes." And I was. I finally felt at ease in my own skin.

The Arrest

It's difficult to describe the progression of addiction. After my first time smoking, I drank and used in a way I would call recreational for a couple of years. Hardly acceptable for a 14 or 15-year-old, but also not pathological. It started to get dicey at homecoming during my junior year.

My friends and I had secured a bunch of hard alcohol. We were saving this for after the dance on Saturday night, but a friend and I jumped the gun and decided to split a half gallon of vodka on Friday night before the football game. We downed it in 15 minutes—so fast that we weren't feeling intoxicated at all as we finished it.

By the time we got to the football game, I was starting to have trouble walking. I had no idea where my friend was. Everyone was telling me to leave before I got arrested.

So, I wandered off. Best I can remember, I took a few laps around the strip mall next door and ended up hugging the toilet in the grocery store. At some point, someone found me and called the cops.

I got cuffed and placed in the back of a police car, all while trying to convince the officer that I was not drunk and it was a big misunderstanding. They called my parents. I ended up blowing 0.19% that night, hours after I had stopped drinking. My friend ended up in the hospital getting his stomach pumped. The fact that I didn't need this type of intervention should have been a clue that I was an alcoholic.

After that, I was off to the races. I had decided alcohol wasn't working that well for me, but drugs were just fine. The next year or so was one non-stop bender, at the end of which I found myself smoking meth at a drug dealer's house. I was a small-time drug dealer, strung out of my mind, and living to get my next fix. My drug of choice was "what do you got."

Although I've done my best to make amends, it's still painful to think about everyone I hurt during that time. When you're in your addiction, nothing else matters. You just have to get high. You may not want to let people down, but you're going to. Because you're gripped by something stronger than yourself. And it won't let go.

Sundown for My Addiction, Sunrise for My Life

On December 16, 2001, I would walk into a facility called Sundown M Ranch in Selah, Washington. Along the long driveway, there was a series of signs. Each sign had one word, and together, the message was, "Welcome To The First Day Of The Rest Of Your Life."

I was skeptical at best, but I was also out of ideas. My best thinking had failed me. I figured I would either die in the next few years or end up in prison, and I was okay with that.

My parents had finally had enough. They dragged me into the office of my counselor at high school and said, "What do we do with him? He's out of control."

My counselor Tena, in her wisdom, told my parents that she couldn't work with me unless I went to inpatient treatment. Outpatient wasn't going to work. I was too far gone.

For some reason (I've come to understand moments like this as grace, the unmerited favor of the divine), I said, "Yes. I'll go to rehab. I'll do what you say."

So, I spent my 28 days at Sundown. At the time, I hated it. The beds were coated in plastic. The little valley we were in smelled faintly of a sewer. I had very little freedom.

But, boy, was it a beautiful experience. I had to be in a place like that to have any hope of getting sober. I had to be away from all the toxic people in my life. I had to be away from my mother. I had to have my decisions pre-made for me. The only way I was going to get high was if I ran away from the facility, which you could do. They wouldn't stop you. There was just nowhere to go.

Treatment is about so many things, but it is largely focused on acknowledging your powerlessness over your addiction, acknowledging all the harm you've caused, and trying to find a spiritual solution to the problem—packed into 28 days. It's a crash course, a launch pad to get you on your way with living clean.

After my intake interview, I was diagnosed as a late-stage drug addict. I was 135 pounds, eyes sunk back in my head. My counselor called me Skeletor.

One of the defining moments of my life came several weeks into my stay at Sundown. I was outside, walking just after dusk. And in one instant, it hit me: *I am responsible.*

If I want my future to be different, I am responsible. If I don't want to repeat the mistakes and wreckage of the past, I am responsible.

Although I had been hurt severely in my life, particularly by my mother, I couldn't use that as a crutch. I couldn't blame. I wasn't a victim. I had to take responsibility if I wanted things to be different.

This realization lit a fire within me that has never gone out. It was as if I had something to prove. Everyone up until that point had doubted me, and for good reason. But there was going to be no more of that. I was going to own up, and I was going to prove everyone wrong. For the first time in a long time, I had the sense that I could do it, that I was worthy.

Grace

I've heard that approximately 1 in 10 people achieve long-term sobriety after treatment centers. I don't know why I ended up being the 1 in 10. Largely grace, I think, but I wanted to be sober more than anything. I was willing to do anything to not relapse, to not re-create the wreckage I had caused. To not suffer like I had suffered. And although I didn't have the language at the time to even think this, I wanted to break the generational trauma.

I ended up drinking shortly after getting out of treatment. I thought I just had a problem with drugs and alcohol was okay. It turns out that couldn't have been further from the truth. In short order, I was back in a dark spot.

The last time I used was February 22, 2002. I had taken a bunch of mushrooms and spent the night in my car in front of a crackhouse having horrible hallucinations. I woke up, and I just couldn't take it anymore. I had completely broken open. At 18 years old. And somehow, through a lot of work, a lot of grace, and a lot of guidance, I've been sober ever since.

The Comeback

I graduated high school with a 2.9 grade point average and a barely passable SAT score. I was informally voted Most Likely to Go Nowhere by my high school class. I didn't think I was stupid, but I didn't know how to excel in academics.

Shortly after getting sober, I enrolled in community college. I just took some basic classes to get things going. Turns out, if I showed up sober, paid attention, and tried, good grades weren't so hard to come by. I started to gain momentum. I started to build some self-esteem. I started to see a future for myself.

The next quarter, I got even better grades. Two years later, I achieved my dream of getting into the University of Washington.

One and a half years later, I graduated from the University of Washington with faculty honors. The world was at my fingertips. I could go to grad school, start a career, do whatever I wanted. It felt like for the first time in my life, I had options.

A Good Life

I followed in my father's footsteps and got into real estate. It was 2006, just before The Great Recession. I got Rookie of the Year for my company that year, thanks in large part to my dad's mentorship. Seven years later, I won an award from the National Association of Realtors for being one of the top 30 Realtors in the country under the age of 30, and even had my face on the cover of a magazine.

To date, I've helped over 750 people buy and sell homes and consistently been in the Top 1% of Realtors nationwide. I've had the opportunity to build a small team and work with amazing people. I have to pinch myself sometimes. It's been a wild, awe-inspiring ride.

When I was 36, my wife and I had our first child. This is significant, especially because I spent most of my life insisting I'd never have kids. I wasn't sure I could do a better job than my mother had. I wasn't 100% sure I could break the cycle. And I just couldn't take that risk. Rather than subjecting another generation to that, I decided the safe thing was not to have another generation.

Eventually though, I started to have this overwhelming desire to have kids, which was a strange feeling. I thought maybe it was just a phase, and it would go away. But it only got stronger.

So, I went for it. I found the right woman, and we had two children. Again, I have to pinch myself sometimes. At this very moment, I'm doing the unthinkable. I've helped co-create a new generation that will not have to experience what I did as a child. They'll have their challenges. Those challenges just won't be a result of me inflicting emotional trauma on them.

Providence

"We want you to share your story at our annual fundraiser. You used to be a client, and you've had an amazing journey. We want to show people what our work can do."

"You want me to what?" I couldn't believe what they were asking me to do.

"It's no big deal, just 1,200 people. The governor of Washington will be there, the CEOs of Starbucks and Costco, some Seahawks players. It's all good. It's a real feel-good story."

Youth Eastside Services (YES), an organization that helped me when I was a kid, wanted to make a short video documentary about my story from start to finish to raise money for their organization. It was a vulnerable spot to be in. A small group of people knew my story, but I wouldn't say I was public about it.

So, I said yes. As part of that, I spoke at the event and introduced the next speaker, a teenager who was currently receiving help from YES.

I realized it had all come full circle. All the suffering had a purpose. Grace and providence were real. It was all about service.

My message wasn't that I was the end all be all of what a person could become—far from it. It was more that we don't know who the next leader in our community will be—the next governor, athlete, father, mother. I wanted to do my part to help that person become what they could be. That is why I took the risk of going on stage and making the documentary.

And that is why I take the risk of sharing my story. I hope that somewhere, someday, someone will hear it and say, "If he can do it, I can do it." Because, with a little help, they'd be right.

To get in touch with Dan Faulkner about his story, real estate, booking him to speak, or just to connect, you can email him at danjr@danfaulkner.com, visit his website at www.DanFaulknerGroup.com, or check him out on social at Facebook.com/DanFaulknerJr, or Instagram @TheDanFaulknerGroup.

Quotable: If I don't want to repeat the mistakes and wreckage of the past, I am responsible. This realization lit a fire within me that has never gone out.

ENA HULL

From Outsider to Empowered

Ena Hull is an entrepreneur, investor, and experienced C-level executive known for developing large, high-performing teams in the higher education and student finance space. As founder of an investment group, she manages multiple tax-friendly, passive cash flow assets for investors. Ena has also served on multiple professional boards.

Contrasting Realities

My early life was a tapestry of challenges woven in the Central Valley of California. Growing up as a Hispanic girl in poverty, I often felt like an outsider among my peers. My mother's ingenuity and my grandmother's home address placed me in a more privileged school district, yet I was constantly reminded of my differences there. My appearance, family background, and changing last names (that's a whole other story!) exposed me to a world of adversity. While my classmates enjoyed packed lunches and laughter, I worked diligently to earn my meals cleaning cafeteria tables.

My family's history as migrant farmworkers colored our daily experiences. Sun-soaked fields, cactus-filled lunches, and resolute spirits were my grandparents' norm. My mother's transition from that grueling-labor lifestyle to a career as a hairdresser left a mark on my own journey. My elementary school years were punctuated by unconventional haircuts and hairstyles like perms and even a Carol Brady shag doo!

Despite discrimination from my classmates and their parents, the teasing only fueled my determination to excel. I found solace in learning and mastering various skills. From learning to play the clarinet to learning to type over 60 words per minute in sixth grade, I reveled in discovering new talents.

Resolved to Succeed

Middle school introduced me to a different kind of prejudice, one born from my mixed heritage. Because my father was white Caucasian and my mother Hispanic, the conundrum of not being "Mexican enough" for some and "too Mexican" for others further strengthened my resolve to succeed academically. These experiences, both painful and empowering, became the bedrock of my resilience.

My college years ushered in a summer of scorching factory work when I took a job on an assembly line churning cardboard. This grueling labor in the factory's oppressive heat stoked my determination to never work in those conditions again. A burning desire to transition into an air-conditioned office environment set me on a trajectory towards success.

Driven by determination, I found a job at the student finance department of my college. This was extremely pivotal in my career. To ensure I would never work in a factory again, I knew I needed to make myself valuable. I focused on mastering the department's computer systems and studied the business model. Quickly, my drive and my ability to adapt empowered me to create my own consulting business where I could use my knowledge to help other colleges.

Hurdles on the Professional Fast Track

This ignited my professional journey. In my 20s, I became the Director of Financial Aid at a Northern California college, where I was responsible for managing a substantial financial aid portfolio and team. My subsequent journey saw me navigating the corporate landscape, facing market crashes, and experiencing both personal and professional successes.

I went on to become a Vice President of the student loan division of Citibank, until markets collapsed in 2008 and I lost my job. Although that was challenging, I was determined to "figure it out," and I went on to become a Senior Vice President at what would then become one of the largest nursing colleges in California. In 2022, that led me to my role in the C-Suite executive position as a Chief Operating Officer in Southern California.

Each post came with a unique set of challenges and triumphs. At every turn, I found unforeseen hurdles forcing me to adapt and evolve. Over a 10 year period while in my leadership roles, I was challenged multiple times with regulatory audits and near company closures. Fortunately for these companies, I had an uncanny knack for resolving issues and restoring compliance. By embracing each obstacle, I transformed my experiences with these companies into stepping stones towards my ultimate goal—making a meaningful impact on the educational landscape.

There Must Be More

In the midst of my successful professional trajectory, I encountered a familiar, yet different, challenge—a challenging work environment that left me feeling hollow and like I was not fulfilling my potential. Recognizing that I was not happy with my position led me to embark on a journey of self-awareness. I sought solace and growth through the Exceptional Women Alliance Foundation. The support, mentorship, and camaraderie of the organization proved instrumental in my personal transformation.

With newfound clarity and strength, I embarked on a quest to redesign my life. Armed with self-awareness, healthy habits, and an unwavering belief in my abilities, I made the difficult decision to resign as a Chief Operating Officer and stepped away from a position that was no longer fulfilling me. This action marked the final chapter of a career journey spanning decades in the education space.

A Life Empowered

My post-resignation endeavors reflect my newfound sense of purpose and autonomy. I've embraced entrepreneurship, consulting, and mentoring. I'm sharing my expertise and guiding other women towards success.

My journey, characterized by its trials and tribulations, has led me to a place of empowerment and fulfillment. I now serve as an Executive Advisor for a private equity firm, a Board Advisor for a technology company, the volunteer Chief Financial Officer of the Exceptional Women Alliance Foundation, and a mentor with the SHE-CAN organization. I also get to pursue new business ventures that use my creativity and talents for passion work. My new career portfolio allows me to revel in each day defined by *my* own terms.

I am proud to say that my quest to redesign my life and, with as much joy and happiness as possible, expect to have "the best day ever" each morning has become a reality for me. I live my life with the intent to have as many blessed days as possible by spending time with loved ones and by pursuing activities that ignite my passion for living life to the fullest. I am a living testament to the power of dreaming, believing, and taking action.

I Am Transformed

In retelling my life experience, I share a profound message of transformation. From the depths of adversity and discrimination emerged a woman determined to create her own destiny. In my journey, I experienced empowerment through struggle, a path illuminated by unwavering belief, and the pursuit of mastery.

Each one of the challenges I encountered along the way served as a catalyst for my growth. The experience of not fitting in, battling prejudice, imposter syndrome, and overcoming systemic obstacles imparted invaluable lessons. Instead of succumbing to adversity, I harnessed it as fuel to propel me towards success. The human spirit is resilient and I have seen how, through steadfast determination, our boundless potential can be unlocked.

Through perseverance, a thirst for knowledge, and the audacity to step out of my comfort zone, I transitioned from a factory floor employee to a C-suite executive and an entrepreneur. This trajectory is a testament to the transformative power of education, hard work, and the tenacity to dream bigger.

I also recognize that transformation is not a solitary endeavor. The support of mentors, peers, and organizations like the Exceptional Women Alliance Foundation played an instrumental role in my evolution. The shared stories, encouragement, and guidance from fellow women reshaped my perspective and propelled me to new heights. This is why I give my time to mentor other women, young and mature—to pay it forward.

I hope my journey stands as a symbol of inspiration for those navigating their own challenges. I wish for it to serve as a reminder that adversity need not define us; it can be a stepping stone towards a brighter future.

To connect with Ena Hull about her investing, consulting, mentoring, or entrepreneurial endeavors, email her at Ena@VentanaPartners.net. She is also a keynote speaker. You can find Ena on Facebook, LinkedIn, and Instagram at @EnaSHull.

Quotable: Adversity need not define us; it can be a stepping stone towards a brighter future.

Scan to schedule a call with Ena.

VISH MUNI

Lifestyle Investor in Motion

Vish Muni is a full-time commercial real estate investor and a fitness and personal development enthusiast who loves inspiring investors to take action through education. He loves traveling, dogs, giving to his community, and creating family memories. He believes we all have a lot more potential than we think and that the quality of our relationships is key to everything.

Growing Up in India

I was born and raised in Bangalore, India, in a family of five siblings.

We lived close to my grandparents. My grandfathers were blue-collar workers, disciplined farmers, who grew guavas and lived a simple life.

We were financially stable, but as a family, we were struggling emotionally. My father could have been different, and given more time, emotionally present. I do not have pleasant memories with him growing up. All I saw was abuse, physical and emotional. It was not easy being present in the house. Growing up in that kind of situation forced me to get a handle on my emotions and taught me to speak little. I managed my emotions by going for a walk or a run and playing soccer with friends. Managing my emotions through fitness became an integral part of my life, and there have been very few days that I have not exercised since.

My father was a blue-collar worker, and my mom was a housewife. My mother and grandparents placed a very high importance on education, and I still remember the challenging emotional moments and sacrifices they made just to get us educated.

Apart from being blue-collar guava farmers, my grandparents were entrepreneurs and owned commercial and residential rental real estate. Along with my other siblings, I was given the responsibility of working on the farm before and after school hours. We would take the guavas to the market, which was 10 kilometers (six miles) away by 5:00 a.m., sell them, and be back home by 6:30 a.m. to get ready and be in school by 9:00 a.m.

My grandparents were extremely disciplined. They spent time creating memories with family. They believed in providing value for money and in giving back to the community. My grandfather donated real estate to build a public school (the school building is named after him), he read the local newspaper to a group of people every morning, and always made us grandchildren understand that we should not take anything for granted.

Clarity on Career

After graduating with a degree in economics and taxation, and having been exposed to farming and real estate investing, I was interested in being an entrepreneur. But I did not know where or how to start. I started my first job after graduation as a trainee working for a chartered accountant (CA) / certified public accountant (CPA), and after two months, I decided never to go back to being an accountant. A desk job and working on numbers all day did not excite me.

My second career was as a software engineer. I worked as a programmer, programming and writing code in COBOL. This lasted a year before I lost interest.

At this point, I was not sure what I wanted to do. Since I did not want to be without a job, I started my third career in IT sales, consulting, training, and implementation, which lasted for 15 years both in India and in the United States. During that time, I founded and ran a US-based Salesforce CRM consulting company.

Being friendly, I always had friends around me in my hometown, and it was difficult for me to go straight home without bumping into a friend and having a drink or dinner. I stressed the importance of relationships. I believed in adding value first, always networking, connecting with people, fitness and personal development, always learning, and that there was no finish line or end date in any of these areas.

A Test and a Blessing

In 1999 at age 32, I was blessed with an opportunity to go work in the United States. Honestly, I wasn't sure whether it was a time to celebrate or to be scared. I decided to say yes and was scared. I had never stayed away from my family and friends or left my hometown, let alone gone to live in another country.

I have always liked challenges and operated outside my comfort zone. Saying YES to this opportunity to work in the best country in the world was a blessing and felt like a test.

My leaving India was painful for my entire family. Many of my friends came to bid me farewell at the airport. That moment was special and extremely emotional. I felt like a celebrity.

When I went to bed in California that first night, I cried for a long time, until I fell asleep. I started thinking, should I just go back to India? However, my inner voice kept telling me that would make me a loser and would be failing this test.

Then, I decided to act in spite of my fear and did a small exercise.

I asked myself, *Is there anyone to blame for my current situation?* The answer was Hell NO. I had to get into the driver's seat and take control of my life.

Next, I came up with 10 negative things about the current situation and then thought of 10 positive things AND who was going to benefit.

Finally, I asked myself, *From this exercise, what lessons did I learn?*

Leaving my comfort zone in India changed my life forever. I still use this exercise in all my speeches in Toastmasters and when I speak about influence.

My Biggest Life Moments

The three events which have had the most impact on my life are as follows.

The first was leaving India. Leaving India made me realize that we all need to step out of our comfort zones to know ourselves and discover our strengths. Has it been easy? NO. Was it worth it? Yes, a million times.

The first year in a new country was a struggle. Being an extrovert who had been surrounded by friends and family all the time, I was lonely and depressed in paradise. It took me a long time to build a similar network of friends and family in my new home.

It began to happen one Saturday morning when I was running by a park in Cupertino, California. I saw a couple of guys playing soccer, and I walked up to them and asked if I could join them. They welcomed me and made me feel at home, and that changed everything.

Little by little, we built that pick-up soccer team. At one time, over 40 people from over 20 different countries were showing up for Saturday morning pick-up soccer. That was the new family I had. We played five days a week, indoor and outdoor, and we traveled.

The second event which changed my life and gave me a bigger WHY was meeting my wife, an internal medicine doctor, and getting married. I met my wife in 2004, and we got married in 2005 in Houston, Texas.

Today, we have been married for over 19 years, and it still feels like we met yesterday. We have a wonderful time together. We both like traveling, gardening, exercising, dogs, socializing, entertaining, and community service.

The third most life-changing event happened in March 2009 when we had our first baby. Some things in life can't be expressed in words, and this was one of them. If you are a parent, you know what I am talking about. Our daughter is a National Junior Honor Society student mentor and an Olympic track (800 and 1600 meters) athlete in the making. We do a lot of races together, including Spartan obstacle races and 5k races.

Following My Passion to a New Career

After being an IT professional and then owner of a Salesforce CRM consulting company for over 15 years, I decided to follow my passion and became a full-time real estate professional in 2020. As a realtor and full-time commercial real estate investor, today I have invested in several syndications with over $40 million in assets under management.

I consider myself to be a lifestyle investor. I invest so I can live the life I want to live. Real estate is the investment method that complements that philosophy.

Real estate investing gives me the flexibility to travel, network, connect with people, add value, continue my personal development, develop my fitness, and give back to the community I live in.

In 2009, my wife and I decided to start a company called Duplexaholics with the intention of buying one duplex a year for 10 years. Everything went as planned for the first four years.

In the fifth year, there were a lot of challenges, including lending limitations, a falling credit score, and maxing out my credit cards by using a 0% APR strategy and multiple lines of credit. That is when I hit rock bottom.

Having been knocked out by the school of hard knocks after 10 years in single-family investing, my comeback had to be strong. That is when I got curious about and researched who these people doing multi-million-dollar deals were and how they were doing them.

That is when I joined a real estate mastermind group investing in multifamily apartment complexes. I educated myself on how to buy bigger deals, was introduced to syndication, and decided to surround myself with people who knew a lot more than me. Now, I surround myself with people who are doing what I want to do and people who push me to continue leveling up and operating outside my comfort zone.

What Lifestyle Investing Gives Me

I am a lifetime athlete. I played soccer in school all the way up to university and continued playing until I got married. Then I switched to non-contact sports—CrossFit, running marathons, and obstacle course racing (OCR). I love to take on fitness challenges.

As a way to give back to the community, I joined Lions Club International (Temple Breakfast Lions Club) seven years back and, for the year 2022-2023, I was elected president of my local Lions Club, Temple Breakfast Lions Club in Temple, Texas.

As a way to keep my personal development going, I joined Toastmasters more than seven years back as well and have gone on to achieve the highest award—the Distinguished Toastmasters Certification. For the year 2023-2024, I volunteered for Division Director Leadership (Toastmasters District 55, Division K Director).

I believe in WRITE, an acronym I coined, to support my lifestyle.

I use WRITE every single day, I influence my friends and family with WRITE, and I speak about WRITE at Toastmasters and Lions Club.

WRITE.

WHY: Every one of us needs to have a why in life. Your why is what drives you every single minute, hour, day, month, year…and my biggest why is my family.

RELATIONSHIPS: Without relationships, nothing in life will happen. I need to cultivate, build, and maintain good relationships with everyone I cross paths with in life. Otherwise, I find life is difficult.

INCOME: Money is important, and we all need money to live, but we only need so much. It is like food on your plate. Depending on how much food you have, you can lose weight, fall sick, maintain weight, or gain weight. Money is the same. It is very important to have a strong why because a strong why will take care of excess money.

TIME: Having a strong why, a perfect relationship, and financial freedom, does not mean anything if you do not have time to spend. Hence, it is very important to protect your time. I am very selfish with my time and very careful about how, where, and with whom I spend it. I need to be in good health, physically, mentally, and emotionally first.

ENVIRONMENT: When I have a strong why, financial freedom, time, and strong relationships with myself and everyone around me, one way I maintain that success balance is through associating with and being in an environment with the right people who support and help me to level up.

You too can live a life of your dreams. Life is a marathon. It is a training in progress and takes time. It is not a one-class or a weekend-seminar fix.

Vish Muni would love to share his experience.
Connect: linkedin.com/in/vishmuni
Ph: 254.444.7300

Quotable: You too can live a life of your dreams. Life is a marathon. It is a training in progress and takes time. It is not a one-class or a weekend-seminar fix.

 Lifestyle by design not by default.

LATINO

Transformation Journey
10 Million Records World-Wide

Latino is a Brazilian recording artist and entertainer. Born in Rio de Janeiro, Brazil, Latino has written over 20 hit songs and sold over 10 million albums in pop, freestyle, and funk melody. He is also a producer with a music studio in Brazil and his current show Latinera.

Growing Up an Artist in Brazil

Sometimes I think maybe I'm a character. One that was built over time. There were three phases in my life: before, during, and after America, where I became a popular artist. I think this was a process, a work in progress, but it didn't have a purpose per se, it just happened.

I had a very tough childhood. My mother married my father, then we went to live in a very humble place. Their relationship did not work out, so she went to live in the United States and left me with my father in Brazil.

My father never wanted me to get serious about the entertainment world, but it was something I always liked. I've always been a very charismatic figure in that sense. This propelled me into my future as an artist.

My father wanted me to go to school and have an ordinary job. I was studying, but it was not something I could take to heart. He ended up kicking me out of his house, as he did not want art in my life. I had to stay at Aunt Marlene's house, who lived in Engenho de Dentro in Rio de Janeiro.

There were eight people in a one-bedroom house of 150 square feet. It was very simple, so I used to stay out most of the time. The street brought me connections for life. I ended up staying in Méier, a suburb of Rio de Janeiro. I slept under an overpass, and there I met pastors who are famous in Brazil today.

I got close to pastor Edir Macedo and the bishops by shining their shoes and helping them set up their sound. That led to me reinventing myself. I lived with the street kids, who sometimes threw tomatoes during the sermons. They were irritated because the services used to start early and wake them up. I somehow started to mediate this fight between the street kids and the pastors until I managed to find a harmonious and prosperous way for them to help us feed ourselves.

Becoming an Entertainer

My mother was worried about me because I lived on the streets. She decided to return to Brazil to pick me up and take me to the United States. I was scared because I did not know English. I was already at odds with my father and hardly spoke to him. That was sad for me, and he was sad about it as well.

At the age of 14, I went to the United States on a student visa. I was studying during the week and mostly doing odd and part-time jobs on weekends. I lived in the US for five years, and during that time, I toured with the illusionist David Copperfield through the northern part of the US and Canada. I worked as a roadie and did little things on stage that the backstage crew would allow. I had the chance to improve my English and get to know more people.

Since I didn't have a Social Security card, I could only get simple jobs that paid three dollars an hour or so. After I got my Social Security card, I was able to work in better places including the Ponderosa & Bonanza Steakhouse where I worked part-time and learned to cook, work the buffet, and even wash dishes. I started staying longer hours there because I loved to cook.

On the weekends, I got involved with a group of graffiti artists and breakdancers. It was the time of breakdance and breakbeat music. I started to develop my dancing skills. I also started to understand chords, compose music, and play the guitar. I became interested in the vocals. At one point, a show in Rochester, New York, called City Limits was filming in clubs, and I had a group of dancers to animate these parties. I used to dance, sing, perform magic, and entertain people. I started making some money on weekends.

At the time, freestyle and funk melody music were in vogue. The scene grew, and I became famous in Rochester as a dancing artist. I was full of energy, 17 years old, and very excited to enjoy life. It was a very rich experience that formed me artistically. I learned to deal with the public, unforeseen circumstances on stage, and changes in scenery. I learned how to adapt my repertoire to the audience. I developed versatility. If I know how to deal with it nowadays, it is because of everything I learned and the experiences I had in the US.

Building a Music Career

For reasons beyond my control, we had to come back to Brazil and, unfortunately, I couldn't finish high school in the US. My father was very sad, and my aunt, who was my godmother and lived with him, convinced him to accept me back home. At first, I went to live in Juiz de Fora with my mother and stepfather. Then, I went to Maria da Graça, which is my childhood neighborhood, to stay with my father and godmother. I stayed there for about a year, but I really wanted to pursue an artistic career, which my father was still completely against. After another disagreement with my father, who wanted me to be in the military or be a doctor, I got a job at Pan Am to make amends.

The family was all happy. I was able to speak English well at that time but, unfortunately, I didn't last six months there. Instead of being focused on my work, I was showing the passengers my songs and dancing for them. When I saw on a passenger's passport that they were an artist (like when I saw a man from Universal Studios), I used to tell them that I was a singer and would start singing in the middle of the line. The supervisor said "Man, I think you are on the wrong job," and fired me.

Once again, I had let my father down. He ended up throwing me out of the house again. Then, I went back to where I was before going to the US, Engenho de Dentro, and sharing 150 square feet with the whole family of eight people.

Back in the US, a Mexican chef taught me how to make a spicy sandwich, which was extremely popular. It was delicious! I taught my aunt how to make it so we could sell it at the beach. We started making some money. The ladies from the Copacabana and Leblon neighborhoods fell in love with it and used to buy a lot. My mother joined us and started selling the sandwiches as well.

I used to use a speaker box and beatbox on the beach. One day, a man asked me if I was a singer. He told me that the Sony Music executives would have lunch in the restaurant across the street from where we were. After that, I would go there every day, from noon to one in the afternoon, to try to find the executive directors of Sony Music in Brazil.

I saved up some money and went to DJ Marlboro's studio to ask him to record a song for me, called "Woman." When I got there, Marlboro said that the melody was very good, but I should sing it in Portuguese. I came home, translated the song, went back, and took it to production.

That's how "Me Leva," the biggest hit of my career, came to be. This song was the story of my first relationship with my first wife. That day, Marlboro invited me to sign with the production company without charging me anything. But he was focused on the other artists. I knew I couldn't rely on him to become a success. I needed to find a way to do it myself.

I made a lot of friends on the beach and ended up meeting an old man who drove a Volkswagen Kombi and sold pamonha, a traditional Brazilian food. This gentleman became my friend and knew that I liked to sing and dance. I convinced him to park his Kombi in front of the restaurant where the Sony executives were and play the song "Me Leva" two or three times during lunch. He did this for about three months.

In my point of view, anyone who heard "Me Leva" would not like it right away because the movement was daring. The "funk melody" was innovative. Brazil did not expect funk as romantic music. Soon it came in handy to be part of a movement called "funk melody," but before, it did not exist.

I met the girls who played music in the elevators of the Sony building. I would bring them sandwiches and ask them to play my music every time the executives used the elevator. We did this for about three months. It was a manipulation that started at lunch, with the music playing in front of the restaurant, and when they got back to work, the music was playing again in the elevator.

DJ Marlboro had a meeting at Sony to show other compilations along the lines of funk carioca, which was the funk movement emerging in Brazil in the early '90s. When they asked about an MC Latino, Marlboro presented them with my work. When he played the song, the executives opened their eyes wide and said, "Man, this is a success! Where have I heard that before? I've heard that somewhere...."

Marlboro did not understand how they knew the music or why they liked it so much. He had only played it on the funk show that had a minimal audience, from five to six in the afternoon, on a radio station that was fifth down the list in audience size. There was no way they were listening to that show. Marlboro came back, called me aside, and said, "Look, Sony wants to sign you as an artist, but here is the thing, you have to sign the exclusive contract with me, everything with me."

One Million Copies Sold

I wanted success at any cost, so I signed the contract. For four years, Marlboro did his part, and I did mine. He was successful as a DJ, and I made my career as a singer. Things were being reborn, growing and evolving.

My first album sold one million copies. It was daring for the market. I was the first funk singer (rap) to release an entire album with hits greater than the artists who were leading sales at the time.

From there, I was reborn a different artist. I released 22 CDs and six DVDs. Today, the market is more about releasing tracks song by song rather than an entire album. Even so, I like to go against the grain.

Five years later, I became addicted to horse racing and lost more than $20 million Brazilian reals, everything I had built. I felt bad I had lost everything. So, I had to start my career again from scratch. I made the charts with "Vitrine," a song that had a very funny choreography, and all the money I earned I had to pay to loan sharks. It was very sad.

At that moment, a pop singer appeared in my life. She had a teen audience. I invested everything I had in her, and I lost my money again.

Then there was another pop singer looking for a chorus for her new song. She called me, and I did the chorus. The song broke in 14 countries, and I made millions again. Having a pop song on the global charts is different from being on the charts in Brazil. I recapitalized and built a studio for myself, so as not to rent studio space, which ends up being very expensive when you spend the whole day in it.

It was a new phase of my career. "Festa no Apê," "Renata Ingrata," "Cátia Catchaça," "Amigo Fura Olho," and other great hits were born in the new studio. "Dança Kuduro" also took off. It is a version of an American song that was featured in a soap opera that was very successful in Brazil. Today, I think that I have become a reference for Latin-Brazilian music. I engaged a lot with wealthy audiences, and I became regarded for my shows at high society parties because I know what kind of music an audience likes. I work a lot with nostalgia. My show today has references from the funk melody era, Latin music, American rap, house, and dance music. I mix it all up in a blender to make my show one big "Latinera."

Latino Today and the Latinera Party

After we turn 50, being able to add value to a party, being recognized, and having a name that's recognized, shows that we know what kind of animation, rapport, performance, musicality, and repertoire that our audience likes. My new goal is to share with my fans a party concept and bring a new experience to the public. I say that "Latinera" is not a normal show, it is an experience. We created "Latinera" so that people who listen to reggaeton, salsa, merengue, or tango and travel to Latin America can also feel that vibe in this show. "Latinera" is a party where I am an integral part. That is, I, Latino, previously a solo artist, became the lead singer of my own band.

Today, I work in several spheres, not just music. I became a business-building artist. I am a broker for several companies in Brazil. We set up a credit recovery company and an insurance company. We meet many demands from entrepreneurs, and we end up connecting with other businesses. There are a lot of people who only think about making a profit, and that's okay, but there are a lot of people here who, beyond making a profit, thank me because they had imbroglios they could not solve, and through their willpower and my engagement with politicians and businessmen, we manage it. We end up being the light in some people's lives.

The key to success is "enthusiasm." If you have enthusiasm for what you do, the universe works in your favor. It's being grateful for the little things because it's through gratitude that your character is revealed to the spiritual world. That is very important. If we do a show and it is very vibrant, and everything goes better than expected, I appreciate it with gratitude. Any little thing that happens to me, I celebrate as if it were a big step at the very beginning of my career.

Gratitude in small things allows God to reveal great achievements to you, because how is He going to give you big things if you are not grateful for small ones? So, let's be grateful, look forward, have the eyes of a tiger, and envision what can go right. At worst, what we cannot lose is enthusiasm.

Follow the Brazilian recording artist and entertainer Latino at www.instagram.com/latino or on Youtube @CantorLatinoOficial. To listen, search **Latino (Artist)** on Spotify or any other music streaming service.

Quotable: I've had ups and downs, but I've learned the key to success is enthusiasm. Great achievements are about being grateful for the little things.

WAGNER NOLASCO

My Journey to America and Living the American Dream

Wagner Nolasco is the founder of Build 2 Rent Direct, one of the largest developers in Florida, with $700 million in delivered inventory. Wagner has over 5,000 hours of volunteer service with the United States Coast Guard Auxiliary. He received the Lifetime Presidential Achievement Award in 2017 from President Donald Trump.

Beginning

My father was a bank executive for the Brazilian Central Bank in a time of violence for the country. In 1991, during a bank robbery, my father was shot five times. It took a year, but he recovered, thank God. After he recovered, my family was targeted for kidnapping. In 1993, we came to the USA.

The hardest thing about going someplace so far away was that I wouldn't be able to see people I loved—my grandma, my uncles, my friends from school. There was no email, no Skype, and no FaceTime, only calling cards. We didn't know how long it would be before we saw them again. But the first time I set foot in the United States of America, I knew I was home.

It took a little while for us to get all the papers and get everything set up. Once we did, we traveled back many times. But now, when I go to Brazil, I miss home, which is the USA.

There are many challenges to overcome to make a home in a new country. In my journey, there were five pillars of transformation: language, culture, patriotism, law, and opportunity.

Language

When I came here, I was 13, and I went to Olympus Junior High School in Salt Lake City, Utah. I was a fish out of water. I couldn't speak a lick of English. In my classes, I was just sitting there, not knowing what was going on. Not being able to communicate or understand or socialize was frustrating for everybody, especially for me. And my whole family was facing the same challenge.

I took ESL classes (English as a second language). A lot of the teachers spoke Spanish, but not Portuguese. Eventually, I did end up learning Spanish, but at the time it was another language I didn't understand. The patience and skill of the teachers really helped me. They showed me that it could be done.

My classmates and teachers really wanted me to succeed. They spoke slowly. They tried to help me by showing me objects and signs. After three months, I woke up one day understanding and speaking English! I walked by the TV, and I understood what they were saying. I was definitely not fluent, but I could understand!

It happened through persistence, opportunities, and patience. Unless you really put it into your mind and heart and you have the support system, it's really hard to accomplish. But I was very fortunate and speaking the language opened up more opportunities for me to communicate, be more useful in my school, and be a part of the community.

I think one of the biggest signs of respect you can show for a country is making an effort to speak the language and understand the culture. You need to transform yourself from the inside out, starting with the language. Learning the language was the first step into my becoming an American.

Culture

Once I had the language, I started to learn about and understand American history: what Americans went through, how much they suffered to be where they are, the American Revolution, how the country was initially organized, the Civil War, and everything else that happened. It helped me understand the people, the heritage, and our great diversity. I fell in love with this country, the culture, and the people that built it.

This country is different from South American countries. I believe people went there to take wood, coffee, and gold. Here, they came to build, form communities, live, raise families, and be generational.

It's amazing how the culture helped me transform my mindset. You can change who you are to better yourself, to become a better human being, and the culture here was a big part of me understanding that.

It's not giving up your identity. It's understanding where you're going and how to be respectful and be a part of that society. So when I say I adapted, I mean that I adopted a culture for myself. I'm not erasing who I am, but I am so in love with the people and this country that I want to be a part of it. It's a choice, not an obligation. Coming to the US, being a part of the community, speaking the language is a choice.

I truly believe if you are willing to come here and you want to be a productive member of your community, understanding US history, the culture, the language, and everything that comes with it, will help you to become a better American.

Patriotism

The day I became a US citizen was one of the happiest of my life. The culture and the history of this country makes me want to be a part of it. It's fascinating, intriguing, and beautiful. It's based on hard work. It's based on farming, fighting for what you believe in, and patriotism. Patriotism is really respect. Once you understand something, then you can appreciate and respect it.

This country has a history. It has blood, sweat, and tears that is fascinating because I come from a country where patriotism is not big on the list. Nobody is going to die for the flag. Nobody is going to fight for their country or pay the ultimate sacrifice for it. Coming here and seeing people that are committed to giving up everything and fighting for something that they believe to be correct.... It gives me a great sense of pride to be a part of that country.

I think that's what the US gives their citizens. You can become part of the greatest nation in the world by understanding the language and culture, by growing your respect and becoming a patriotic person. Either you are a patriot or you're not. I think it's a choice that's made by your heart, by your beliefs, and how much you absorb. I think it's fascinating how culturally the language and the patriotism shaped me into who I am.

I feel volunteering is the least that I can do for this country and my community. God gives us so much, that sometimes we have so much more to give, that by holding our talents back, we're really doing a disservice to God and to ourselves. We work, we're parents, but we still have more time and gifts to give away. I have donated more than 5,000 hours of service to the United States Coast Guard auxiliary. I have become a police officer to serve my community.

My soft spot is definitely for kids and the elderly. So I had the pleasure to serve as a police officer and as flotilla commander for the Orlando Coast Guard. I also worked in international affairs for the US Coast Guard. I helped sign international cooperation agreements between 22 islands in the Caribbean and the US. That exposed me to another thing that I'm very proud to be a part of, the rule of law.

Law

Here, the law serves everybody equally. It doesn't matter how much money you have, the level of success you've reached, your profession—everybody is equal. This rule of law is what keeps our country so strong, organized, and desirable to the whole world. You know rights are going to be respected regardless of your race, religion, or beliefs. Unless you've experienced not having that freedom, you won't understand the privilege we have here.

There are countries you can visit where you cannot even be yourself. You can't choose your religion. You get treated by the courts differently if you're rich. You can't express your sexual preferences or sometimes even be out about your race, your hair color... everything gets scrutinized by the government. It's very sad for me to see a country that respects money more than people.

Even in Brazil, when I was growing up, there was some of this. Brazil at that time lacked security, policing, training, equipment, and effective sentences for criminals. If you know you're not going to get caught, if you know the police are not going to get called, then would you do it? Even if it's not right, people will do it. In Brazil there is a saying that goes, if I commit a crime and nothing happens, well that's the career I choose because it's easier. That's the sad part. Crime was promoted in a way. People chose to steal, rob, and kill. And politicians were one of the biggest examples—they took from poor people. This was the climate where my father was shot in an armed bank robbery and the climate which we left to come to the US.

In the US, we have the freedom to be who we are and are treated equally in the eyes of the law.

Opportunity

I think, in this land of opportunity, you can be anything you want. You can be as successful, or not, as you wish. Here, you have the opportunity to be everything you want to be and have dreamed of. I would say to people who were born here and haven't experienced traveling to another country or living abroad, that for the immigrants who come here, it's definitely the land of opportunity, as long as they put their minds, hearts, respect, language, appreciation, and patriotism into it.

Time, in my opinion, is the biggest gift that God gives us. God gives us 24 hours of opportunity a day. Whatever happened today, it's not coming back, and hopefully we always have the next day, a fresh start.

I did a video in Portuguese, sharing an exercise that really blew my mind. I got two friends and I asked them, would you take $10 million if I gave it to you? What would you do with it?

One friend said, "Yes, I would invest, retire, help my family, and do, you know, whatever."

And my other friend said, "Same thing. I would use it to buy a house and help my parents."

Then I asked: "What would you do if the condition for each of you to receive this $10 million is you won't wake up tomorrow?"

They each said, "Oh, no, I don't want the money."

I said, "Are you sure? You don't want $10 million?"

"No, no, no!"

And I said, "So you have today, and you will probably have tomorrow. And you're not willing to accept $10 million today if you know you're not waking up tomorrow.... So why are you not appreciating every second of your day?

"Why are you not enjoying every minute with your family, your coworkers, and everyone in your community? What are you doing not calling the people you love? What are you doing being angry about traffic, honking your horn, and just being miserable?

"Why would you do that when you have the chance to have a fresh day tomorrow?

"Why are you wasting the time God gave you if you're willing to give up $10 million so you can have tomorrow? How much is $10 million worth to you? Clearly, tomorrow is worth more!"

People sometimes invest their time in making money and then use their money trying to buy back their time and their health. I think this is crazy.

Every season of my life, I do something that's special to my heart. I volunteered for the Coast Guard; I volunteered as a police officer; I have done a motorcycle trip from Florida to Alaska flying the flags of the US and all the services represented by the armed forces. I don't know what my next challenge will be. I think now it's bringing the message of financial freedom to people. I would love for people to understand that if they have an opportunity to invest well or to get a financial education, they can have financial freedom and the choice to do whatever they want with their time—the most precious gift God gives us.

Financial freedom is so important because it is freedom of choice. In my case, real estate gave me financial freedom. I invested in rental properties that brought me monthly income, and with that monthly income, I have the choice to continue to work or to not set a new goal. How much is enough for you? Or how much would you like to make on a monthly basis? Generate a plan or look for a professional who can help you generate a plan so you can achieve your monthly financial goal. Then you can choose to keep your W-2 job or become an entrepreneur, retire, spend more time with your kids, travel, go fishing, or go motorcycling to Alaska.

Take action. If you have something in your heart, you have to act upon it. Get educated, read all the books you want, go to seminars, but take action. An idea is just an idea unless you implement it.

Building Communities, Sharing Opportunities

The real estate development industry is always changing. If you don't change, you're gonna stay behind. For example, two years ago, the market was really hot. We were selling pretty much anything and everything we could build. Now, we have to be better and bolder. We have to build with less, control better for cost, and deliver products more quickly. You have to continue to evolve to be successful. You have to be respectful of your clients and make sure you are always trying to create the next best product for your clients. For me, that means bringing quality at a great price in a timely manner.

Right now, we're building what is essentially a steel-frame house in a box. We've been developing this product in China for two years. We have partners at 52 overseas factories to bring all the components together. We are always trying to make something better. With this new product, we can put a house together in six and a half weeks.

We're building 104 homes in Alabama intended for low-income families. Our biggest challenge is finding a product that will be affordable for families in every city in the US. We really would love to provide that. It's really about finding a product that will be able to scale at a very, very low price. It's critical right now. Many people can't afford to live, and they deserve dignity.

I just started speaking internationally. I would love to continue to learn and to teach financial education to kids and other members of my community locally and internationally. There are a lot of people that would love an opportunity to come and invest in the US. They just don't know how. We are still the strongest country in the world, the most desirable country to come to in the world, with the best currency in the world. So I want to serve the Latin American community and teach them how to become financially free as well as the Americans here in our local community.

My goal is for people to experience what I have experienced. But how can you share the feeling of coming here and living this with somebody who has never done it? It's tough.

You can't really share a feeling, but you can demonstrate it. I try to live the example for people and tell people it's possible for them too. I want to empower because sometimes you can have all the education, but unless you are empowered to act, you're not going to be able to do it. Sometimes you need someone to hold your hand, lead by example, show you it's safe, and motivate you.

Zig Ziglar said if you want to build a company, build the people. The people will build a company. So, if you want to build a community, you build the people, and the people will build a community. If you want people to become financially independent and have financial freedom, you have to train them. You have to educate them, prepare them, and give them the confidence that it's achievable.

Wagner Nolasco is a developer, real estate investor, syndicator, and founder of Build 2 Rent Direct in Central Florida. Connect directly with Wagner Nolasco about real estate development, sales, and investment syndication.
(305) 684-2222
Instagram: wagnernolasco.official
Email: wagner@b2rdirect.com

Quotable: Take action. If you have something in your heart, you have to act upon it. Get educated, read all the books you want, go to seminars, but take action. An idea is just an idea unless you implement it.

Scan for more info.

HEATHER ROXBURGH

Overcoming Addiction
How I Rebuilt My Life Through Real Estate and Resilience

Heather Roxburgh leads an award-winning real estate team in Salt Lake City, Utah. She is passionate about helping people achieve their real estate goals and mentors agents and fellow business leaders about growth and marketing presence.

Falling Into Addiction

If I had known what was in that little Ziploc bag when my coworker at The Driftwood Lodge offered it to me, I might have thought twice about trying it. Needless to say, there are plenty of moments in my life I would change if I had the chance, but believe it or not, becoming addicted to methamphetamine isn't one of them.

Welcome to Hurricane, Utah. It's a small town at the bottom of the state surrounded by red rock and nosey neighbors. Everyone knew my family, so everyone knew about my dad's alcoholism and the pressure of divorce. When the inevitable happened, the ink drying on the divorce papers and my mom moving the rest of the family up to Salt Lake City, I was left with nothing but problematic friends and even more problematic decisions on the horizon.

I stayed in Hurricane and lived with my dad. He remarried, and his new wife, also an alcoholic, was not fond of me so she made it her personal goal to make my life a living hell. She would lock me out of the house regularly, make false allegations against me to the police, and on occasion, get into physical altercations with me.

Some could say, when it came to the drugs, I could blame my parents' divorce. Or maybe my dad's volatile temper. But, let's be honest, I am the only one responsible for my destructive behavior and poor decisions. At the age of 15, I became addicted to meth.

I dropped out of high school and moved into a small apartment with my boyfriend hoping to escape the chaos of my home life, but I should have known that running away from my childhood home would only bring me closer to my addiction.

It began with one line, one hit from a pipe. It immediately took over my body and controlled every aspect of my life. Meth became my new reality, a way to disconnect—and it was the perfect escape from the hurt and pain that consumed my body. What I didn't know was how dangerous this drug was and how quickly it could take over your mind and control every decision you make. I was a normal teenager that quickly turned into a strung-out drug addict.

Not Your Average Nuclear Family

If becoming addicted to meth wasn't already chaotic enough, imagine my surprise when I discovered I was pregnant at 17. I was young and uncertain, my boyfriend even more so. Although I didn't use while pregnant, I was still deep in the world of drugs and dealing.

My daughter was born in January of 1994, and within months of her birth, our lives began to spiral. We got evicted from our apartment, so we moved into my boyfriend's parents' home while they were away on a mission with The Church of Jesus Christ of Latter-day Saints. Shortly after moving, our house got raided by the police, and we were arrested for a multitude of drug charges related to meth. I bailed myself out of jail and so did my boyfriend, but that was only temporary for him. His multiple arrests finally caught up with him, and he was sentenced to prison for a year.

If things weren't bad enough already, I learned that I was pregnant again. I could barely take care of my daughter, let alone another baby, so my mom and stepfather packed up their family and moved back down to Southern Utah to help me. In February of 1995, my second daughter was born, and as soon as I delivered her, I was back to my old ways.

A Moment of Clarity

One day, I was sitting in the living room with my two girls. I was rocking my newborn as my one-year-old terrorized the house as near-toddlers do. I glanced between my girls with a fierce love for them—but also tremendous guilt. These two girls never asked to be born into a world of drugs and addiction. They didn't deserve to be in this environment.

At that moment, for the first time in a very long time, my thoughts were somehow clear, and I realized what I had done. The three of us were lying in the bed I'd made for myself. These were my babies. I was responsible for them. *What am I doing? How can I expect to raise my daughters when I'm surrounded by my friends using meth every day?* My thoughts shifted from my girls in the living room to my sister and our group of friends in the backyard. I knew this wasn't my life. Not anymore.

At that moment, my lightbulb turned on.

The Journey to Sobriety

In Hurricane, Utah, there was nowhere for me to turn when it came to getting clean. Nowhere to go, nowhere to run. With my boyfriend in prison and my two babies sleeping on a pull-out couch next to me, I saw no clear path in front of me—so I decided to head in a new direction.

The path to sobriety included a long car ride north to Salt Lake City where I moved into my mom's empty home. There was no way to scrub my past clean as long as the red rock of Hurricane kept my memories fresh. Needless to say, I left a lot of things behind that day.

My boyfriend was still in prison. He had nine more months until he would be released, and I promised myself I would be clean the day I picked him up. I had nine months to strip myself from the identity that I'd built—and it wasn't going to be easy.

When people tell you getting clean is hard, please know, that is a vast understatement. I managed to wean myself off meth over those long nine months—it was by far the hardest thing I have ever done and the most difficult nine months of my life. To this day.

I will always hold close to my heart the people who helped me through this time in my life, especially my mom and stepfather. They are my heroes and the most caring people I know. They sacrificed so much and never gave up on me even when they should have. I wouldn't be standing where I am today if it were not for their unconditional love and unwavering support.

The Uphill Battle

Nine months later, a new life was born. A new Heather.

If you know me, then you know I am likely the most stubborn person you have ever met. If I have my sights set on something, I will stop at nothing to achieve it. When I set a goal to be clean by the time my boyfriend was released from prison, I was determined to reach it. And by God, I did it. I was finally clean, one week before he was released.

I consider that to be the greatest accomplishment of my life. I set a goal—I made an active choice to leave my old life behind and craft a new one—and I did it. I had dug myself into the trench of addiction, and I was determined to find a way to climb out.

I chose to stand myself up, to choose courage over comfort and move forward.

I chose to leave the only life I knew behind and move to Salt Lake City to build a better life for my girls.

I chose to wean myself off one of the most addictive drugs that exists and become sober.

Even though my decisions are what brought me to the darkest days of my life, they were also what brought me to sobriety nine months later.

From Addicted to Agent

Would I go back and change anything about my life? Oh, there are a few decisions that come to mind. But would I change the course that brought me to where I am now? Not in a million years.

Not everything works out in life. Even after waiting almost a year for my boyfriend and father of my daughters, it was clear that he had no intention of getting clean. I knew the moment I picked him up from prison that I had to leave him; I was not about to go back to that life. That was my next impossible hill to climb. But, one year later—I left our little apartment with my daughters and never went back.

After I got out of the trench of addiction, I got a part-time job. During an annual review with my boss, I asked her for a 50 cent raise to help make ends meet. (I was making $6.00 an hour.) She denied my request and told me to be happy at my job because it was the best job I would ever get.

Her words infuriated me, and I was determined to prove her wrong. She lit a fire in me that day that honestly has never gone out.

When a victim's advocate position opened up at the police department, I knew I would be a great fit. However, it required a high school degree and a clean criminal history—I didn't have either one of them—but I was **determined** to find a way to qualify.

I attended night school at an adult high school and quickly got my diploma while I worked with an attorney to get my record expunged. I eventually got the job as a victim's advocate and spent the next eight years working with victims of violent crime. This job developed my empathy toward people in distressing situations—which I knew all too well. This position at the Midvale Police Department introduced me to the importance of relationships and establishing strong connections with clients.

More Grit than Sandpaper

When I discovered a way to combine this mentality with selling houses, I knew I'd found my next calling.

I began my real estate journey in 2006—completely unaware of the housing crash that was around the corner. But even during one of the greatest recessions of American history, I was determined to stay in the game and build my business. Even as other real estate agents dropped like flies around me, I bolstered my business and grew into my unrealized potential.

Helping people discover their real estate dreams and then achieve them has provided so much purpose in my life. It helped me finance a life for my girls and establish a launch pad for their future success. It allowed me the chance to build relationships with people and form connections that now fuel my passion for growth.

Today, I manage an award-winning real estate team and have the opportunity to mentor fellow agents about the many ways to grow their businesses. I am a huge advocate for investing in real estate and find joy in helping others achieve their real estate goals. I also have an immense love for marketing, so I built out a second business to help real estate agents develop marketing content and strategies. There's nothing more fulfilling than helping fellow agents and like-minded business owners discover their potential.

When I decided to become successful in real estate, I knew it would only be a matter of time before those dreams became a reality. After all the trials in my early life, my grit and determination keep me moving forward—step by step—until I reach success. Sure, you fall now and then and scrape your knees, but it's the choice to stand back up and try again that makes the journey possible.

The Heather Roxburgh I am today would not be possible without the 15-year-old meth addict from Hurricane, Utah. The life I lived allows me to prosper in the life that I have. There is always hope for a "happily ever after," and I hope my story will have the chance to help others write their own.

Heather Roxburgh is currently the leader of a real estate team in Salt Lake City, Utah. If you are looking to achieve your SLC real estate goals or would like to have Heather speak at your event or podcast, you can reach her by emailing heather@theroxburghgroup.com, calling 801-913-6454, or visiting her website and social pages: www.theroxburghgroup.com Facebook.com/TheRoxburghGroup instagram.com/theroxburghgroup

Quotable: From battling adversity to embracing opportunity, my journey from drugs to success is a testament of resilience and transformation.

Scan to reach out to Heather Roxburgh.

GEORGE C. OZOUDE, MD

My Journey to Becoming the Best Doctor in a Broken System

Dr. George C. Ozoude is an orthopaedic sports medicine surgeon and real asset syndicator in Houston, Texas. He is founder and medical director of Movement Orthopaedic Institute, Houston's first 100% direct-pay orthopaedic practice. He is also founder and CEO of Time Health Capital, a private equity syndication company with a $50 million portfolio that builds financial freedom for physicians through real asset investments.

The Best Doctor *IN* the World

Movement is life. And I've approached life with innate curiosity and a drive for constant personal growth and development. It feels as if I am constantly evolving and progressing, whether it's forward or backward. However, the most pivotal moment of transformation for me occurred when I discovered the concept of letting go of the rope....

I was born into a Nigerian family in Houston, Texas, but I've always considered myself a New Yorker since we moved to Queens when I was just four years old. Growing up in New York City shaped my early years, and I have fond memories of our cozy home in the middle-class neighborhood of Hollis. My parents, hardworking immigrants, instilled in us the values of family, integrity, and education, creating a strong foundation for my siblings and me to explore the world and pursue our dreams.

Like many boys in the city, the sport of basketball became an integral part of my life. Gathering around the living room TV to watch basketball with my family became a tradition that remains strong to this day. I played in Catholic youth leagues, AAU teams, and summertime park tournaments—these moments are some of my fondest childhood memories. I continued playing through high school, even nurturing ambitious dreams of playing in college and beyond. While I wasn't half bad, I also came to recognize my limitations on the court.

After realizing early that a career in the NBA was unlikely for me, I chose sports medicine as my career path. Medicine had always been a part of my upbringing, with my father working as a general medicine internist. The desire to help others was ingrained in me by my parents, and I held a deep respect for the honorable work carried out by healthcare providers.

Thus, my journey in medicine began in 10th grade when I discovered the various career possibilities in sports medicine from a book I read in the school library. From physical therapist to team physician, the array of options thrilled me. I aspired to achieve the highest level of knowledge and expertise, setting my sights on becoming a sports medicine surgeon. It seemed like the perfect fit.

With unwavering determination, I dedicated myself academically, anticipating the immense effort required to navigate medical school, residency, and fellowship training. I meticulously tested, interviewed, and networked my way into a reputable employed practice in the city where I was born, Houston, Texas.

Once in practice, I assumed the responsibility of caring for student-athletes at 10 local high schools as their dedicated team physician. My reputation as a skilled sports medicine physician and surgeon grew rapidly. For the first few years, I couldn't imagine myself happier or in a more fulfilling setting. I had achieved the majority of my goals.

Unveiling the Flaws of the Corporate Medical System

For the longest time, I believed that following the standard medical career path was the only option. However, as I began to free up mental space and reflect on aspects of life that had continued on while I had focused intensely on my training and social position, I realized that my perspective was incomplete.

My innate curiosity led me to a period of discovery during my first several years in practice. And in that short time, I learned things that fundamentally shifted my worldview. I gradually became aware of the unacceptable realities that I had unknowingly subscribed to within the corporate medical system.

This realization evoked a powerful response within me—disillusionment mixed with disdain. The system I had placed so much faith in was failing not only me but also my patients. The insurance-centered model presents numerous flaws, including the denial of diagnostic tests, medications, and surgeries, which hinder appropriate patient care. Additionally, volume-focused clinics prioritize quantity over quality, restricting the time necessary to address chronic conditions adequately. The model contributes to the decreasing affordability of quality care for patients, often leading to personal bankruptcy due to high medical expenses. Furthermore, the alarming rates of physician suicide and moral injury highlight the detrimental impact these flaws have on healthcare providers within this broken system.

My immediate instinct was to reject the whole system and question everything I thought I knew about my career. However, with more thought, I came to peace with the reality of the corporate medical model I was entangled in and set out to strategically create the new reality I desired.

I felt like I matured. This growth opened the second chapter in the story of my life. I transitioned from a calculated employee striving to be the best doctor "in" the world to an empowered physician courageously forging the path to become the best doctor "for" the world.

The Best Doctor *FOR* the World

Today, the world needs independent doctors more than ever. We need doctors who can deliver top-quality care to patients without devastating their households financially. We need doctors and staff who are themselves healthy, secure, and fulfilled.

This kind of medical landscape can only be realized outside the confines of the conventional US healthcare system. It necessitates stepping beyond the perceived safety net and familiarity of the corporate medical model. The only way to truly succeed in this endeavor is to make the effort without relying on that safety net.

My physician brain tends to suppress my willingness to take such risks. In general, every action and decision in medicine is based on doing the least harm. It relies on a measured and well-reasoned decision-making process, backed by scientific evidence and a proven track record.

This approach fosters a certain level of familiarity and comfort in the day-to-day. It even instills routine confidence. However, I'm grateful to have realized that this mindset also limits growth. If I'm not growing, I'm standing still, which is the opposite of movement. And to me, that's akin to death.

I felt like I was losing my purpose as a physician in the corporate model. Yet, this sense of loss was happening to allow me to rediscover my purpose. I am meant to step out of my comfort zone, challenge the status quo, and set new precedents. I am meant to be different, to go against the grain, and to blaze new trails.

To accomplish this, I had to embrace the concept of risk-taking… calculated risks…and embracing failure as a means of learning and moving forward. And to do this, I had to let go of that safety rope. It's an incredibly difficult notion for a highly trained medical professional to accept. However, when the purpose is greater than the fear, the decision becomes clear. And I'm grateful for that clarity.

Financial Freedom for Physicians

The path forward for me involved building alternative streams of income through investment opportunities. My goal became financial freedom and time freedom, which would allow me to continue my medical career as an independent physician with no overriding obligations to insurance companies, healthcare systems, or the government. My sole obligation could be to my patients.

To successfully invest, I had to delve into the world of real estate, real assets, and businesses. I needed to cultivate a network of colleagues and partners to collaborate with.

Finally, once I had acquired enough knowledge, I had to take the leap and invest my funds to embark on the journey of growing passive income. I explored various avenues, from stocks to start-ups. It was through local meet-up communities and podcasts that I first discovered real asset syndications. I settled on these investments because they offered the least volatility and required minimal active management. This choice made the most sense for me as a busy employed surgeon. I was willing to risk losing $50,000 to determine if it was the right move.

Since my first investment in 2016, I have ventured into 25 similar deals to date, ranging from multifamily residential properties to energy and medical office spaces, even agriculture. Moreover, I made another leap of faith and have transitioned to independent private practice with an affordable direct-pay model, free from any insurance company or government interference.

I feel I am truly on the worthy path of becoming the best doctor for the world. I founded Time Health Capital to meet the financial literacy needs of fellow physicians who are still experiencing the unbearable friction of a broken corporate medical model. The majority of us entered healthcare intending to do good while thriving in our personal and professional endeavors. We are a special group deserving far more than the disheartening realities of the current system. Now, my greatest happiness comes from assisting others in making the courageous leap without the rope.

To connect with Dr. George C. Ozoude regarding investments, or to learn more about his direct-pay medical practice, you can reach him at george@timehealthcapital.com or 979-464-9135. Visit his website at www.timehealthcapital.com or www.movementorthopaedic.com. George is on all social media platforms and most active on LinkedIn at https://www.linkedin.com/in/george-ozoude-md/

Quotable: I transitioned from a calculated employee striving to be the best doctor "in" the world to an empowered physician courageously forging the path to become the best doctor "for" the world.

 Connect with George C. Ozoude, MD

DEANNA BONE

From Foreclosure to Multi-Millions
How I Overcame My Parents' Unspoken Lesson

Deanna Bone has dedicated herself to helping families build wealth one house at a time for 20 years. Her business thrives on referrals, and in 2023, she exceeded $200M in total sales. Deanna is devoted to her three grandkids with autism, and she donates a portion of each real estate transaction to autism awareness.

My Parent's Unspoken Lesson

My parents always struggled with money. My dad made a lot of it, but they didn't know how to manage it. They taught me how to use my house as an ATM and how to keep doing that to get myself "out of trouble" financially. I would watch my parents refinance the house, pulling out all the equity to pay off credit cards, but then turn around the next month and use those same credit cards again. Before long, they would have the credit cards at their limits, plus a new, higher house payment eating ever faster away at the same funds they had available before. It was a very stressful cycle to get caught up in.

In October of 2000, my dad told me he had only months to live. In that short time, I watched my dad, age 57, die of cancer with fear in his eyes. As the main breadwinner, he worried about how his family would survive when he was gone. I do believe the cancer was caused by stress over debt and my parents never having learned the power of investing in themselves first so that they could breathe at the end of the day.

Watching my dad go through the pain and struggle, not from the cancer but from the burden of debt, during his last few months of life was something that kept coming back to me over my next 20 years. Little did I know, I would also fall into the same trap.

The Recession Is a Terrible Thing to Waste

I was told the 2008 mortgage meltdown caused over a third of the homeowners in Arizona to lose their homes. Right along with them, that same mortgage meltdown caused me to lose my house to foreclosure.

Years later, one of my mentors, Brian Buffini said that 2008 wasn't a recession, it was a depression. Looking back, I have to agree with that. That depression taught me that no one should be ashamed of their challenges or failures. That's also the time I found out how important it is to share my story to build trust and integrity with my clients.

I had a powerful real estate business through 2007, and then, just like that, a wall hit us, and the real estate industry died in Arizona. As the main breadwinner in my family, I went from making six figures to no figures in what felt like a day. Just like my dad, I had made a lot of money, and just like him, I did not learn how to save.

I remember the day I came home and, as I was driving into my garage, I saw a foreclosure notice on my house. I ran as fast as I could to remove it before any neighbors saw it. The next indignity was a call from American Express. They were going to sue me because I could not make a payment for the sixth month in a row.

As soon as I ended that call with American Express, I dropped to my knees to cry and feel sorry for myself. At that same moment, a client called me to say they had just come home to a sign on their garage. The bank was foreclosing on them, and they didn't know what to do. At first, I was thinking, *I just received one too. How could I help?*

Believe me when I say this moment was both a curse and a blessing. The curse was I knew the full weight of what the bank could legally do and I was not sure how to get through it. The blessing was, at that moment, I knew something had to change.

My Greatest Struggle Became My Greatest Strength

The biggest decision I had to make was to either stay in real estate or, as most real estate agents do when the market changes, move on to another career. I knew real estate was my calling, so I said to myself, *If this career is your calling, then pick yourself up, start over, and build your business again.*

That day, I hired a business coach from Buffini & Company on a credit card that was almost maxed out, without knowing how I was going to pay that credit card bill. The first obstacle we worked on was honesty. I worked on being honest with myself and my clients by sharing my story. I shared that I understood what they were going through, that I was going through it as well, and that we would learn together and make it through this. Around my clients' kitchen tables, I embraced honesty and openness as I shared my story. One client and one story at a time, I built my career into a strong career of referrals that I have today.

While working through $500,000 in debt, I then faced my own fight with cancer. I was diagnosed with endometrial stromal sarcoma. As with my dad's case, I do believe the stress of debt caused my body to break down and allowed the cancer to grow. The first thing doctors tell you when you get cancer is to get rid of stress. That was not so easy while I was struggling with the same questions my dad had: *How will my family survive once I'm gone? How will they pay off the debt I've created?*

Through two surgeries, two years of treatments, and many personal prayers and discussions with God, I healed, and my life started to make more sense as I got clearer about what I am meant to do while I'm here on this planet.

The Other Side of Foreclosure

From the day the bank foreclosed on our home, all I wanted to learn about was how to invest in my family's security so that I never had to live the way my dad did his last few months of life. I didn't want myself or my husband to ever have to keep working because of debt if life threw us the notice that our time was about to end.

Within 18 months of the foreclosure, my husband and I purchased our first post-foreclosure home with only 3% down, which we had saved one dime at a time. The equity of that home allowed us to purchase a second property, and then that equity allowed us to purchase a third property, and on and on.

One success for me was the day I was able to gift our youngest son the downpayment for his first property from a savings that I call the "Thanks Dad" account. Every time I deposit or withdraw from it, it's a reminder to thank my dad for his silent lessons on money.

I grew from a negative $500,000 net worth to a multi-million net worth in five years. I'd never have grown my portfolio that much in five years without the power of real estate.

These are the lessons and stories I share with my clients when they come to me to buy their first, or even their 20th, home. I know my dad would be very proud of me and my story. I was able to come out of the fire of foreclosure and debt to give hope to other families. With everyone I meet, I share the power of home ownership and the wealth your home can build if you treat it right and not like an ATM.

The REALTOR® on Your Financial Advisor Board

Today, I believe that the fastest way to build security and wealth is through real estate. My goal with each client is to go over their net worth and share how, as I've learned along the way, buying a home can be a better investment than just putting money in a savings account. There are many ways to build your wealth through real estate, and I'm here to guide my clients and teach them that they should not skip the most important step in financial stability: investing in yourself first. At the end of the day, it's important to build your security and wealth to ensure your family is protected.

I work with many CPAs and financial planners on investment plans for my clients. I want them to understand that I'm here for more than when they want to buy or sell a home. Each time you pick up the phone to discuss your strategy for building wealth with your CPA and financial planner, your next call should be to your REALTOR®. I have clients reach out to me each January to get the correct value on their homes so they can accurately validate their net worth alongside their 401K, IRA, SEP, stocks, bonds, etc.

Foreclosure Lessons

Have you ever looked at your life and said to yourself, *Why is it that every time I take a step forward I end up taking two steps backward right after that?* Well, I sure did.

Looking back, I see that as I went through my obstacles in life, I was really taking one step back and two steps forward. This is the biggest lesson I learned about myself. I thank God every day for the blessings of my challenges and for the advisors I had along the way. If you are open to it, a good advisor will give you opportunities to learn great lessons that will work in all areas of your life. My goal is to be one of those advisors with everyone I meet.

Don't be ashamed of your foreclosures in life, no matter when they come. Learn from them, rebuild, and then teach the next person you meet what you did. I cannot wait to be connected with the next person who wants to build security and wealth one home at a time.

Deanna Bone's mission statement is helping families build wealth one house at a time. If you're interested in learning how you can build your wealth through real estate, contact Deanna Bone to schedule a private consultation. You can send her an email at Deanna@SouthwestHomeTeam.com or via social media www.instagram.com/DeannaBone.

Quotable: Around my clients' kitchen tables, I embraced honesty and openness as I shared my story. One client and one story at a time, I built my career into a strong career of referrals that I have today.

Scan to download Deanna Bone's business card.

ADEBAYO FASANYA, MD

Overcoming Challenges
An Immigrant Physician's Path to Success in Finance and Medicine

Dr. Adebayo Fasanya has been a practicing physician and real asset investor for over five years. As the founder and CEO of Dr. Breathe Easy Capital, his focus is on increasing financial literacy among physicians and helping others achieve financial independence through investing. Today, his team has over $140 million in assets under management. Adebayo is also a husband and father of three.

Discipline, Hard Work, and Academic Success

My mum was a teacher in Nigeria and she made sure we were disciplined individuals. She would often tell my brother and me, "You can't be doing bad in school while you are a teacher's son." It worked! We were both number one in our respective classes.

My dad was an accountant since his early 20s. My mum was a grade school teacher with multiple side gigs—she made cakes for weddings, and she had a hair salon where she worked in the evenings. This was my first glimpse of entrepreneurship. When I was growing up, most Nigerians were well-educated and also had side gigs. So, I have kept with the tradition, even when I moved to Canada and later to the USA.

My mum left for Toronto, Canada, when I was 13 years old, and my dad lived in a different state in Nigeria due to a transfer for his job. Our parents wanted us to have structure and a mother figure, so we moved in with my aunt (mum's sister) and her family. With my brother and I, we were nine boys. With my uncle and my aunt, we were 11 people living in the four-bedroom apartment. I always remember that time as a time of bonding. Not one moment did I ever feel we were suffering.

We boys played soccer together, we wrestled, we made peace, and I felt we grew strong in mind, body, and spirit. We competed academically in a non-toxic way. Everyone wanted to beat the standing record set by our eldest brother. I was the first-born in my family but transitioned to number five of the nine at my cousin's. We grew up as brothers. No line was drawn between us, and till today, we are all brothers.

A typical day in the life of a teenager in Mokola, Nigeria, will sound atypical to most people in the Western world. We would wake up at 4:00 a.m. and walk two miles to fetch water from a nearby borehole. Then we'd walk back home, sometimes making the journey twice if it was our turn to get our parents' water. We had no washing machine for dishes or laundry and hand-washed everything. While this routine may have been tedious and challenging, we also felt a sense of accomplishment very early in the day. It taught me the value of structure, discipline, and hard work, which have been instrumental in my journey as an entrepreneur.

This discipline also translated into my academic life. I realized that being disciplined with my time and studying consistently could help me achieve academic success. As a result, I was able to maintain good grades and earn scholarships that helped me fund my education. I was even able to skip a few grades in the process.

I was accepted to a school of veterinary medicine at 15 years old, and I was in my third year when my mum sponsored my brother, my dad, and me to come live in Canada.

Lessons Learned in Door-to-Door Selling

Having fantasized about the fun lifestyle I saw in movies, I was very excited about the prospect of coming to a developed country. When I arrived in Canada, it was fun for a few days as we were welcomed by family and friends. Most importantly, I was very happy to reunite with my mum.

My mum did well for herself, but I quickly saw that for us to do well as a family of four, she would need help. My dad was a chartered accountant in Nigeria, but he couldn't find a job in Canada. I had to get into college fast and I needed a job for the summer.

We had arrived close to the end of April, and the application for college at the University of Toronto had already closed for the year. Armed with just a few days of orientation to the country, I embarked on a journey to convince the University of Toronto dean to let me into school for the year.

Attending the University of Toronto had always been a dream of mine. It was a well-acclaimed university in Nigeria. The name came with credibility. In fact, in 1999, one of our house representatives lied about graduating from the University of Toronto to help him get a high-ranking position. Of course, the lies were found out, and he lost his seat.

I took public transit to the campus to talk to the dean. I was granted an audience, and I explained my case—how I regarded the University of Toronto as the number one university in the world, how sad I was when I found out that application season had ended, how I would be a great addition to the university if given the chance, how I was number one in my class in high school, and finally how my transcript from veterinary school showed good grades too.

To my amazement, he said, "Okay, I will make a case for you." That's all I needed to hear. A few weeks later, I got my admission letter.

That was one problem solved. Next, I needed a job for the summer.

I applied for a job making boxes for a chocolate factory and supplemented those hours with a sales job selling ADT security systems. I believe this job was pivotal in my development as a person because I was paid $275 for every system I sold, whereas the factory paid seven dollars an hour. That worked out to be about the same amount of money per week.

I slowly transitioned into the sales job full-time. There was lots of rejection. I might knock on 100 doors in a day and get rejected at all of them. Often, when I was about to give up in the late afternoon, I'd think to myself, *Let me knock on the last three doors on this street before I quit*, and that's when I'd make the sale. I am not sure if I just put more energy into the last few, but I was usually reinforced by that.

Selling security systems door-to-door taught me valuable lessons that prepared me to become a more effective entrepreneur. I learned effective communication, quickly introducing myself and explaining the benefits of the security system. I learned to adapt my communication style to different individuals and how to ask the right questions. I discovered that success was not solely based on my personality or product but instead on my willingness to persevere. Managing my leads, tracking my sales, and following up with customers taught me the importance of creating systems and processes. I came to understand the importance of providing value to my customers. As a salesperson, I was not just selling a product but also providing a solution to the homeowner's unique security needs.

I made over $8,000 that summer from the sales job and that allowed me to help my parents in a significant way.

This reminded me of a story my parents told me. When I was about eight years old, there was a tough month at the bank for my dad. My mum was a teacher moonlighting as a cake maker and hairdresser, but that month, there was not enough. I told my parents I had money in my piggy bank. They were not ready for what they found. I had saved all my pocket and lunch money for years and had 700 Naira (equivalent to about 24,000 Naira in today's money) in my piggy bank. It was just enough to pay the rest of the rent that month. I felt proud I had saved the day. Perhaps that was also positive reinforcement for me to always want to be financially responsible.

My Journey in Medical Education

I started university that September and pursued a degree in mathematics and biology. During my time at the University of Toronto, rather than continuing my training in veterinary medicine, I decided to pursue human medicine.

I graduated with distinctions and a double major after three years. I applied to a Caribbean medical school because their cycle from application to admission was shorter. I enjoyed the two years on Saba Island, which was part of the Dutch Caribbean.

I ultimately pursued a residency in internal medicine with a subspecialty in pulmonary and critical care. I chose internal medicine because of the intellectual challenge and exposure to a wide variety of patients and diseases. I was particularly inspired by my internal medicine rotation, which called for students to provide solutions to diagnostic problems that were initially very puzzling and required a whole-body approach to patient care.

My choice also arose from my interest in the sophisticated mechanisms of the body. I have since gained a deep appreciation of the fact that humans are more than the sum of their physical mechanisms. I have come to understand the need for a holistic approach to patient care and that each person is worthy of dignified and individual understanding. A career in internal medicine represents a decision to apply scientific knowledge to advance the wellness of other human beings. I am committed in a personal way to this humanitarian tradition.

I am passionate about medicine and extending the availability of healthcare, having witnessed the sad results where it is lacking or insufficiently accessible.

My pulmonary critical care fellowship is an extension of my inclination to go where the action is and treat the most important organ in the body. *When you can't breathe, nothing else matters!* I have always felt strongly that this saying is true. This saying is also where I found my name, Dr. Breathe Easy.

From Medical School Debt to Financial Freedom

Growing up, it was common knowledge in Nigeria that there is one thing you cannot trust anyone else with—your money. Being frugal came easily to me. However, the concept of building wealth did not solidify in my mind until I finished medical school.

I was fortunate enough to come across White Coat Investor. I slowly digested the materials on the site, and I quickly found myself reading books, blogs, and other websites and watching YouTube videos on finance.

As I became more knowledgeable, I started telling people about the basics of personal finance and encouraging my friends to build their knowledge too. In residency and fellowship, my colleagues often did not know what a 401K really was.

After medical school, my student loan debt was in excess of $200,000. With interest, over time, it settled around $300,000. The matter was compounded when I met my wife, Mrs. Breathe Easy, as she too had some student loans she acquired from a nursing degree. We got married on February 14th of my graduation year.

We had our work cut out for us. We lived as minimalists, in a two-bedroom apartment we shared with a roommate. In Summit, New Jersey, that was the only way to bring the rent cost down to $700 in a good area of town. In residency, I was unable to moonlight in another job and thus unable to pay down much of the loan.

During my fellowship, our program allowed what was termed "extra resident coverage." This allowed me to earn extra income as we transitioned to being a one-income family for a time. It was not easy to work the additional hours as my pulmonary critical care fellowship itself was very demanding, and as was building a life with my wife and kids, but I buckled down and got it done. We started paying off the student loan debt from my fellowship. Every dollar after the basics went to the loans.

By the end of my fellowship, we had about $150,000 in debt remaining. We dumped my stipend, my sign-on bonus, and almost every dollar we had into the loans. My job also paid about $36,000. Within six months after fellowship training, about five months into my real job, we were debt-free.

Through determination and a commitment to financial responsibility, I transformed my financial situation from overwhelming debt to a debt-free life.

Sharing the Wealth

A few months after fellowship training, I launched my blog inspired by my journey, Dr. Breathe Easy Finance, and established Dr. Breathe Easy Capital, my private equity firm, to provide guidance and support to fellow professionals seeking financial freedom. As an immigrant physician, I understand the unique challenges in navigating the financial landscape of the Western world. My goal is to share the knowledge and experiences I have gained, to offer a perspective rooted in my background and a deep passion for improving financial well-being.

My partner, Dr. George Ozoude, and I do bi-weekly, educational webinars to educate other physicians and other high-income earners. We also offer diverse investment options for those who want to join us. We have done oil and gas funds, multiple multifamily deals, and multiple self-storage deals, and we have two luxury senior living construction projects ongoing.

I am very excited about this journey of educating other physicians while creating generational wealth for my family in the process. By teaching others, prosperity can only multiply.

Connect with Dr. Adebayo Fasanya regarding investments, or his coaching program, by joining his investment club and bi-weekly webinar series (https://drbreatheeasy.invportal.com/signup). Adebayo is active on social media and most active on LinkedIn at
www.linkedin.com/in/adebayofasanya
Email: bayo@drbreatheeasy.com
Website: https://www.drbreatheeasy.com

Quotable: I transformed from water-fetching teen and door-to-door salesman to a balanced physician and real asset investor helping others achieve financial freedom. You can transform your life too by joining the right circle.

 Schedule a one-on-one with Dr. Fasanya.

SHELLY SLOCUM

Standing at the Crossroad
of Misery and Success

Shelly Slocum is a realtor, speaker, trainer, and author of Amazon #1 New Release Love and Inspiration from Mom. *Her most important job has been being the mom of two wonderful daughters. In everything Shelly does, her goal is to help people move toward success and happiness. As a cancer survivor, her bold mission is to change the world one inspired person at a time.*

A Suspicious Nodule

"It could be nothing, and it could be something."

I was sitting knee to knee with my primary care physician going over the results of a follow-up CT scan. She said, "The nodule in your lung has grown and changed in consistency."

As the doctor spoke, my world started to spin. I felt sick to my stomach and closed my eyes. I could feel my heart pounding in my chest. When I opened my eyes, she took my hand and continued. "The radiologist noted that the nodule is suspicious of adenocarcinoma, which is a type of cancer."

I took a deep breath and closed my eyes again. Everything in my body felt heavy. It seemed like the walls of the small patient room were closing in on me. The sound of the word cancer hung in the still air.

Incidental Finding

Just over a year prior, I had gone to the emergency room with excruciating pain in my left kidney. After a CT scan, they discovered I had a large kidney stone. The radiologist also noted an "incidental finding," a small nodule at the bottom of my left lung. At the time, the ER doctor told me, "Because the stone is so large, you have a 50/50 chance of passing it. And, don't worry about the nodule, half of the population has a nodule in their lung which can be from any number of benign things. Just make sure you do a follow-up scan in a few months to keep an eye on it."

On his advice, I didn't worry. I passed that excruciating kidney stone, and three months later, the world shut down with the COVID pandemic. Because of that, I wasn't able to get another CT scan for over a year. But, I still wasn't worried. I was healthy and felt great. The day after I finally got my follow-up scan, I received a call from the doctor's office asking me to come in and go over the new scan results—that's when I got worried!

As I sat with my doctor, I asked, "Lung cancer? How can that be? I've never been a smoker."

My thoughts drifted back to college when my roommate and I believed that all the cool kids smoked. Of course, we wanted to be cool. So, one night, we decided to learn how to smoke with a pack of menthol cigarettes, because that seemed especially cool. We coughed and hacked and smoked until we made ourselves sick and concluded we should figure out another way to be cool. After that night, we never smoked again.

Could one night of smoking cause cancer? I wondered. It didn't seem possible considering some people smoke their whole lives and don't get lung cancer.

(I have since learned that while smoking increases your risk of getting cancer, between 10-20% of lung cancers occur in non-smokers. That is a shocking statistic!)

I realized that the doctor was still talking, and my attention came back to the small, stifling room. I heard her say, "I'm referring you to a pulmonologist at National Jewish Hospital, the best lung hospital in the country. Again, Shelly, hopefully it's nothing."

It was all I could do when I left her office to get to my car without becoming a complete puddle. In the elevator, I had a thought that the people who were sharing space and time with me had no clue about the news I had just received. *Don't make eye contact, just get to the car.*

When I closed the car door, I learned what it means for the floodgates to open and cried like I had never cried before. When I finally gathered myself, I called my husband to tell him about the appointment, and he said, "Whatever it is Shell, we will get through it together." At that moment, I was so grateful for my husband, my family, and my strong faith.

Pity Pool

So what do you do when you get bad news or when bad things happen? Well, we can have a pity party, and believe me, I did. I had a long weekend of *poor me, why me*, wallowing in self-pity. It was a miserable weekend. At some point, though, I remembered something my sister-in-law once told me, "It's okay to dip your toe into the pity pool, but you can never get in and swim."

Truth be told, I am a terrible swimmer, so I knew I didn't want to hang around the pity pool for long. And people who know me, know that's not me. I'm a "glass half full" kinda gal most of the time.

By the end of the weekend, I decided to put my optimism to work and made a plan. Moving forward, no matter what the outcome, I was committed to looking for the lessons and blessings, big and small, every day in this trial. I also decided that every time I heard the word cancer, I would turn it into an affirmation. When I heard "cancer" I'd say to myself, "Oh yes I can-sir!"

Don't get me wrong, I was still praying that it wasn't cancer, but I chose to focus on what I could control and stay as positive as possible. From that point on, every doctor I spoke to—thoracic surgeons, the pulmonologist, the oncologist—all said they would be surprised if it wasn't cancer. In my head, my response each time was, "Oh yes I can-sir!"

The Next Best Thing

After the pity weekend, I reached out to my dear friend, an anesthesiologist, and told her what was going on. I asked her what she would do. She said, "Regardless of what the nodule is, because it has changed, I would get it out as soon as possible. I want you to talk to the very best thoracic surgeon I know. I would trust him with my life." When she told me his name was Dr. Cross, I knew I had found another blessing.

Within three weeks of my primary care appointment, I was on the operating table with Dr. Cross at the helm of the surgical robot, and my friend, the anesthesiologist, at my head. The plan was to cut out the nodule and have it biopsied while I was asleep. If the nodule was benign, they would close me up, and I'd be good to go. If it was cancer, they would remove the lower half of my left lung and all of the lymph nodes surrounding it.

After nearly seven hours, I awoke from surgery to my husband's face. I smiled, expecting to hear him say it was all clear. But instead, he frowned and told me it was cancer.

A tear rolled down my cheek as I felt the pain and sadness of my reality. Then, I thought, *Oh yes I can-sir!*

I left the hospital on Good Friday (another blessing) just three days after my surgery. I was half a lung and two chest tubes lighter and breathing with no oxygen assistance. It was weird and scary, especially the first time I had to climb the stairs to get to my bedroom and realized I could only go two steps before I was gasping for breath.

Within a few days of being home, we got the much anticipated results of the lymph node biopsies, and praise the Lord, the lymph nodes were all clean! I had prayed it wasn't cancer and got the next best thing. We caught it at Stage 1. For this type of lung cancer, at Stage 1, surgery is considered curative. No chemo. No radiation. Hallelujah!

Luck or Choice

It has been over two years since my surgery, and the scans continue to show that I am cancer free. "Oh yes I can-sir!"

Many have told me they admire how I navigated this cancer journey with optimism and strength. In the past, my husband has joked about me having Polly Anna thinking, which is pie in the sky, blind optimism. And to that I say, "Oh no, I have Shelly Anna thinking, which is where reality and optimism meet." I had the opportunity to live out my Shelly Anna thinking everyday through this journey, choosing to face reality with optimism.

Some people have called me lucky: lucky that I caught it early and lucky that I didn't have to have chemo. While I believe it was a blessing that we caught the cancer at Stage 1 and surgery was curative, I honestly didn't feel lucky at all.

When she found out I had cancer, my college roommate said, "Shelly, you are my healthiest friend. You take good care of yourself. You eat healthy and exercise. If you got cancer, the rest of us are doomed!"

In my opinion, if you gauge life according to a "lucky scale," someone who takes good care of themselves and still gets cancer doesn't seem very lucky. And then, if you consider the fact that it was non-smoking lung cancer, that seems really unlucky. When someone tells me I'm lucky, I respond with how I truly feel. I was blessed to have an excruciatingly painful kidney stone because it saved my life. I was blessed to have a friend who connected me with the best thoracic surgeon who cured my cancer. These are just two of the many amazing blessings I have chosen to focus on.

I contend that life is not about luck. It's about choice. Stuff happens to everyone, and sometimes that stuff is really bad and hard. We don't get to choose what happens to us, but we ALWAYS get to choose how we respond!

After my diagnosis, it struck me: I had been cast in the leading role of a story about a cancer patient—a role I never wanted. On the stage of life, sometimes we're cast in a leading role based on choices we've made, and other times, we are innocent bystanders thrust on stage. In the moment, how you got there is actually irrelevant. The important thing to remember is, when you are center stage, you get to choose how you play your role. Will you play a victim who looks at life as a series of unlucky events you have no control over? Or will you approach the role with optimism and seek blessings every day, even in the toughest times? It really is your choice.

A Beautiful Reminder

After my surgery, I knew the recovery was going to be challenging. I also knew that I needed something to focus on while I was healing, to keep my spirits up and to stay optimistic. Within a week of being home from the hospital, I had seen enough television for a lifetime. Suddenly, I felt a push from God telling me that this was the perfect time to publish the words of inspiration I had written for my daughter. Overcoming cancer could be the fuel that propelled me to fulfill the dream of publishing my book.

Several years before my cancer diagnosis, one of my daughters lived through a torturous experience. When that happened, I dropped everything in my world, moved to where she lived, and did whatever I could to support and love her back to health. Over a period of months, she did intensive therapies. Together, we spent hours at a meditation garden and walked along the beach. I believed that everything we were doing was working together to help her heal.

I also know that putting 100% of the focus on yourself, no matter what has happened in your life, is never a good thing. When you begin to take the focus off of yourself, true healing can take place. For that reason, I knew a creative outlet could help take the attention off of my daughter and give us something to focus on during our downtime. We worked on a sewing project, creating two patchwork Christmas tree skirts—one for her and one for her sister. These amazing skirts are a beautiful reminder under their Christmas trees every year, that we have the opportunity to turn something bad into good.

The Beginnings of a Book

When my daughter was strong enough to go back to work, I wanted to continue loving and encouraging her. Every day for a few months, I texted her an inspirational quote along with a couple of tips on how she could apply it in her day. I ended each text with "Love, Mom."

Over time, she got stronger and more optimistic. Soon, she was better than she was before. She encouraged me to write a book using all of the inspiration I had shared with her, to help others going through a tough time who might not have someone to lift them up.

After three months with my daughter, I went back home with aspirations of publishing a book to inspire others. Then, life got busy and the book went on the back burner.

Well, after my surgery, four years later, I was suddenly not too busy. So, I accepted God's challenge to get my book published. Little by little, I began to finalize my manuscript and navigate the publishing process.

One year and one month after my surgery, I launched my book, *Love and Inspiration from Mom*, which includes loving words to inspire a happier you. Jack Canfield, co-creator of the *Chicken Soup for the Soul* series, wrote the foreword and calls it "a warm hug in a book." With this book, my mission is to share a mother's love and change the world one inspired person at a time.

We Get to Choose

In the book, I say, "Isn't it amazing how two people can experience a similar illness, accident, or tragedy and one becomes miserable and depressed and the other uses the experience to become a better person? The difference can come from many things: support, attitude, faith. But when you stand at the crossroad of misery or success—YOU pick!"

My life, like most, has been sprinkled with many opportunities to choose between misery and success. The amazing gift in each opportunity is that we get to choose how we respond. We can choose to let it keep us down, or we can choose to focus on the lessons and blessings in each of life's challenges to help us transform into the person we have always wanted to become.

No one escapes this life without pain and struggle. I don't profess to understand why that is part of the human experience. I just believe, with all my heart, that in each trial we face, we have the opportunity to grow and transform, if that is what we choose!

To connect with Shelly Slocum for inspirational keynotes or success training, please connect with her at www.loveandinspiration.org or email inspirationfrommom@gmail.com. Shelly is a certified trainer for Jack Canfield's Success Principles and helps people achieve more success and happiness in life and work. Her book *Love and Inspiration from Mom* is available on Amazon.

Quotable: In each trial we face, we have the opportunity to grow and transform, if that is what we choose. When you stand at the crossroad of misery or success—YOU pick!

DALE YOUNG

From **WHAT** to **WHY**
Mentors on My Journey to Calling and Legacy

Dale Young is an executive coach specializing in teamwork, leadership, and calling. As an entrepreneur, Dale is familiar with the daily overwhelm, whirlwind, and chaos. He coaches each entrepreneur and business leader through their chaos into clarity to pursue their calling. Dale is also the author of The Identity Key *and a professional speaker.*

Lessons from Dad

My dad and I had a very complicated relationship. He provided for the family and was physically present. However, he was absent emotionally. I can understand this intellectually, but for many years, it left a hole in my heart.

Dad was 45 when I was born. Mom was 36. I have two siblings, a sister that is 14 years older and a brother that is 12 years older. Being the "late-life miracle" and a "momma's boy," I always got the feeling from Dad that I was an afterthought, unwanted, and not good enough. This was compounded by the fact that I was a shy introvert and a thinker, the opposite of Dad.

When I had just started first grade the school announced a special evening meeting for the Cub Scouts. I didn't know anything about Scouts, but my brother had just joined the Army, and I associated the Scouts with the military. I wanted to be like my brother because he was Dad's favorite. I convinced Mom that I wanted to go to this Cub Scout meeting.

It ended up that Dad drove me. I don't remember the meeting because of what happened afterward. On the way back home, Dad stopped to talk with somebody. There was nothing to keep me occupied. After what felt like hours (probably less than 10 minutes) I went up to Dad and pulled a couple of times on his pants leg.

He barked out, "WHAT?"

And I timidly said, "I'm tired. Can we go home?"

Silence.

In my memory, it feels like a cold blast of freezing air was emanating from Dad. He marched me to the car, and we drove home. I went to bed wondering what I had done wrong.

We never talked about it. In fact, I don't recall ever talking to Dad about anything going on in my emotional life. And yet, his approval was what I wanted the most.

When I was nine, Dad started a lawn mower repair business. He started teaching me to work on lawn mowers. I had very little interest in lawn mowers per se, but I always wanted to learn new things, and I really wanted my dad's approval, so I jumped into it. By age 12, I could take a lawn mower that wasn't running, tear it apart, find what was wrong, fix it, and put it back together. And it would run. With no parts leftover! Did I get any praise or appreciation from Dad?

Silence.

I knew something wasn't right, and it hurt, but I could not have put into words at the time what it was. I've since learned that my primary love language is words of appreciation, and that is what I needed but did not get. Ironically, I later found out through my brother that Dad would brag about me to other people.

Although I didn't know the term at the time, Dad was my first mentor. I learned both good and bad things from Dad.

Three things I learned from Dad:

- Persistence—you can do almost anything when you stick with it.
- Money gives you options.
- Feelings are irrelevant.

An Exciting and Profitable Offer

After college, my WHAT had developed to be: make a lot of money and have a good time. Then, a friend I knew called to tell me he had taken a new job. Then he asked, "Dale, have you ever thought about going to Australia?"

I thought back to fourth grade. Our music teacher had taught us "Waltzing Matilda" and told us about kangaroos, koalas, and platypuses. It had always been a deep-seated desire of mine to someday see these things.

It turned out, the company he went to work for, E-Systems, was a defense contractor working for the US government. They were hiring and wanted someone with exactly my experience to move to Australia. They would supply travel there and back, plus housing and utilities, plus a 30% bonus on the base pay!

I applied. They flew me to Dallas for an interview. They offered me a job on the spot, and the base was more than I was making at the time. It was a no-brainer.

Australia

In January 1982, I moved to Australia. My first boss was great, but he was replaced in 1983 with the worst boss of my entire career, who was a liar, a fraud, and a poser. I decided to move back to the States in December 1984. Interestingly enough, this worst boss was fired six months later.

After two years back in the States, an opportunity came up, and I was able to return to Australia. I had a series of bosses but no mentors.

In 1992, our office announced that the government was going to start taxing the housing and utilities benefits we had been enjoying. A group of us were sitting around the lunch table griping about this tax, when out of my mouth came: "You know, we really shouldn't be griping. After all, **this is JUST a job, not a career.**"

At that moment, I realized my **WHAT** had changed and my heart wanted something much bigger.

In the next four years, I moved back to Dallas, Texas, and changed jobs, all while looking for my next big thing.

Lessons from Gary Tatsch

That's when Gary Tatsch came into my life. We met at a DFW Unix User's group meeting; I was helping run the group, and he came in looking for IT talent. Gary offered me a computer consultant job, which I accepted. Over the next 13 years, across four companies, he was my boss and mentor.

In late 1998, Gary was recruited by a company to start a new division that would sell hardware and do consulting. I joined him. We moved a lot of hardware and were profitable. A year later, the company wanted to get out of the hardware business and focus on website development. Gary negotiated a deal to roll the division into a new company, take the existing hardware clients, and pay them a referral fee for the first year.

In January 2000, I, Gary, and eight others created a new startup company, Applied Solutions Incorporated (ASI). Gary was president, I was vice president. As a new company, we started with no revenue. But as a team that had been together for a year with a pre-built pipeline in the hardware business, we hit the ground running and ended the year with millions of dollars in revenue, albeit a relatively small profit. It was enough for us to place number 10 in the *Entrepreneur Magazine* Hot 100, the 100 fastest-growing privately owned companies in America.

Lessons from Hugh Jones

In 2001, a group of us in the company were involved in a vigorous debate about how to proceed. Tensions were high. Voices were getting louder and louder. Several people were getting red-faced. It felt like a thunderstorm was about to break out in the room.

Then a quiet, firm, crystal-clear voice echoed from the back of the room. "Gentlemen, you are in **VIOLENT AGREEMENT**."

Even though he said it only once, it was as if that phrase was still reverberating around the room. I know it was echoing inside my head.

Violent agreement.

The argument was over. The way forward was clear.

The clear voice from the back of the room was Hugh Jones. Hugh had joined ASI to mentor Gary and me. At first, I wasn't sure about Hugh. He was often blunt and he told me things about myself that I didn't want to hear. As it turned out, those were things I **needed** to hear.

Hugh had a whole vocabulary of phrases that would grab your attention. In addition to "violent agreement," some others were:

- Communication is a bilateral responsibility.
- Lead with facade and fill with substance.
- Leadership commands, not demands.
- Management is adult day care.

Although I worked with Hugh for less than three years, I would go on to refer to the wisdom I learned many times.

Three things I learned from Hugh:

- When everyone else is losing their head, the leader keeps his and focuses on the next right move.

- A short, memorable phrase can communicate a deep philosophy—and becomes a verbal shorthand.
- Feelings are critical. The leader takes care of their people.

Between Gary and Hugh's mentoring, my craving for personal development had exploded. Prior to that point, I had read a lot of technical books. Now, I was devouring books on leadership and self-development by John Maxwell, Jim Collins, Stephen Covey, Patrick Lencioni, Rick Warren, Bob Buford, Bob Beaudine, Zig Ziglar, John Eldredge, and a host of others.

Lessons from Gary Tatsch, Part Two

Despite Hugh's guidance and hitting number 23 on the Entrepreneur Hot 100 in 2002, we ended up shutting down ASI in September 2004.

Gary took over as a division lead for Stonebridge, another company in the same industry. I was his right-hand man with no direct management responsibilities. Within a couple of years, we sold a major consulting contract to a company in Houston. I put a team together and delivered some great outcomes. As a result, the contract was annualized for the calendar year 2007. That year, this one contract contributed almost 10% of Stonebridge's revenue.

The 2008 recession hit the company hard in 2009, and Stonebridge had to reduce the headcount. Gary recommended that they keep me, since I was managing the major contract and the team. Gary was let go, and I was assigned a lot of his responsibilities. After 13 years, I had a new boss. Gary got a job within a couple of months.

Three things I learned from Gary:

- There's likely a way to turn what looks like an impossible situation into a win. Be creative.
- Give your people plenty of room to grow and they (usually) will.
- Don't let a few bad apples sour your faith in humanity.

My Transition to Calling

These mentors and others have led me on a path of continual growth and self-improvement. This has had a major impact on my life. In 2011, I started training as a life coach. I have had multiple mentors on my coaching journey: Chris McCluskey, Dave Mead, Michael Marx, John Ramstead,

Kim Avery, Kyle Wilson, and many others. Their mentorship not only accelerated my growth but also launched a desire in me to start passing on the lessons I've been privileged to learn. There was yet another level I was being pulled toward.

In November 2017, I heard a book review of Simon Sinek's *Start with Why*. This led me to read the book and to view and recommend his TED Talk of the same name multiple times. **WHY** was the core question that everything kept circling around. And yet, as big as it was, it still wasn't big enough.

Finally, in 2022, the word **CALLING** took center stage. To me, **calling** is an upward pull, something that is not of yourself, and it adds a necessary spiritual component to the equation.

In November 2022, I saw a diagram in a flash—a "God download" as Kyle Wilson likes to say. Although I had seen it, it took me two weeks of struggle to get the words correct. It took another two weeks to put together the basics of a presentation that enabled me to talk about and explain the framework of this message.

Keys to Finding Your Calling

◆ = CALLING

Scan to Download a Colorized Version

Copyright © 2022 by Coach Dale
https://CoachDale.com
License: CC BY-NC-SA 4.0
https://creativecommons.org/licenses/by-nc-sa/4.0/

Abilities Others Affirm — Passion — Desires Of Your Heart — Career — Mission — Provides Income (or impact) — Purpose — Makes Your Heart Cry

A colorized version with more detail is available at http://CoachDale.com/calling.

This is my gift and message to the world. I feel like God gave this to me to pass along, not to keep. To that end, the diagram and the framework are licensed under the Creative Commons license, which allows use and modifications with an acknowledgment that it originated with me. This is part of my legacy.

In the months since this God download, I have developed and tested a coaching process using this framework. I've named it The Calling Experience, and it integrates the calling framework with my previous coaching experience to bring remarkable clarity to the future path and calling of each of my clients. It's exciting to see the progress! I look forward to helping others get clear on their unique calling and the next steps in their journey for years to come. That is my calling!

To find out more about The Calling Experience, the results that have been achieved, and whether it might be right for you, send an email to dale@coachdale.com and mention The Calling Experience. Website is www.CoachDale.com. Follow Dale on LinkedIn.com/in/CoachDale or Facebook.com/CoachDaleYoung.

Quotable: What's the difference between an inheritance and a legacy? One word of two characters:
An inheritance is something you leave TO someone.
A legacy is something you leave IN someone.

 Coach Dale — The Calling Experience

JANA HUBBS

From Educator to Entrepreneur
Investing for Legacy

Jana Hubbs, co-founder of Legacy Investors.US, tackles the special needs housing crisis as an experienced entrepreneur in investment real estate. With expertise in special education and real estate, Jana and her husband, Randy, raise and manage capital for real estate ventures globally, including single, multi-family, and luxury resort properties.

Where the Journey Began

I was born in Boise, Idaho, the youngest of three children and the only girl. My dad's parents were full-blood Basque. The unique and diverse culture of the Basque is rooted in a region where France meets Spain on the scenic coast of Biscay at the end of the majestic Pyrenees Mountains. When my grandparents married, they left their homeland, arrived at Ellis Island to become US citizens, and migrated to a community popular with Basque immigrants in Jordan Valley, Idaho.

The culture in my family was very male-dominant, and there was an underlying expectation that I would become someone's wife to take care of the household. Although I knew I would marry and raise a family, I knew there was much more value I could add to other people's lives.

Through the years, I was exposed to many people who had disabilities.

One of my best friends, still today, I met in third grade. She was completely deaf and wore hearing aids to assist with her hearing. I never saw her as different, only as a friend of mine. When I was in middle school, my family moved to a different neighborhood. Soon after, a family moved in across the street, and their little boy, Doug, had Down syndrome. We developed a good relationship, and I worked with him on school activities and communication.

My oldest brother, David, had a learning disability which was identified when he was in fifth grade. Although my parents understood his learning difficulties, my dad had difficulty accepting this diagnosis because of the shame associated with it as a Basque male.

David married young and soon after had a boy who was born with a severe case of cerebral palsy. This affected his ability to walk, and his communication stopped progressing at about a four-year-old level. Watching him grow up was a powerful experience and forever changed my life.

Although my father loved his family, he was the ruler in our house, and it was never wise to argue with him. Through my years of growing up, I learned how best to communicate with him, listen, read his face and body language, and get him to understand my hopes, desires, and needs.

When I acquired my driver's license, I worked in various industries: fast food, meat wrapping, and as an escrow officer at a bank. My goal was to solidify my independence from my father's plans for me. Because of my desire to go into teaching and my experiences with my best friend, Doug, David, and my nephew JJ, I found my calling in special education.

One evening in particular, I had the courage to look my dad in the eyes and say, "Dad, there's always a fork in the road, and if I take a different path for a while against your wishes, know that I will always end on the right path." Although that didn't sit well with him, he accepted my statement and goal in life, and as a result, I earned his respect.

Discovering My Gift

After graduating high school, I attended Columbia Basin College and eventually transferred to Central Washington University to study my passion, teaching individuals with disabilities. This university specialized in behavior modification, where we learned how to set goals and objectives for individuals and complete task analysis and reverse task analysis.

We also learned about our inner selves and what traits and behaviors we needed to modify to be more successful. I was told I had a gift for figuring out how to offer tools, skills, and coping mechanisms that created functional skills in each individual or group I worked with. I became obsessed with reading books on communication, self-help, psychology, and counseling to understand these concepts better and practice what was lacking in my childhood.

My role as a special education teacher was to provide coping skills to help people deal with their disabilities and family training to help the family and the individual when it became time to transition to the next level of their life. As a high school teacher, I taught students life skills, prevocational skills, and vocational skills by teaching reading, writing, and math through life survival skills, including woodworking (building and refinishing furniture), simple plumbing, cleaning and organizing household spaces, and grooming. The goal was that once a student graduated, they would live as independently as possible and function at a job as a contributing member of the community.

After three years teaching at the high school, I was recruited and hired by the Educational Service District 123 to train teachers and parents in rural districts how to develop prevocational and vocational skills with students in each of their communities. I also approached local businesses in each community to develop job sites for students with disabilities. After that, I coordinated programs from preschool through high school in these districts, which allowed me to look beyond the present and help staff and parents set goals for the future when their students would transition to the next level in life. This was extremely important because it gave hope and encouragement to each family.

Always Ask, "How Can We?"

It's difficult to talk about my successes, especially after being married to my husband, Randy, for 42 years. We've grown into a "we" or "us" versus an "I" or "me" approach. I hope my awareness of various approaches stimulates others to help solve what we have identified as a crisis in this country.

Throughout my years, I developed different approaches to working with individuals with disabilities. It wasn't about one approach or about me. It was seeking the key that would unlock the learning door for each individual based on what they were all about socially, emotionally, intellectually, and physically. I studied facial expressions, body movements, gestures, and how they understood or expressed language. The other factors that played into working with children and families were response time, processing time, and wait time. These techniques allowed me to create success with individuals and groups that no one believed could happen.

One student whom I worked with, along with his family, was originally not allowed on the steps of the school due to his severe disability and inability to communicate and because the staff didn't know how to teach him. After several years of working with this young man in his home, teaching self-help skills and communication through pictures and a communication board, his parents were able to move him into a living situation where he was provided with the guidance and support he needed while he was also allowed to continue to develop skills for independence. Transitioning out of the parent's home should be a natural process that allows parents to age without worrying about what will happen when their lives are over. Unfortunately, this is still a massive issue in our country.

Another child I worked with was three years old and severely autistic. My first goal was to identify what the parents wanted most for their child. In this situation, they both wanted to hold and cuddle their little girl. Due to the child's aversion to touch and eye contact, we developed a program to increase her tolerance for sensory touch and increase her sense of communication through touch and sight. After four months of working with the child and family, this little girl sat on her dad's lap for the first time. He was so elated that tears of joy rolled down his face. Driving away afterward, I was overwhelmed with emotion and excitement because we had achieved what initially seemed impossible.

From Problems to Solutions

Throughout my teaching and administrative work years, I met with various agencies and individuals within our community. I always had a vision to identify "what's right, what's right, what's wrong." My supervisors always knew that if I identified a problem, I also had solutions to consider.

In working with agencies designed to assist people with special needs, it always disturbed me that their caseloads were extremely high, waiting lists were extremely long, and our graduates and adult population would end up living at home or with relatives and losing valuable skills they had once acquired.

What seemed to be an industry-wide problem was certainly not the ideal situation. Throughout my career, this haunted me because nobody seemed to be looking for a solution. This ultimately became the driving force for us to create our Special Needs Housing Model.

The Balancing Act

After Randy and I began having children, I took a position in a local school district where I could offer teachers, administrators, students, and parents incentives to create a better educational system for each student. During my 23 years as the Director of Special Education of the Pasco School District, I continued to develop programs and look for ways to enhance learning environments that would further an individual's development of functional lifelong learning skills.

My passion for special needs individuals was so strong that it was vital for me to lead by example. I was in classrooms or homes of individuals with disabilities for at least 10 hours per week, modeling, demonstrating, and helping staff and parents to develop the skills required for teaching individual students with disabilities.

The Transformation from Educator to Entrepreneur

Outside of our careers, Randy and I worked on our real estate hobby: rental properties, remodels, and increasing our knowledge and experience. We decided early on that we didn't want to retire on a teacher's salary, so we set a goal to purchase a property yearly. During the 1990s, we started flipping properties to get capital for our buy-and-hold investments. During that time, when we realized there was much more to learn about real estate investing, we began to read books and focused on getting more educated. Because we were actively involved in our careers and raising our children, often, our real estate hobby happened after the kids were tucked in bed. Because Randy, who was also a teacher, had three months off in the summertime, he put that time to use in working on flips and managing our portfolio.

As we moved into the 2000s, we realized it was time to treat our real estate hobby more like a business. Having been through the crash of 1980 and having witnessed several other market dips along the way, we observed the massive run-up of people clamoring to get into real estate investment, and we began to pull back on our acquisitions in 2006. Fortunately, we were able to dodge the 2008 crash, and we used that time to position ourselves to capture the multi-family opportunities that became available in the aftermath. During this recovery period, we grew our business to the point that we needed to start thinking about exiting our careers and going full-time in our real estate business.

It was time to open the door to the next chapter in our life. I retired in 2015, and Randy soon followed. We were now full-time investors and continued to acquire multi-family properties in the US and internationally.

Discovering My New Identity

When people ask the opening question "What do you do?", we usually answer by identifying with our job or career. I had to figure out what hat to wear now that I was retired. It was uncomfortable, and I felt lost. I knew my skill set but had to navigate how to add value to our real estate business.

I have always loved numbers, accounting, and working with people, so I ultimately settled into my comfort zone, running the finances for our business and working with the various management companies, banks, attorneys, and vendors on our team. It was a relief to finally find my role and new path.

Leaving a Legacy

In 2018, Randy and I set a goal to create our legacy project. This project is what keeps me going, and knowing it is coming to fruition touches my heart. By working to solve the special needs housing crisis in the US, we are impacting the lives of so many people across the nation. This is our big, hairy, audacious goal (BHAG), and parents and guardians of people with special needs as well as investors, can be a part of our mission.

Specifically, the population we are working to provide adequate housing for is physically and developmentally disabled children and adults. Mostly, these individuals were identified sometime during their school years and went through special education programs in their respective school districts. This is not as much for profoundly medically challenged individuals as it is for individuals with special needs who need supported living and employment in a home where they can be as independent as possible given their skill sets.

This need has existed for an eternity and continues to be a crisis. The federal government and politicians have done very little to change the system, which forces adults with disabilities to live below the poverty level. There are nonprofit organizations and programs in different communities that build or rent facilities for adults with disabilities. However, the problem with this is that there are many strings attached to these programs and far too limited funds to be able to serve this growing population.

We have discovered that the solution is a for-profit model where parents/guardians and investors cannot only reap the financial benefits associated with this model but also make a social impact on the community and create a lifestyle that our children and adults with disabilities so deserve.

Randy and I are very excited about our new legacy project. We followed our "why" from the start by going into teaching so we could make a positive impact on students. Now, we are taking that experience to a new level by helping those parents and guardians, as well as investors, make an impact and a profit in their communities and target markets. By sharing our knowledge, we will help those who, like us, want to make a positive social impact and leave a legacy.

Jana Hubbs and her husband, Randy, have created a for-profit model to solve the special needs housing crisis. Both have extensive backgrounds in real estate investing and teaching. To get a free copy of their eBook and learn about their online course: Solving the Special Needs Housing Crisis in the US, contact: Jana@legacyinvestors.us or visit www.legacyinvestors.us.

Quotable: Pursue your passion and discover your why to leave a lasting legacy!

 Randy & Jana Hubbs' "Legacy Investors.US"

DUSTIN REICHERT

Breaking Through Me

Dustin Reichert is a retired deputy sheriff and a recipient of his agency's Purple Heart. He is a professional speaker, team-building specialist, and PTSD advocate. He is the author of the book 10-88! Officer Down and founder of the program Breaking Through You! He has facilitated events all over the country for groups of all sizes and types.

Nostalgia and Triggers

Every year, I take at least one trip to Houston, Texas, to visit Brad, one of my best friends from high school. I love going back to visit when I can, and there is something so nostalgic for me about the state of Texas. I moved with my parents to the Houston area after I graduated high school.

It's interesting that it is nostalgic for me to visit, because there was a lot of loneliness and pain living there. Part of it was missing my Minnesota friends, but the other part was losing my grandparents, an uncle to suicide, and my brother to a car crash. One of my Texas friends was murdered during a robbery too. Then, I was devastated when I lost my little girl Tyealeen at just over two months old because of a heart defect. It was hard to enjoy life down there. It felt like life was working against me.

I moved back to Minnesota after four years to be closer to friends and family and pursue a career in law enforcement. I think it's easier to visit Texas and enjoy it nowadays because I'm so far from that time in my life. Plus, I get to visit Brad and his wife and also visit Tyealeen's gravesite to tell her I love and miss her.

One of those visits was in February of 2019. I love live country music, and there was a band I really wanted to see playing near Brad's house. The band was playing at a bar in unincorporated Grimes County, Texas. The sound engineer was doing a sound check for the opening artist when, suddenly, the loudest feedback I had ever heard came across the speakers. I was standing at the bar, and my right ear was facing the stage. I felt instant pain shoot through my ear—but really, through my soul.

As much as everyone in the bar groaned, I did not. I fell immediately silent. My eyes were rapidly bouncing across everything in the room but focusing on nothing. My fists clenched so tight they were large stones. I felt tears roll down my cheeks. It took me a few moments to realize what was happening. That moment of jarring sound had triggered my PTSD.

I looked at Brad and said, "Let's go play a pool game. I'm going to pace. I'm going to cry. It won't make sense to you. Don't say a single word to me. Just let me settle this down."

Brad has been an amazing friend for decades, but he didn't really understand PTSD or the impact of post-traumatic stress injuries. Most people don't. Heck, most of us who suffer from PTSD don't understand it or sometimes even realize it. I had the benefit of at least knowing I had it and tools to manage it.

This was a powerful trigger though. It startled me that I reacted so strongly. Thankfully, one of Brad's best qualities was his willingness to do what I needed and allow it to calm down. He was the perfect person to be there at that moment.

A few months later, I was at lunch with my wife and my mother. The restaurant we were at had concrete floors. About 20 feet away, a staff member dropped an empty metal pan. It was loud. It startled a lot of people, but it did more to me. My ear started hurting again. I didn't realize I was triggered until I felt my mother's hand touch mine from across the table. I was frozen. My fists were clenched tightly on the table. She later told me my eyes were bouncing all around the room with my head straight.

My Dream Job, 10-88 Officer Down

I should probably step back and tell a little more about why this monster is even inside me.

After moving home from Texas in 1994, I immediately worked towards my career in law enforcement. I was first sworn in as a part-time deputy sheriff at the Ramsey County Sheriff's Office and later full-time with the Anoka County Sheriff's Office. My hard work paid off.

I worked as a patrol deputy and eventually a detective on the Anoka-Hennepin Drug and Violent Crimes Task Force. I was the first drug recognition expert (DRE) for our agency, and eventually, a DRE instructor. This all gave me a lot of experience. I absolutely loved being a police officer. I loved the interaction with the public. I loved removing criminals from the street. I loved helping people in need. And fast driving legally didn't hurt either!

On May 13, 2003, I was working in the city of Andover when my partner, Sam, got a call about loud music disturbing the peace. It was Thursday night, and we would often go to those calls alone since we were a smaller department, but this neighborhood had a history of problematic people and Sam was only on her second day on her own.

Upon arrival, we heard music from inside the residence. It was the Bee Gees playing, which is rare for a loud music call. It was just before 2:30 a.m., and there was obviously no party occurring, except for Sam and I doing a little disco dance in the driveway.

The next 60 seconds would change my life forever. As Sam knocked on the door, I was looking through the large front window. A man surfaced from the kitchen, disappeared, and then returned with a gun in his hand. The residence was a duplex, and the front door was near the middle of the structure. Sam and I re-positioned ourselves against the wall at the midpoint between the units while yelling commands as he opened the door.

Realizing that if he started shooting, we would both likely get hit, I took a big step away from Sam. At that moment, I realized there was no cover and I was now committed to directly confronting him. He was five to eight feet away, in an elevated position. As he opened the door, he pointed the gun at my chest, and by the time I pulled my trigger, he had the gun pointed between my eyes. In our exchange of gunfire, I struck him in his torso, fatally piercing his lung. He hit me with two forty-five caliber bullets. One hit my upper right arm and the other hit my pelvic region. The second round dropped me immediately.

I heard Sam yelling over the radio, "4A57 shots fired! Officer down! Shots fired! 10-88!" 10-88 was our code for an officer in need of emergency help.

Next, I would hear the tones only played when an officer is in trouble followed by an unbelievable amount of help coming. Although I felt like I was going to die face down in front of that window, they were able to rescue me and get me to the hospital.

The first round hit my right arm, exploding half an inch of my humerus bone, half of my biceps and triceps, and causing injury to my radial nerve. The second round struck my pelvic region and surprisingly traveled cleanly through my body, only causing internal scarring. I spent five days in the hospital before being sent home to heal.

A Lost Man

Over the years, I've come to learn that the physical injuries pale in comparison to the years of PTSD.

Most people think my PTSD was from the gun battle only. But it's more complex than that. What happened after my body healed from the shooting is a long, complex story which I detail in my book *10-88! Officer Down*. To sum it up, in my experience, many law enforcement administrations do not support officers in cases of officer-involved shootings the way the public thinks. Even with my shooting being clearly justified, both by law and policy, higher-ups in my agency, people who were once friends, gave me no support.

After months of stress, including waiting to hear if I was cleared by the agency, the pressure was getting to me. It felt political. But I just tried to keep my head down and work on my assignments. Since I wasn't talking about my situation to them, my partners came up with their own conclusions and rumors spread. My undersheriff told me to stop riling everyone up, which I wasn't, but he didn't believe me. I was then assigned to the crime lab, which was in the basement and away from all other deputies.

I was at my lowest. I was isolated. I still hadn't had a chance to fully process the shooting itself. I felt shamed.

I had weekly meetings with my undersheriff, and feeling the pressure of how I was being treated, I had a thought I needed to share. I told him I had never understood how an administration could push an officer to put a gun in their mouth. I explained I wasn't suicidal, I liked life too much, but that now...I understood.

He stared at me blankly. Instead of helping me, they put me on medical leave and ordered everyone not to visit while on duty or discuss Sheriff's Office business with me.

I was lost. I met with my attorney for a strategy meeting. With tears rolling down my cheeks, I asked her, "What if I'm ready to be done?" My arm was not healing the way I had anticipated. The mental stress was taking its toll on me, and by then, I had been diagnosed with PTSD. I knew I could no longer do the job that I loved, not just physically or mentally, but in the manner I would be proud of.

I was broken. It was time to turn in my badge. I retired May 3, 2005, almost two years after the incident.

Invisible Wounds

When that pan dropped at the restaurant, I was triggered. But, when my mom touched my hand, I felt comfort. I felt someone could see my PTSD for the first time.

Those two trigger experiences I described weighed heavy on my mind. It was my first realization that the treatments I had gone through weren't permanent. That terrified me.

I had previously gone through a treatment called eye movement desensitization and reprocessing (EMDR). It looks like an eye test we do for drunk driving arrests, but different in technique and outcome. My therapist explained in lay terms that it was like downloading traumatic memories locked in my short-term memory to my long-term memory.

It was powerful. I did multiple sessions over several months and finally felt peace. I felt healed. That is why I was startled that this monster was back.

I now had to question if I needed more help. I thought maybe there was hearing damage from the shooting, thus the pain and triggering with loud things. But I went to the hearing doctor, and my hearing was perfect. It was kind of strange being disappointed in that outcome. This was the beginning of an understanding that PTSD would be with me for life.

The more struggles I had, the darker I got, the more I drank, the more I didn't care about myself. I avoided riding my motorcycle because I was getting too involved in risk-taking—a direct symptom of PTSD. I felt a darkness, but I didn't know what it was. I wasn't suicidal, but I was terrified of what the stage after the darkness might be. I didn't want that for me, but I especially didn't want that for my family and friends.

In 2023, I went back to therapy and found the perfect therapist for my personality. She diagnosed me with complex PTSD, more commonly known as cumulative PTSD. It is related to cumulative traumatic exposures rather than a singular event. Police officers see the worst of everyone's days, the worst of mankind, people that want to hurt and kill them, horrible accident scenes, and more. Generally, an average person will experience one to three serious traumas in their lifetime. Police officers will experience more than 700 such traumas without even being involved in a critical incident.

As I continue to manage this, I will continue therapy, including EMDR, and refresh my tools. Strangely, I look forward to releasing memories my mind has shielded me from. I also recently went through a treatment called a stellate ganglion block (SGB). The neurosurgeon uses an ultrasound-guided needle to inject ketamine directly into the stellate ganglion nerve areas, which research has shown plays a significant role in our fight or flight system. There is no intoxicating effect. Instead, it resets the fight or flight system. I went through three sessions over a year and felt a distinct emotional impact. I am in the most peaceful place I have been in years.

Walking on Fire, Not Through It

Over the last couple of years, I've been trained and mentored by Dave Albin, the man who facilitated firewalks for Tony Robbins for 20 years.

I have been developing a program called Breaking Through You! It involves a speaking component and sharing my story but also includes breakthrough experiences curated to help you break through your barriers. I facilitated my most recent program this last May. I asked everyone to lean into it, to find their breakthrough moment. As I told them my story, I explained that my story isn't any more or less important than theirs, it's just an example. The program would normally include one or two experiences for the group, but for this one, I included all four: board breaking, arrow breaking, glass walking, and firewalking.

I could tell my message and the program resonated with the attendees. Although not everyone participated in all the activities, whatever they participated in, I saw amazing breakthrough moments. And that triggered a breakthrough feeling for me. I was once again helping people.

I had been symbolically walking through the fire of life for the last two decades, burning up inside. Of all the fire walks I have participated in, this one...this one wasn't just one I facilitated. This wasn't just any fire I walked on. When I took my steps across those hot coals, the sense of relief I felt at that moment was more than I had ever had.

A mistake I continued to make over the years was thinking again and again that momentary relief was a fix. The last few years have reminded me that no one single fix is THE FIX. Instead, it's a journey. Just like someone managing their weight must always work on diet and exercise or a marathon runner must always train to be marathon ready, so must I, and others with PTSD, continue to work on mental health. Because doing a little work along the way to keep me healthy is much less damaging and much less work than trying to play catch up when the darkness hits. And so the journey continues.

Dustin Reichert is the author of *10-88! Officer Down* and the facilitator of Breaking Through You! With over 15 years of experience as a speaker, team-building expert, and professional hypnotist, he is available for speaking and to facilitate special events. You can find out more at www.DustinReichert.com and www.BreakingThroughYou.org. Reach out to him at info@DustinReichert.com or 763.325.4242.

Quotable: Just like someone managing weight must always work on diet and exercise, or a marathon runner must always train to be marathon ready, we must also work on ourselves to maintain mental and physical health.

 DustinReichert.com

MANDY JUNGE

Enduring Devastating Loss but Choosing to Be Happy

Mandy Junge is currently an executive assistant. She has a long history in property management and is a passive real estate investor with her husband Greg. She is a health enthusiast and loves the beach and traveling. Mandy lives in Florida with her husband of six years and their dog, Buster.

A Happy Childhood

I grew up near Seattle, Washington, with two loving parents and a sister. Sometimes my sister and I would fight and sometimes we would get along, like typical siblings. My father worked hard to support our family and my mom worked part-time, while we were in school, and took care of us and the household the rest of the time. She was always at my school events, including daytime assemblies and football games where I was a cheerleader. She even chaperoned a school band tour down to California. My dad would take us skiing on the weekends, and for bike rides after dinner, and we'd take family trips together. Every summer, my parents would drop us off with my grandparents and they'd take us camping for a week.

Despite my parents' divorce in my senior year of high school, the dream I had always had was not tainted. I wanted a life similar to what I had growing up: two or three kids, to be there and support them in everything they did, and to have a close family.

Growing up, I loved school and the friends I had. Our neighborhood was full of kids my age, so we were always outside playing when we were younger. When my alarm went off in the morning, I would jump out of bed and was always excited for the day ahead. I loved being in band, on the drill team, and a cheerleader my senior year of high school. I got really good grades too. I had to study for them, but that was a great achievement for me.

When I turned 15, I got a job at an amusement park and water park with my best friend. I quickly became a barista there and loved it. Eventually, I got a job at a coffee shop and remained a barista for over 12 years.

My Dream Life Begins

In college, I met my now ex-husband. We moved to California after we graduated and eventually got married. We had good jobs and a nice starter house. The next step in my dream was to have kids. That journey soon started but the path turned out to be nothing I could have ever imagined.

At nine weeks pregnant, I lay on the table for my first ultrasound. There was an embryo, but no heartbeat. I was devastated. The doctor did not have an explanation for why it happened, but we were told to wait two months before we tried again.

Four months later, I was eight weeks pregnant, and we had a heartbeat at the first ultrasound. I was ecstatic! It was really happening.

The following month, at my 12-week checkup, there was no heartbeat. Another devastation. Again, there was no explanation for why it happened. The doctor told us to wait three months before we tried again.

Five months later, at eight weeks pregnant, we had a heartbeat once again. This time I was excited but cautious.

The second ultrasound showed a growing fetus and a strong heartbeat. My dream of having a baby was finally coming true. I couldn't be more excited. We began to tell friends and family. Gifts started coming in. We were thinking of names and preparing to have a baby.

After four months, I could start to feel the baby move, and my stomach was growing. *This time it's really happening. In five months, my life will be everything I'd ever wished and hoped for.*

Loss and Devastation Changed My Life

Twenty-one weeks and five days into the pregnancy, I woke up for work and thought I had gas pains. By the time I got to work, the cramps were worse.

My manager's previous career was in early childhood development, and she had a couple kids of her own, so when she showed up to work, I told her what was going on. She felt my stomach and said it didn't feel like labor pains.

A couple of hours later, I started bleeding. I called my now ex-husband to tell him what was going on, then went directly to my doctor. Luckily, I had an appointment already scheduled that afternoon, so they got me right in.

When they realized I was going into labor, they put me in a wheelchair, pushed me across the parking lot to the hospital, and admitted me. After several hours of contractions, laying at a decline, and being given a drug to stop the contractions, I went into full labor.

I was eventually given an epidural for pain, and I had my precious baby girl that evening. She was born too early to save.

At 21 weeks and five days, 12.8 ounces and perfectly formed on the outside, Katherine was beautiful. The doctor put her in my arms. After several seconds, I said to the doctor, "She just took a breath, she's alive!" The doctor informed me that was just her body shutting down. I held her in my arms for 45 minutes while her organs stopped working. Her lungs continued to periodically gasp for air, and I was crushed each time.

That was the worst day of my life.

This time, they told me I had an incompetent cervix. I could get pregnant again, but I would be on bed rest through the whole pregnancy. Anything they suggested, I would do, if it meant being able to have a baby.

Anger Sets In

Shortly after that, my now ex-husband and I started fighting more and he lost his job. We were barely intimate, so having a baby seemed impossible. We just weren't on the same page with life anymore. I was becoming unhappy in my marriage, and we never got pregnant again.

Every time I would see a newborn or a pregnant woman, I would cry. When I saw young girls, troubled girls, or anyone I thought might not make a fit mother having a baby, I would get angry, thinking that they could easily have kids and I couldn't.

For years, on the anniversary of Katherine's birth, I would drink a bottle of wine and cry while I looked through the box the hospital gave me. It included pictures of my precious baby, the gown and hat she was in, a blanket, a little heart pillow, and her feet and hand prints.

I was changing from the happy person I had always been to a person who was angry, bitter and jealous. This was not the plan I had for my life or the person I had always been. I needed a change. Otherwise, I was afraid this negative worldview would be my life forever.

Inspiring Words That Changed My Life Forever

One day, I was having a conversation with my dad, and he told me, "You only get one life. Make the best of it."

It was a much deeper conversation, but that was the nugget I needed to hear. I never wanted to disappoint my parents, and I felt like he had given me permission to leave my unhappy marriage and start a life that made me happy.

I got a job offer in Arizona and decided to take it. I didn't really know anyone out there and was moving farther away from my family, but I needed the change. I packed up a moving truck and started my new journey.

Things didn't work out with that job, but I was determined to make a good life for myself. I met a lot of friends, got another job, and was enjoying life.

At that point, I was still young enough to have kids. I decided to leave it up to my future partner. Although I was terrified to go through another loss, if my partner wanted a family, I would try again. If he didn't want kids, I was okay with that.

After being in Arizona for a few years, I met my husband, Greg. We met on a dating website that my dad convinced me to join. We fell in love pretty quickly, and I moved in with him after four months. Again, my dad suggested that to me since my lease was up. Greg must have read his mind because he suggested it also.

We got along so well, barely argued, which was a nice change from my previous marriage, and we loved and supported each other. Greg did not want kids, and I was okay with that.

After four years of dating, and getting my dad's permission before he passed, Greg and I got married. He is an amazing man.

A New Mindset

Life doesn't always work out the way you plan, but I decided to make the best life I could with the cards I was dealt. After I changed my mindset and no longer dwelled on the fact that I wasn't going to have kids, the anger, jealousy, and bitterness went away. I felt better than I had in years. This one life I have was turning into something amazing.

I married an amazing man, we have great friends and family, and we always seem to be traveling and finding our next adventure. Our life has been about making great memories. We love traveling to new places together, especially islands where we can do fun water activities or just relax on the beach.

Many of our friends have kids, and we get to enjoy them. Spending time with their kids is great, but we are also happy that we can go home and not have the responsibility of taking care of them. When we make weekend or travel plans, we can do what we want. We don't have to think about childcare, if a vacation is right for kids, etc. I have always been a silver-lining type of person, and I do that even more now.

It might sound strange to people who have children, and I would have a different mindset had I been able to have kids of my own, but staying positive about the life I've been given is the best way for me to live.

This transformational mindset of being happy can be used in any situation, not just having miscarriages. In any circumstance that didn't turn out the way you planned, you can look at the positive outcome.

Since I was a kid, I wanted to be a doctor. I even went to college for almost four years studying toward that goal. When I found out my lifelong dream wasn't going to happen because I pass out in hospitals and can't stand cuts, blood, etc., I had to find a new career path. I got my degree in business and have chosen jobs that make me happy.

Whatever happens in life that doesn't go according to your plans, you can find the silver lining so you enjoy the one life you are given.

Jim Rohn said, "Happiness is not an accident. Nor is it something you wish for. Happiness is something you design."

Designing my happy life is exactly what I'm doing.

To contact Mandy Junge about her story or share your similar story with her, please email her at mandyrjunge@gmail.com or friend her on Facebook. She's always available to listen if you need a sympathetic ear.

Quotable: Life doesn't always work out the way you plan, but I decided to make the best life I could with the cards I was dealt.

DEAN SHUPE

Serial Entrepreneur, Real Estate Investor, General & Landscape Contractor

Dean Shupe is a serial entrepreneur. He has been a real estate investor since 2012 in single/multifamily and land with 220+ flips/units/doors in four states and a contractor license in two states. Dean and his wife Samantha have started eight successful companies. Besides business, Dean enjoys time with his family and outdoor activities.

Break the Old Stigma

Do you remember when your family, teachers, and professors, maybe not in so many words, said, "You must get good grades or you will go nowhere in life and amount to nothing?"

This brings back so many memories for me, like not being capable of paying attention to the teacher or understanding the assignments. I failed nearly every test, and would stutter and turn bright red anytime the teacher called on me. In high school, my grades were terrible: 1.33 average GPA. Through the years, I struggled. I was in the dark about the real issue, which is so clear to me today.

I was born in Northern California between Sacramento and Lake Tahoe, and my childhood was far from easy. I started wearing glasses when I was 18 months old. With my bottle cap lenses and huge eyeballs, I was known as four eyes. My mom was working three jobs to keep up with the bills while married to an absent, alcoholic husband. My older sister was raising me and my brother. It was hectic, to say the least.

At the age of five, I was left by my biological father and adopted by his best friend. I quickly embraced that I finally had a father figure, a man that actually cared about me, put a roof over my head and food on the table, and took care of my mother. I called him Dad from day one. We moved to a better neighborhood in a new town with a fresh start.

Through grade school and middle school, I had a speech impediment and would be pulled out of class for speech therapy. But I played lots of sports and had lots of friends. As I got older, I began to care less about school and sports. High school came, and the real trouble began. I quit sports and started hanging around with the wrong "friends." A few of my grades started slipping which led to me constantly being grounded. My grades were so bad that I would have to bring a progress report home every Friday. If I had A's, B's, and C's, I wasn't grounded that weekend. If any grades were lower, that meant I was staying home.

Well, after a few weekends of being grounded, I was tired of being in trouble. So came a great idea. I had a classmate sign all my teacher's names and grades: A's, B's, and C's every week. When the real report cards came out at the end of each semester, my grades would once again read one B, the rest C's, D's, and F's. This would confuse my parents. I would tell them, "I must have failed the final."

Being the youngest of five, with two biological siblings and two step-siblings who all excelled in school, I quickly became the bad kid in my family. At times, I had low self-esteem and felt that people did not understand me.

My actions began to affect my family. My mother would call for meetings with the school principal, all my teachers, and myself. My mom wanted to know what was going on with me and my grades. I was not making the right decisions and definitely was doing things that would make NO parent proud. I was smoking weed, drinking alcohol, and running amok.

As how I felt about things crumbled into self-destruction and feeling lost, at the age of 17, I attempted suicide in my bedroom. In 2005, at 17, I met and started dating Samantha. She was with me through ups and downs and today is a woman I'm very proud to call my wife. Six months after we met, college came. I committed to signing up for college classes in hopes of impressing my family. One semester later, I dropped out. Everyone thought that I was the biggest idiot and now I really was not going anywhere in life. I was working at Lowe's and was popping pills, and drinking alcohol excessively.

Make It or Break It

I started working at a print shop, printing wine labels. I quickly excelled as a top press operator. A few years passed, and my boss at the time called me to his house. He said, "I am starting a new company and I want you to be the first person to come work for me. Mind you, I was the youngest employee at the time. We turned that new company into an eight-figure business by year two. He would tell me that one day I would take over the business.

In 2015, after eight years in the industry, I decided to step away. I told my boss, "I have more to offer than what I can do in this 30,000-square-foot building. It's time for me to do my own thing." While that job taught me so much about business and made it possible to purchase my first three real estate properties, it was my time, and I had a bigger calling.

I heard a lot of noise from doubters and naysayers. Coworkers were saying, "You'll be back." The family was saying, "You have a great job. What are you doing?" My boss and his wife said, "Everyone is replaceable, but Dean, you're not replaceable." One year after I left, they sold the company.

Second to None

As I set out to start my own business, I knew I'd be good because I knew I had no choice. There was a reason my old boss chose me to be the first person to work for him and launch his business. My work ethic and grit were second to none.

Growing up, my dad was a tough cookie. It was tough love, and he was known as "The King" in the neighborhood. No friends ever wanted to stay the night because he would make us wake up on the weekends at 6:00 a.m. to replace the roof, renovate the bathroom, build a retaining wall, pour concrete.... The list goes on. These early life experiences were my foundation in LIFE, DISCIPLINE, and SURVIVAL, a foundation I relied on as I started on this new journey.

My wife and I acquired a California landscape contractor license and quickly built a reputable and successful company that did high-quality work and was trusted throughout the community. We became one of the top landscape companies in El Dorado County, California.

When our daughter entered this world in late 2019, our lives changed in the blink of an eye. When she was born, since I had been left by my father, I had a fear of abandonment for my daughter. Childhood flashbacks came and scared me to death like a reoccurring nightmare. I realized that I could not imagine how a father could leave their child.

Pandemic

With our landscape company growing as we were managing our real estate portfolio, COVID-19 hit in March 2020. After canceled contracts and government instructions to shut it down, we had to lay off workers. As landlords, we were being stripped of our rights. We had a three-month-old daughter counting on us. We were not allowed to go outside and make money. We would literally be sneaking around to conduct business; we had no choice. With an unsure future, we had no clue what was to come.

We realized that the government could shut anything down at any time. After laying off employees, we realized that I was my business. I was limiting myself by digging in the trenches and only taking on a workload that I could physically handle. The question popped into my head, How can we conduct business from anywhere throughout the USA or across the world?

I thought, I need to start working smarter, not harder, as I am too smart with my brain to just be working with my hands. It clicked. I had been thinking too small and I was restricting my potential. How can I get in front of anyone, anywhere in the world, whether to sell them a product or service or simply inspire them?

New Ventures

In September of 2020, we decided to sell our business, our real estate portfolio, to relocate our family to Boise, Idaho. This was the best decision and has led us to our most successful life as parents, spiritually, and in business.

As our mindset shifted to go bigger, Samantha and I built new businesses and ultimately expanded them across the United States. This required me to get on social media for the first time in 10 years. I hadn't cared to show anyone what I was up to or the empire I was building. Now, I knew I could no longer hold myself back. I needed to get out of my comfort zone and start showing the universe what was going on in my world. I've got a lot to offer!

Samantha and I also started attending real estate conferences across the USA, building our network worldwide, and building lifelong relationships and friendships with some of the biggest names in real estate and business. This has allowed us to stay knowledgeable, relevant, and on top of our game in the industry. We used to think it was not what you know but who you know. No, it's WHO KNOWS YOU. Our business expanded from county-wide to country-wide, across the United States of America.

Do What They Say

"They" have always said you must get good grades, you must study, you must pass the test, you must go to college, and you must get a good job. But I'm proof that just because you don't do well in school doesn't mean you're not going to go anywhere in life. Just because you don't go to college, doesn't mean you won't be successful.

Does this mean go out and be reckless? Absolutely not. You still must be a hardworking and upstanding citizen. Whether you decide to get a degree or work for yourself, you can be successful with anything in life you set your mind to. You need a solid foundation, starting with family, health, work ethic, productivity, and passion! Don't listen to the fear and hesitancy of others who have never done the things you've set out to do.

Now, as a grown man, I realize how much I love and appreciate my dad. He was tough on me because I pushed the envelope. I bordered the edge and he was trying to reel me in. When I turned 19, he told me that he was so hard on me because he saw a lot of himself in me. He had been charged with 14 felonies and seven misdemeanors at one point in life. He didn't want me to turn out the same way. The smarter and older I got, the more I understood that, with the trials and tribulations I had as a kid, I did most of it to myself as I was making poor decisions.

Along with teaching me how to be a good father and husband, I am most GRATEFUL for my parents teaching me three key components to being successful in life: work ethic, a good FICO score, and buying a house. When I was 17, they co-signed a car for me. A year later, they told me to sell it and buy my own car with the credit I had built. At age 24, as I was going to rent an apartment, they said to go buy a house. I was confused as I could not afford it. We ended up using a USDA loan, 100% financing, and it ended up being cheaper to buy than it would have been to rent an apartment. That was 2012. I sold that house in 2021. You can only imagine the appreciation that property made over those nine years!

Through life and business ups, downs, and all arounds, I have gotten smarter and tougher each step of the way. I am certain that I would not be the man I am today if my biological father hadn't left me. If I had gotten good grades, I would probably be working a nine-to-five. I embrace my

ADHD, and without a doubt, this is my superpower! Every day, I become a better version of myself as a Christ follower, father, husband, and business owner. By the grace of God, I am here today to tell my story.

Recently, my brother told someone, "Dean is lucky to be where he is today because of where he has been and the choices he made growing up." This is because I didn't give up, I didn't play the "poor me" card, and I continued to tune out the noise of haters. Today, Jesus and my family come first! Samantha and I have built eight successful businesses. Moving states has allowed us to open our mindset and live our best lives. Our motto is, ENJOY LIFE MORE (ELM).

I focused on inspiring the underdog, like I once was. I have not taken a sip of alcohol in over six years and do not overuse prescribed medication. As a major advocate for youth, I donate time and funds to charities that help children, including children of the homeless and less fortunate. As a survivor of a suicide attempt and having a nephew who committed suicide, I am on a mission to help as many people with similar situations or thoughts. There is so much life to live. Even in dark times, you must stay strong.

My Challenge to You

Want to be successful in life? Be different. Take massive action. Run good businesses. Be relational. Understand business and put the right people in place. Work on your business, not in it. Be willing to diversify, adapt, and pivot. If you want extraordinary results, you must do "unordinary" things. Stay the course! Your results in one, five, and 10 years are a direct reflection of your choices today. Keep grinding, start successful businesses, get that cash flow, and most importantly, BREAK THE OLD STIGMA; be in control of your time and do what you love.

When your clock runs out, how did you live? Or did you even live at all? Life is short, and there is no time for bad days and negative people. Stay positive every day in every situation. Be in the now and be present, you're not guaranteed tomorrow! Your best life starts with faith, health, and family; everything else falls into place. Give your children unconditional love. Give people grace.

To learn more about real estate acquisitions, renovations, value add, property stabilization, out of state investing, along with construction and landscaping, contact Dean Shupe, who has over 11 years of experience.

allin1enterprises@deanshupe.com
Facebook @dean.shupe.1
www.deanshupe.com

Quotable: If you want to change, you must be willing to take action. Your results in one, five, and 10 years are a direct reflection of your choices today. Let's go!

Scan to catch up with Dean.

RON WHITE

2x US Memory Champion
Creator of the Afghanistan Memory Wall

Two-time US Memory Champion Ron White is a speaker, author, and trainer. He has been featured on Stan Lee's Superhumans, *National Geographic's* Brain Games, *CBS's* The Morning Show, *and more. Ron is the creator of the Afghanistan Memory Wall, his tribute to fallen soldiers in Afghanistan, where he served in the US Navy.*

The Call That Started It All

In 1991, I was a telemarketer for a company that cleaned chimneys.

One day, I called up a guy and offered to clean his chimney, and he said, "We don't want our chimney cleaned. We're trying to sell our house."

So, I said, "Well, if you're trying to sell your house, you need a clean chimney."

He laughed and said, "I don't know about that, but I need a good telemarketer." He taught memory seminars, and not long after, he hired me as a telemarketer and then as a speaker on the topic of Memory.

It was hard. The first year in business, I made $7,500 for the entire year. That was 1992.

The BIG HARD Lesson

In 1998, things were going decent. I was making $25,000 a year, but I was still only 24 years old. I was dating a girl, and she ripped my heart out and stepped on it. I had to get out of Texas. So, I looked at a map and picked the farthest city away from Fort Worth but still in the United States I could find: Seattle.

I got in my car and drove to Washington. The first six weeks in Seattle, I made $20,000. I had barely made $20,000 in a year. I was succeeding, and I was focused, but then, I started being a big mouth and talking.

I often played pool with my buddy at a bar, and there was a guy there who I never saw playing pool with anybody. I kept seeing him, night after night. One night I said, "Hey man, I see you here every night. Why don't you come play pool with us?" From there, he listened to me talk for two or three days. He just listened and asked me questions. I kept saying, "Oh man, I just made $20,000. You know, I'm gonna make $10,000 next week."

Then, he told me his story. He told me that he owned all these restaurants, that his best friend was the manager at Microsoft, and that his other best friend was the basketball player for the Seattle Supersonics. The next thing I knew, he wanted to be my business partner.

He moved me into a $4,000 a month apartment in downtown Seattle on 1st Ave. I was 25 years old, I was making $20,000 a month, and this guy was my new business partner who was a multi-millionaire, supposedly.

Then one night at dinner, it was me, him, and his date. He turned to his date and said, "Did I ever tell you what happens when the person with money meets the person with experience?"

She was like, "No, what happens?"

He said, "The person with the experience gets the money, and the person with the money gets the experience."

It immediately sent chills down my spine because I knew he was talking to me, but I didn't know why. I couldn't put it together.

A couple of days later, at 2:00 a.m., my phone rang. He said, "Ron, the IRS, I just got a letter from the IRS. They're seizing your bank account. You're making so much money—they just drained it."

What?!

The next morning when I woke up, my account was empty, and I believed his story. This was the beginning of a series of events where this guy took money from me.

Then, the landlord of the condo he had moved me into called me and said, "Ron, you need to get your stuff out. Thomas hasn't paid the rent for this month. It's two weeks late."

I said, "What do you mean? He owns this condo."

And the landlord said, "Look, he doesn't own any restaurants. He's a con man. Google his name." I should have done it three months earlier. He was a con man.

Homeless and No Money

Now, I was broke. I didn't have one dime to my name, and I was getting evicted, had to be out by the end of the day. I had woke up that morning in a $4,000 a month apartment, and at the end of the day, all my stuff was in my vehicle, and I was homeless and had no money.

I went to his condo. He had been evicted and wasn't there. I called one of our common business associates. I said, "Tell me where he's at."

"Ron, he's in a hotel. I just loaned him money to check in."

So, I went to this hotel, and I sat outside for eight hours waiting for him to walk in or out.

When he did walk out, I started following him. I followed him for about eight blocks, and then I grabbed him from behind. I pushed him up against the wall, and I said, "Thomas, did I ever tell you what happens when the person with experience meets the person with muscles?" And it was just as if he had taken a laxative. I threw him as hard as I could. He hit the ground, and when he came back, I lifted up my hands. He lifted up his hands, but then he put his hands down, and he wouldn't fight me. I couldn't fight someone who wasn't going to fight back.

I let him go.

I was broke. My business partner took my money and was a con artist. I didn't have a house. I didn't have money. I didn't have anything.

Living in My Car

I took a job as a waiter at a Red Robin restaurant. I would get asked, "Ron, you wanna pick up my shift tonight?"

Always, I said, "Yeah, I'll pick up your shift. I don't have anywhere to go." I would take food from the restaurant to eat.

I lived in my car for six weeks. I paid $30 a month for the gym. I would wake up every morning, go to the gym, shower, and leave. The people at the front desk were like, "Hey Ron, why do you leave 10 minutes later in a suit?!"

During that time, my friend Frank Massine called me and said, "Ron, there is a speech in Lake Tahoe another speaker, Brian, can't do. They only want to pay $2,000."

I'm like, "$2,000? Are you kidding me? Yes, I will do it."

Well, Seattle to Lake Tahoe was at least a 12-hour drive. I had to buy my plane ticket up front, but I didn't have $300 for a plane ticket. I started looking at my tires the week before the event. I was thinking, *I don't know if I have enough gas, but if I do have enough gas, the metal is showing on these tires. The wires are sticking out. But I gotta go. I gotta make it.* I remember walking into Red Robin that day to work a double and telling myself, *I have got to make $250 today or I can't make this trip. I won't have the gas.* I'd never made $250 in a shift before.

I walked out with the $250 almost exactly. I almost wanted to cry.

When I got into the parking lot, I saw my car was gone.

It had been towed. I had all these unpaid parking tickets. It was $80 to get it out. Now, I only had $170—not enough gas to get there and back, but enough gas to get there. I'd figure out the rest.

I drove the 12 hours to Lake Tahoe, I gave the speech, and they gave me a $2,000 check. I cashed it and made it back to Seattle.

Through a series of lucky trials like that, I was able to build my business back up. Eventually, I moved into a hotel where I lived for a year, and then I moved back to Texas.

It All Comes Together

After I moved back to Texas, September 11th happened. I was 28 years old, and I joined the Navy Reserve.

My business was still up and down. I had money, but it wasn't going really well. I had a top-secret Naval clearance because I was an intelligence analyst. At the same time, I was a security risk to the Navy because I was $40,000 in debt to the IRS, so I was going to lose my security clearance. It was a really stressful time.

One day, my friend Chris Widener said, "Ron, do you realize Kyle Wilson, the founder of Jim Rohn International, lives 10 minutes from you?"

I said, "Yeah, I know that, but what am I supposed to say to him?"

He said, "Take your CD series over there, and he'll sell it. I'll tell him you're coming." I was sure Kyle would have no interest in selling my CD series, but Chris said, "Just do it."

I walked into Kyle's office, stuck one leg in the door, handed the CD series to Crystal, and asked her to please give it to Kyle.

She said, "Oh, he's here. Do you want to talk to him?" No, I did not want to talk to him! I was scared.

Two or three days later, Kyle called me and said, "Ron, I want to buy 1,000 sets of your Memory in a Month CD program." I hadn't sold 1,000 sets in my life! This was the biggest day of my life, income-wise.

Two weeks later, Kyle had sold them. He called and said, "Ron, I need 2,000 more."

A couple of weeks after that, I was at a restaurant with my friend Brian when Kyle called again. He said, "Hey Ron, I'm going out to Shreveport this weekend to a casino and want to see if you want to go. I don't know you really well, but this would be a chance to spend some time together." I was all in.

We drove out there and became friends on the way. We ended up making that three-hour drive each way three or four times over the next several months.

I remember very specifically, on one drive back, Kyle said, "Ron, what's wrong? What's on your mind? Is everything going okay?"

I said, "Kyle, look. I have a security clearance in the Navy. And if I don't pay my $40,000 IRS debt, I'm going to get kicked out of the Navy."

Kyle listened to me, and I could see the wheels turning in his head. I was certainly not asking for a loan. $40,000 was out of my realm of possibility for a loan. When we got back to Dallas, we pulled up to his offices, Jim Rohn International, went into the office, and Kyle had Hilary write me a check for $36,000 (the amount we decided I needed). We made a deal that day that Kyle would sell my program, Memory in a Month, and instead of paying me the commission, he would just deduct it out of the money I owed him. Within six months, it all was paid back. We have had a great friendship and ongoing business relationship to this day.

For me, that several years of no money, living in my car, waiting tables, and showering at the gym was a time of resilience. The day I drove back from Lake Tahoe on bald tires, having not been sure I had enough money to get there, let alone back, I saw the skyline of Seattle pop into view, and I just started laughing. I couldn't believe I pulled it off.

And then, when I met Kyle, that was another really hard time. With his help and guidance, I was able to get through that.

A lot of times, people tell me, "Ron, I want to do what you do. I want to be a speaker. I want to get paid $15,000 to give a speech (which is my fee these days), and I want to travel the world and speak."

I tell them everything I've done. I start laying it all out, and they cut in: "No, I don't want to do any of that. I want to do what you do now." If you don't want to go through the hard stuff, forget about it. The hard stuff of building your business and coming up with solutions and the character that's built in that is the only way you can handle success.

Training for the US Memory Championship

In 2007, still in the Navy, I was deployed to Afghanistan. When I got back, I decided I wanted to do the US Memory Championships, and I hired a coach, United States Navy SEAL TC Cummings.

He taught me a lot about discipline. He had me memorizing cards underwater. He had me memorizing cards at bars. He had me changing my diet, getting up early, and training like a Navy SEAL would train for war, but I was training for a memory tournament.

I won back-to-back years and became the two-time US Memory Champion. And in the process, I set the record for the fastest to memorize a deck of cards in the United States. (Later, that record was broken in 2011.)

Afterward, I wanted to do something more special with my memory, something I was passionate about.

You Are Not Forgotten

Being a veteran and having served in Afghanistan, I decided to create a tribute for everyone who died in Afghanistan so they would not be forgotten.

There are 2,300 fallen soldiers. I memorized their rank, their first name, and their last name in the order of their deaths. It took me 10 months to memorize and be able to write out and spell each correctly (there are multiple spellings of so many names).

With this list, I created The Afghanistan Memory Wall, a project where I travel the United States, writing out these 7,000 words from memory on a wall. It takes about 10 hours to physically do it.

The core message of the tribute is that they are not forgotten. I'm humbled by all the friends and family that come to witness while I'm doing this in different cities and at some major events like NFL games, Nascar races, MLB games, Independence Day at the National Mall in Washington DC, and on Veteran's Day. I have countless stories that shake me to my core of how The Afghanistan Memory Wall has made an impact on friends and family of fallen soldiers.

The wall is also a testament to discipline. When I was memorizing that wall for a year, I lived in solitude. I took a book filled with each soldier's name with me everywhere I went. When I was sick, I was memorizing. When I was tired or on trains or airplanes, I was memorizing.

Living in my car, being close to going out of business, almost getting kicked out of the Navy, serving in Afghanistan, training for and winning the US Memory Championship, and then creating The Afghanistan Memory Wall are all a part of the transformational path and journey I've been on the past 20 years. I'm thankful for it all.

 Ron White is a professional speaker, a veteran of the United States Navy who served in Afghanistan in 2007, and a two-time US Memory Champion who held the USA record for fastest to memorize a deck of cards for two years. Ron's memory program Black Belt Memory can be found at www.blackbeltmemory.com. Follow Ron on YouTube, Facebook, and Instagram at Brain Athlete. Email: ron@ronwhitetraining.com Podcast: www.americasmemory.com

Quotable: If you don't want to go through the hard stuff, forget about it. The hard stuff of building your business and the character that's built in that is the only way you can handle success.

KIMBERLY R. FAUCHER, MD

Physician, Veteran, Investor
A Spiral Path Thru Meaning and Purpose

Kimberly R. Faucher, MD has 30 years of active duty Air Force, private medical practice, and business experience. As the founder of Open Sky Associates, an investment firm focused on multifamily syndication, Kimberly builds communities and creates wealth. Currently, her assets, valued at $91,000,000, are in California, Georgia, and Texas.

Some Assembly Required

I met a young woman recently. She had been in a car wreck earlier in the year. She was not obviously injured, but she went to the emergency room to be on the safe side. As part of her evaluation, she had some x-rays. One was of her neck. There were no fractures, but they did note that her bones were way out of alignment.

She later had some bodywork done. It turned out that, after one visit, a sensation she'd had her entire life, a sensation she did not know did not belong, vanished. She had what she now knows was a headache since she took a big fall on her head at the age of four. She reckoned that was just how a body felt. She had no reference, until that sensation was gone.

It is troubling to me how often we don't know what we don't know.

Stumbling Away from Ghosts

I remember a lot about living in San Francisco, The City of Love. Being four when I arrived, my memories are powerful but somewhat hazy—hippies in Golden Gate Park, Haight-Ashbury, and fire truck sirens when our entire apartment had been set ablaze by the neighbor's basement grow lights. Running home from school every day to avoid getting beaten up. Making soup and Cheerios with beer instead of milk with my sister.

My first-grade teacher, Ms. Lee, came to visit my family one night. I was excited and wondered what made me so lucky. Whoops, she was there to criticize not congratulate. I was channeling Ramona the Pest at school, and she was somberly listing off my delinquencies—misdeeds such as swatting at a bee in the post-recess line up, tapping my shoes a bit too loud in the hallway on the shiny wood floors, and getting up during work time to use my classmate's pencil sharpener. Her visit prompted a doctor visit. His visit prompted skipping second grade.

Most of us can picture a time in our childhoods when we were uncertain and afraid. Through the cruelty of strangers, the misguided choices of wobbly kinships, and the isolation of shame (because we are often told to stay quiet), we keep on paying for that fear with pain and self-doubt.

The powerful truth is we can, repeatedly, decide. The root of the word decide is to cut. We remember and reassemble the past and our meaning we assign. Deciding and reassembling the past, we embrace the virtues and strengths from the crucible of our experience.

Life Is Built by Action

After four years in The City of Love, we returned to San Diego. My dad had left San Diego as a grocery clerk, and he returned as a dentist. We moved from the projects to a suburban rental with a garage. Instead of the 10-cent lunch program, we packed peanut butter and jelly in crisp brown bags. My mom took up tennis. My two little sisters and I came home from school to ride our bikes, which had not been stolen from the stoop like they were from our project porch. We took off for miles and for hours until it was time for dinner. We went shopping once a year for clothes, and usually at the grace of my grandmother, we were no longer buying our clothes at the Salvation Army.

My parents bought a set of encyclopedias. I had never seen anything like it. This was long before the internet. I felt the lure of all that knowledge. I would stay up past my bedtime reading with a flashlight under the covers. I was especially drawn to the collections of shiny pages. I remember going back often to the ones about astronomy, maps of explorer expeditions, and the human body.

We had neighbors with tract homes and well-kept unfenced yards. I met many of them as I walked around the neighborhood. I remember eating their tangerines and petting their cats. My sister and I would park our bikes on the lawns of strangers, and they would invite us in. I asked to be allowed to go with them to church. Not just one church, I wanted to go sit in all the different ones and see what went on. I was a real Harriet the Spy.

My favorite memories of living in California were the trips. The upside of our lingering cash flow problem was that our family fun was almost exclusively camping. The ocean, the sand dunes, and the Sierras. This was when there were not 13,000 visitors a day to Yosemite and you could get a campsite, a horseback ride, and a river raft excursion. At one point, I dreamt of being a park ranger. I wanted to understand the social systems of the wild, to breathe in the peace of nature, and to be outside. And outside for me really meant being at the limit, at something better, beyond boundaries and confines.

Then, after merely three years, when it seemed we were on the verge of financial stability, we moved again. In Seattle, school was no less awkward. But one thing was different, they had sports for girls. They also had ski school. My sister had the audacity to ask if we could take lessons, and my parents said yes!

As my dad attended graduate school, my mom became familiar with the care and feeding of the aged and infirm from 3:00 p.m. to 11:00 p.m. for minimum wage. I became familiar with how to make a plate of dinner— main dish, side, salad—with an emphasis on hamburger. Hello, Rice-A-Roni and an assortment of Kraft box dinners.

By the time I was in high school, we had lived in 10 houses in 10 different neighborhoods. Despite the barriers to my entering any kind of peer group, I loved school. I loved learning, playing sports, and the variety of classes I could take. I took the hardest science and math. I loved English. I took art at every opportunity, including pottery, watercolor, architecture, and photography. The art teacher invited me to become the student curator at the community museum. I did not see that coming. I had never heard of such a thing. I regret not having the boldness to say YES and I wish she simply would have asked again.

After two years of taking skiing lessons, a friend invited me to apply to become an instructor. I applied, and I made it! I was surrounded by mostly adults who had been skiing for decades and a handful of amazing high school skiers. For a few years, I helped eight-year-old skiers learn to control a fall, organize their equipment and their bodies to speed down a slope, and share the wonder of the winter mountains. I, on the other hand, became aware that at any given moment I was either joyously immersed in the moment and able to confidently swoosh down a black diamond mogul field or overcome with self-doubt and merely able to white knuckle and scrape through a gently sloping, blue square run.

My biology teacher and a few classmates told me I should be a doctor, probably as a result of my volunteering to get something out of the teacher's eye and their familiarity with my unsolicited but nonetheless surprisingly helpful words of wisdom on all manner of subjects. No one really seemed to know what becoming a doctor would entail, and it seemed not even the guidance counselor knew I was the class valedictorian. I received invitations from 35 prestigious colleges.

Reconsideration Takes Courage

Senior year took a couple of turns. I tore the ligaments in my knee playing soccer. My dad tore apart the family. Instead of agonizing about college choices, I was agonizing about the dissolution of my parents' marriage.

I decided to attend the local university, to stay near home, to be team mom.

I shared in her sadness, aloneness, uncertainty, and fear. I helped her study biochemistry after she got into nursing school. I had no false sentiment about "until death do you part" or people staying together in quiet desperation, but I was outraged as my dad remarried and traveled Europe to speak, an expert in his field, while we struggled to pay the bills yet again.

The University of Washington turned out to be a very competitive school. Quietly, I took all the necessary classes and the entrance exam to apply to medical school, and I got in. In anticipation of having no help paying the tuition, I also applied to the military academy where I would pay in time instead of dollars. I graduated with zero debt, and I chose a field I love with not one iota of concern for whether it paid enough to pay back educational expenses. I have none. In fact, at 23, I bought my first house.

For the next 13 years, I met people from all walks of life. I traveled the globe. I served on medical missions. I designed teaching curriculums, refined clinic processes, assisted the legal consortium, and led quality programs everywhere I went. The year I completed my service, I was living on Chesapeake Bay in Maryland and working at the Andrews Air Force Base for Air Force One. And I was preparing to have a baby.

During my pregnancy, I worked full-time, hiked Quiet Waters Park, swam laps at the gym, and read *The Little Prince* to her. I craved tacos and pad thai. After 21 hours of labor on the fourth of July, a perfect little girl latched on the second she was handed to me. Olivia was a very easy baby. My life was forever changed.

Saying goodbye to our beautiful house on the beach, I took a job in a large practice, returning to Seattle to be near family.

The moment Olivia arrived, she was attached, within my arms or a babypack. I talked to her all day every day, and by the age of one she had a 100-word vocabulary. When she started school, I packed her lunch with little notes on the skin of the banana or the orange. We went to museums, plays, and concerts. We hiked, talked, made art, took photos, learned to ride horses, cooked, camped, and traveled. We tracked the seasons and we tracked the stars. We did everything. I wanted more than anything for her to be and feel safe, unconditionally loved, respected, empowered, and cared for.

There was one thing that started to nag me. I realized I was no longer okay with working long hours and being on call overnight. I also realized I was a long way from accumulating the savings I would need to work less, let alone retire, anytime soon.

When I was choosing medical schools, joining the Air Force made sense. There had been no wars for years, and avoiding debt was liberating. The opportunities for leadership and advanced tools progressed my growth. While I was being underpaid as a doctor, the logic was that I was also not paying taxes. There was a hidden flaw. I realized later that my financial stability was precarious. If I was not at work, I was not earning. I was also not part of the local medical community, not accumulating any wealth, and had no prospect for any pension, IRA, 401K, or social security.

Have a Compass

Writer Maria Popova notes, paraphrasing the wisdom of writer Italo Calvino, what makes life worth living: love, kindness, the devotion to justice, the unconscious surrender to joy, and the willingness to do the difficult, delicate, work of rising to our highest potential. With each of Olivia's childhood landmarks, I became even more acutely aware of the imperative to prioritize time and my values.

To that end, I worked hard, saved, started investing, and did not buy the doctor mansion or the boat. After savoring Seattle and the richness of urban life, I had a dream to experience the rest of Olivia's childhood in the country, have horses, and enjoy a sunnier climate. To live a life closer to the rhythm of nature, a life I was not trying to escape on the rare free weekend. I was going to start a holistic solo practice in a rural California community that needed a gynecologist. I had plenty of passive investment income.

Well, in the spring of 2008, I got a call: "It's all gone, stolen, seized."

I had no safety net, but it was no time to panic. There was no turning back from the decision to uproot everything. I had two rental homes and was about to close on my little ranch. I simply needed to do the next one thing. I needed to get to work, start the practice, show up for my daughter, and show up for the patients.

In the summer of 2008, everything began to unspool for almost everyone. Although I had lost most of my life savings for a different reason, there was comradery in the shared trauma. The economics of the great recession exacerbated my struggle. I learned how critical it was to trust myself, to maintain calm self-confidence, take the time needed to learn what to do, and most importantly, take action.

Margaret Thatcher said there is no freedom without economic freedom. After my medical practice had legs, I committed to investing time and money with luminaries in the fields of wealth, taxes, and property investing to begin again on the path to economic sovereignty. Investing for passive income and starting my investment company was born of my understanding that there was no amount of actively working for income and saving that was going to allow me to achieve personal freedom, let alone, generational wealth.

Over a decade later, I have built a financial livelihood and personal freedom. I am currently practicing gynecology in California, and I am the founder and investment manager of Open Sky Associates, an investment firm focused on multifamily syndication. Our goal is achieving wealth creation through targeting growth markets for cash flow and tax-advantaged investment performance. In everything I do, my underlying goal is to empower women. I want women to feel confident and to have the tools to optimize their well-being for the journey that lies ahead of them.

Olivia graduated from Smith College and moved to Austin for her PhD in astrophysics. We still talk every day and always have the next adventure in the works.

Kimberly R. Faucher, MD is eager to share how investing for passive income is like having an Air Force Special Tactics Squadron working for you, protecting and performing day and night. For more information about coaching or investing, reach her directly via hello@openskyassociates.com.

Quotable: There was no turning back. I simply needed to do the next one thing. I needed to get to work, start the practice, show up for my daughter, and show up for the patients.

Scan to contact Kimberly R. Faucher, MD.

PATRICK MURRAY

The Pivot Point
From Building Walls to Building Teams

Patrick Murray is an entrepreneur, leadership coach, and real estate investor with a passion for empowering others. As a loving husband and father, he cherishes family and community. Patrick's expertise lies in creating and scaling service industry businesses. He skillfully transforms leaders into catalysts for positive change while helping them find their full potential.

An Entrepreneur in a College Classroom

I have always been an entrepreneur and a self-starter with passionate energy.

I fought my deepest desire to be an entrepreneur and went to college to double major in music and business because that's what I thought I should do to be successful. I had fun beating the system with overlapping credits to cancel out unnecessary classes, I used my meal card to go on weeklong hunting excursions, I drove home from Cleveland to Pittsburgh every weekend to service my lawn care clients, I took a semester off to travel the continent of Australia, and I added another minor to my paper degree. And, I finished in three and a half years, much to the amazement of my lovely mother who has always been my biggest fan.

Upon finishing college, I realized I was still an entrepreneur who didn't want to work for corporate America. During finals week of my senior year, I came up with and registered the name Local Roots Landscaping for my weekend lawn care business. Upon arriving back in Pittsburgh with my degree in hand, I continued mowing lawns with my best friend Kenneth. And we continued mowing lawns, installing landscapes, and creating outdoor living spaces until turning our first venture together into a $10M outdoor construction business after just 10 years, where it sits today as one of our four businesses.

An Entrepreneur in the Early Stages of a Landscaping Company

Growing your first business is an experience unlike any other, and it's an experience you can only have once. The lessons learned can be plotted in stages on a timeline of gross revenue—not because money is everything in business but because money tells a story. The process I have gone through and continue to go through, can be broken down into these stages of gross revenue, but even more so, it can be broken down into eras marked by how my brain defined value, self-worth, and success.

In the early stages of my business, my goal was ultimate freedom, self-sufficiency, and an endless hustle. The hustle felt good. It felt honorable to work hard to make more to grow more for myself. Kenneth and I worked tirelessly through 80-hour weeks to grow our landscaping business from $0 to $350,000 in just three years with essentially no employees. We absolutely hustled seven days a week and saw our revenue double and triple year over year, yet the goal of freedom was nowhere in sight.

In three years, the business had become a small monster that didn't allow us time for friends, vacations, or rest. This was the opposite of what we started out to create. I had thought that owning my own company meant freedom, wealth, and control. This business thing was hard work. Those thoughts stewed and my angst grew.

An Easy Path to Wealth

While we had seen some significant success, I was tired, and I was becoming impatient that we weren't seeing all of this success that "everyone else" was talking about on Instagram with their brand new businesses. It was just around this time that Kenneth and I were given the opportunity to invest in a shrimp farm in South America with a mutual childhood friend. This would be our opportunity to make it, to get rich and travel the world with little to no input or hard work compared to what we were doing with this landscaping thing.

I couldn't have made a worse judgment call. Within one year, we lost all of our savings and were back to square one, or even worse, negative one. All of the hard work and the resources we had obtained in the first three years of business had been washed away in a matter of months due to poor stewardship. And along with it went all the hope of an easy path to quick riches and easy comforts.

This experience revealed to me quite a bit more than my hope to become wealthy. It revealed the self-serving and broken mindset that I was so deeply invested in. It revealed the demons of power, control, and love of money in me which I wasn't able to see until this eureka moment that forced them out.

Up until this point, I was pursuing a life where the sole benefactor was me, myself, and I. At this pivotal moment, I began to see clearly that I wanted to rebuild, redefine, and grow in ways my mind wouldn't have been able to comprehend before. So, I began.

Rebuilding and Regrowing

Kenneth and I came out with a fire under us to grow the most ethical and impactful business we could possibly imagine at Local Roots Landscaping. We wanted to show ourselves that we had what it took to come back from the loss. We had to prove it at all costs.

So, we started the hustle again. We started building a team. We started doubling our revenue year over year and we didn't want to stop. We grew and grew. We were no longer annoyed at the hard work it took day in and day out because we knew that success doesn't come without a cost. We removed all limits, all excuses, and all boundaries.

In fact, we removed every single boundary and were growing so fast and so uncontrollably that we didn't realize our bodies and our minds couldn't keep up. We were burning the candle from every angle. I was experiencing anxiety attacks so strong they kept me in bed for days, relational issues with my wife and family, and relational issues with Kenn both as partners and best friends.

We hadn't realized the difference between growing a business and scaling a business. In just under three years, we had accomplished growing our business so tall and so narrow that the slightest wind would have it tipping over and crumbling to its demise. Even worse, all of the other parts of my life were also on the brink of collapse. Something had to give, and it was our pride.

A Book, Some Advice, and the Ability to Accept It

I received a copy of *The E-Myth* by Michael Gerber which challenges the idea that entrepreneurs should be hands-on technicians. Instead, it suggests that building a successful business requires creating systems and processes that allow the business to run smoothly without constant personal involvement. By working on the business rather than in it, entrepreneurs can achieve growth, efficiency, and lasting success.

Kenn and I decided to hire a coach to help us work through this concept and really bring it to life. We knew we had the skills, passion, and grit to build a business that would be self-sustaining and life-giving, but we needed some tools and pointers to bring out our true potential. We put down our pride and admitted that we needed some serious and intentional help if we wanted to hit our goals in a timely and healthy manner.

When we started with our coach, we were a company that had us wearing every hat while consuming every inch of our brain space at all times. After just two years of accepting a few tools and advice on how to deploy them, we had turned this life-consuming monster into a well-oiled, systematized machine that was working for us.

We created systems and processes that were scaleable and autonomous. We attracted strong, new talent. We created a company culture that for the most part doesn't exist in the landscaping industry today. We were creating outdoor living spaces on par with those created by the top firms in our industry. We doubled our revenue twice over those two years and have since doubled again. During this timeframe, we learned that we could either have control or we could have growth but we couldn't have both. We relinquished control and got results we never thought possible.

Even better was the fact that my marriage, my brain, and my life were restored. I was firing at full capacity and experiencing opportunities and dreams that had been locked away in hustle culture, a mindset that had made my mind its home long past its welcome.

Success to Significance

Business growth has surely been a bumpy road. Thankfully it has smoothed out in some significant ways that have allowed me to begin multiple businesses in real estate, retail, and coaching. The race to the top was something I thought we were supposed to do in business. Then I realized that there is no top, no end, and no single accomplishment that would ever satisfy my entrepreneurial heart.

While business growth is exhilarating, it has been the personal, relational, and mental growth that really took my life to the next level. When the fog cleared, I saw that the satisfaction I could gain from my personal success was limited and even deflating. Once I got a taste of significance and the ability to pour into others to help them reach their goals, dreams, and potential, I never again thirsted for my personal success the way I longed for the success of others.

It has become my mission to support others in reaching their full potential while helping to improve and sustain their mental, financial, physical, and spiritual health. On repeat. Daily. It is my passion, my driving force, and my calling.

Systemizing my business through working with a coach and shifting my mindset had a major impact on all areas of my life, including my health and relationships. When you can let go of the need to control everything in your business, it opens up so much freedom and growth. Because of my passion for building systems and creating thriving workplace cultures, I am now a coach and speaker. I aim to help others get out of the grind and open up their potential. There is a way to do much bigger things and make a greater impact on everyone you encounter!

If you are interested in learning more about Patrick Murray and how his personal experience might guide you through your current stage of growth, please reach out to him at Patrick@frwrdcoaching.com and see what he is doing at www.FRWRDcoaching.com. He would love to connect with you to discuss what it looks like to take your businesses and relationships to the next level.

Quotable: My marriage, my brain, and my life were restored. I was firing at full capacity and experiencing opportunities and dreams that had been locked away in hustle culture, a mindset that had made my mind its home long past its welcome.

 Scan to move FRWRD together!

STEFFANY BOLDRINI

From Brazil to a Startup in Silicon Valley and Self-Storage Investing

Steffany Boldrini is a serial real estate investor and entrepreneur. Born and raised on a small ranch in Brazil, she landed in Silicon Valley at age 18. Steffany shares her knowledge through her podcast, Commercial Real Estate Investing from A-Z, *recently named one of the best commercial investing podcasts by* Business Insider, *and enjoys giving to organizations that help animals in need.*

Humble Beginnings

I was recently at my sister's house in San Jose, California. She had a container of pistachios on her kitchen counter, and right away, it took me down memory lane to when I was a kid in Brazil.

Pistachios were so fancy for us. I only ate them at my dad's house when he had fancy guests over. My parents got divorced when I was seven, and my mom, my two sisters, and I lived in a two-bedroom, one-bathroom house on a small ranch. We didn't have much besides that ranch.

Mom always saved money and sent us to private school because public schools in Brazil were bad. Brazil's economy has never been stable, and the downs were quite low. At one point, inflation was so bad that we couldn't buy bread in the afternoon for the same price it was in the morning. My mom was a horse vet, and when there were no jobs due to the economy, she had to take a job at a cattle auction house which required her to work in a very loud environment until 2:00 a.m., something she couldn't stand, only to wake up early in the morning to take us to school. At some point during that time of economic uncertainty, we even had to ask my dad for oil to cook.

It's funny how God always has a plan beyond our wildest imagination. One life-changing day, my mom took us to a computer show in our small town in Brazil. We walked around admiring all this technology and saw this very nice, black computer, the nicest and most expensive one in the entire show. While my mom was always frugal and never bought herself anything nice, something in her made her buy that black computer.

It was a huge hit in our home. We all wanted to be on this computer. But of course, mama got the most time on it. She started chatting in the AOL chat rooms with strangers across the world, and it was there that she met my stepfather, an American man who was everything she had always dreamt of. They started dating and, long story short, eventually decided get married. That's what led to the miracle of him bringing us to live with him in the United States of America, in California's Silicon Valley.

Welcome to the USA

I remember vividly my first outing to a strip mall with my mom. She pointed at the door of the Kodak store (yes, blast from the past), which had a sign that said "Hiring." I didn't even know what that meant, and my mom proceeded to translate it to Portuguese. I then started noticing that sign everywhere. Everyone was hiring. Everything was so beautiful and clean. The roads were so pretty. There were so many nice cars around. I was ecstatic.

My first job was at Mervyn's, and the thrill of getting that very first paycheck of $146 was unforgettable! The first thing I bought was a CD player for my very own room. Until the age of 17, I was sharing a bedroom with my two sisters. It was so easy to make money in the US. I got a promotion within one month. I was frugal, except for that CD player, saved money, and lived at my parents' until the age of 27.

Fast forward to a few years later. Surrounded by the entrepreneurial spirit in Silicon Valley, I was inspired to create a startup. I had no idea how to build a company. I was working seven days a week, many days into the wee hours of the night. All I knew was my passion for natural, organic products and sharing them with the world. But I had no idea what I would go through for that dream.

Startup Life

Creating a startup was brutal. I was not an engineer, and in Silicon Valley, business founders are somewhat looked down upon. I talked with more than 40 engineers over several months and had no luck finding a co-founder. I then realized that I had to create something myself to get some traction, and only then find a co-founder.

I started doing YouTube videos of these products, begging reporters to write about my company. After about a year of growing my YouTube channel and WordPress website, I pitched my company at a co-founder conference, where I finally met someone interested in my project.

The problem was that he was in the US on a work visa, and he could not quit his full-time job until we had money to pay his salary and sponsor his visa. I would work all day and then meet with him at night and on the weekends to build the product. There was no time for me to work out or date.

I remember one day I was having dinner at a restaurant with my family, and I ended up having a meltdown. I just cried and cried. Things were not moving forward. I was disagreeing with my co-founder over some things, and we couldn't raise money from investors because we didn't have the growth they needed to be interested. How could we get growth without money? Isn't that why angel investors are called "angel" investors?! It was a very humbling experience.

Brutal Lessons

I decided to join a startup incubator that taught me the very basics of creating a company: creating an LLC, creatively selecting a good company name, branding, interviewing potential customers, finding your product-market fit, marketing, and pitching investors. We would meet weekly and had homework due the following week. We had about 50 founders at the beginning of the program, and each week, we had fewer and fewer. People gave up every week because it was so hard.

There is one particular day I will never forget. We had about 20 founders left. One of the founders didn't have time to complete the assignment for his company. The leader of the incubator, let's call him John, reminded us that the rules were clear from the beginning: if you don't complete your homework, you are out. But the other 19 founders didn't want John to let this founder go. It was so harsh. Just give him a break. We all stood up and said we wouldn't accept it. John said, "Okay, fine. If you want to help him out due to his poor performance, then write all your names on a piece of paper, we will put them in a hat, and whoever I pick will be kicked out of the program instead of the founder that didn't do his homework. One unlucky founder's name got picked, and he was kicked out of the program.

At the end of each weekly meeting, we would go out to a dive bar to talk shop. That bar had so many peanut shells on the floor I don't think it was ever swept. That night, I was so mad at John for letting

233

any founder go that I was giving him the death stare. With a beer in his hand, he came to talk to me. He said, "I know you're mad at me for doing that, but do you know why I did it? In the startup world, you will have to make extremely difficult decisions, and if you don't make those decisions, someone else will make them for you, and you won't like it." Mind blown. Life lesson learned.

People think it's easy to create startups because they only read about the success stories. They don't hear about the thousands that fail along the way. Sweat, tears, fierce competition, endless "hockey stick" growth requirements by investors before, during, and after they give you any money, and years of your life spent on it without a guaranteed outcome, sometimes your best years! You get to see your college peers rising in the corporate world, making money, and having their nights and weekends off, while you blindly follow your dream and work crazy hours, most of the time without pay. It's a known saying that founders never quit, and you never know when it's really time to let go, because founders don't quit!

After three years, we weren't able to raise funds, and it was time to move on and close shop. Do I regret giving my all for "nothing" in the end? Not one second. I am incredibly grateful for the opportunity and all I have learned along the way. This experience made me an incredible startup employee at my next job because, after building your own company, working for another company is like taking a vacation. You work during the day, you have your nights, weekends, a paycheck, and holidays, and you don't have the stress and responsibility that the CEO has. I met so many incredible people along the way. I also learned that everyone has a boss, which gave me a much better perspective as an employee. Now I understood that the CEO's bosses are the venture capital firms, the VC firms' bosses are their investors, and so on. It also made me not sweat the small stuff, like a cracked windshield, because nothing was harder than building a company.

For my next job, I wanted to join another startup where I could help grow the company and be part of a team. I looked for startups that had several engineering openings because this meant they had a good product. But they also had to need someone with my skill set: hustling. I found a company that had 100 employees and several engineering openings. I needed one final check—my engineer friends—to tell me if the product that this company was selling was good. Once they confirmed it was, I said, "Great! I want to work there."

The company didn't want me for the role I applied for, so I had to start from scratch. Almost in my 30s, I accepted an entry-level sales job. *No problem*, I thought, *I will show them what I'm capable of and I will get this job.* Eight months later, I was promoted to that job!

It was a truly wild ride. Everyone at that company was fantastic, and I ended up being the number one salesperson. Finally, I was making some money! Tech sales was my career for the next few years. But, once you have the entrepreneurial bug, it never leaves you.

Once an Entrepreneur, Always an Entrepreneur

I had a close friend who was a real estate investor, and while I was learning about and making some investments in startups as an angel investor, it became very clear to me that real estate investing was a much better form of investing, at least compared to angel investing. The chances of you losing your money entirely are significantly less, your property appreciates over time, the government gives you tax breaks, rent increases over time, you get to use the bank's money to invest, so you leverage your own money, it's a great hedge against inflation because it goes up in value over time, and over the last two centuries, about 90% of the world's millionaires (in today's dollars) have been created by investing in real estate. I decided to learn everything I could about real estate investing, and ended up leaving my wonderful sales career for another entrepreneurial adventure.

Happiness

I've been investing in real estate full-time for nearly six years, and it has been another wild ride. Has it been easy? No! But it's been easier than building a startup!

Throughout my learning journey, I came across self-storage and found out that it does well in both good times and bad times. That has become the asset class my firm focuses on. The first few years were difficult because there were no deals available, at least from brokers. Two years in, I managed to find my first deal. I ended up meeting wonderful people and partners in the industry and evolved into doing syndications and raising funds from investors. We will also be building our first facility in California this year.

Does it feel like I have made it? No. Far from it. I'm not only far from reaching my financial goal, but also I just entered my 40s and haven't met my soulmate yet. But, what I do know is that if I wait for life to be perfect in every aspect to be happy, I never will be.

Over the past year, I have been exploring working from different cities for a few months at a time. The trip to the latest city, Newport Beach, was one of the longest drives I've made, with lots of traffic along the way. When I finally got to the new place, I was completely exhausted. As I was unpacking four months of clothes, groceries, my dog's items, and everything in between from my very full car, I nearly cried. *Here I go again*, I thought. *Still single, driving to a new city where I know no one, unpacking, making new friends from scratch, and figuring out all of this alone, again.*

At the end of that night, I took my dog out for her walk and was reminded that where we were was half a block from the ocean. We walked to the beach, and the moon was full and shining above the waves. I thought, *Wow, I can bring myself here, to one of the nicest cities in the world, with the best dog ever, living half a block from the ocean for the next few months. What a blessing.*

It was a great reminder that life is never perfect at all times, in every area. Young, old, married, single, employee, entrepreneur, at all points of our life, we are all dealing with something. If we don't stop to look around us and appreciate all the people in our lives, our career journey, the family member that "if they only behaved this way, then I would really love them," we will never be happy! It's wonderful to have goals, but it's even better to savor the journey.

Pistachios

As I stood at my sister's counter eating those pistachios and reliving this journey, I remembered how incredible this country is, a country where anyone can become anything they set their mind to.

This story was written in honor of this great country that has welcomed me with open arms and given me so many opportunities. Since I landed at San Jose International Airport on August 8, 2000, not a day has gone by that I haven't counted my blessings, and I won't stop anytime soon. I am forever grateful and truly honored.

Get in touch with Steffany Boldrini, CEO of Monte Carlo Real Estate Investments, about real estate investing opportunities at admin@montecarlorei.com or www.montecarlorei.com. Learn more about investing from her podcast, *Commercial Real Estate Investing from A-Z.*

Quotable: Life is never perfect in every area. If we don't stop to look around and appreciate all we have, we will never be happy! It's wonderful to have goals, but it's even better to savor the journey.

Scan to join the investing club.

BILL MALCHISKY

Thriving Through Perseverance with Chronic Illness

Bill Malchisky is the president of Effective Software Solutions, LLC, an author, international presenter, and entrepreneur. He brings global software consulting experience to his client opportunities as a senior solution architect. Additionally, he is an HCLSoftware Lifetime Ambassador and has achieved IBM Champion status for nine consecutive years.

It Was All Going So Well

Upon graduating college, I landed an entry-level position with a prestigious company on Wall Street. I took this position not because it was the most lucrative—it was not—but because it provided the greatest opportunity to learn. I appreciate the metaphor of being a distance runner rather than a sprinter. For me, long-term potential outweighed short-term gains.

Many nights at work, especially in the winter, I would sit on the large window seat looking out at the New York Stock Exchange and just soak in where I was and what I was accomplishing. I found it deeply moving and motivating.

I was on my way upward. The job was a good fit, and I did well. My internal clients nominated me for several significant accolades. This level of achievement in one's first year was quite rare, it made me exceptional but also an outlier.

It became apparent that at least one person above me was concerned with how quickly I might rise, so I was forced out.

The company's outplacement office helped me land my dream job, which due to a company reorganization, vaporized overnight. Needing cash, I picked up a few short-term tech gigs. Doing well and being let go would repeat itself in the next few years. That's how I found consulting.

After initial challenges in building a consulting business, I decided to start my own company. Now, I was in control of my destiny and moving forward steadily again. This decision started me on a path of experiences, memories, and relationships which would create a life-long journey of growth, contacts, successful projects, and accolades for which I am thankful.

Life Tests My Resolve

Five years post-graduation, I was debt-free, had a significant sum saved in the bank, was in a great romantic relationship, and was riding the consulting wave through Y2K and into the new millennium.

Five years later, I had more debt than when I graduated college, the consulting market was dry in the wake of the 9/11/2001 terrorist acts, and I was quite ill. My symptoms had cost me that great relationship and made me physically unable to do the same type of consulting work. My life had quickly turned a full 180 degrees, and circumstances weren't letting up.

The illness got worse with few answers after the initial diagnosis. What happened? I started having problems getting out of bed. I felt incredibly tired each morning—which for me was out of character. It was harder to catch my commuter train. I would finish tying my necktie once I was onboard and sleep. This progressively got worse over the next few months. I went to multiple doctors who all came back with the same diagnosis: stress.

In my heart and soul, I knew that was inaccurate. I went through so much stress early in life, and I knew how I responded. In six months, I had gone from solving complex puzzles to struggling to write a check in the doctor's office. A sinusoidal curve of life: from graduating from a top technical institute, succeeding in my first job, and starting a business to my current cognitive decline. So, I kept searching for answers.

By this time, I was in a fog for almost 23 hours per day. What seemed like a few minutes to me was, in fact, hours. I had about one hour of absolute clarity, and I made the most I could of it. I stopped taking on large, complex projects with well-known financial firms. Right at a time when people knew me and my reputation and wanted me, I disappeared.

I started doing computer system installations, which worked with the fog as this was typically done at night when businesses were closed. If a two or three-hour evening job (as agreed and invoiced) actually took me eight hours, no one would know it, and the work got done. I didn't make much money during this time, but I kept my credit rating and paid my bills.

In the middle of this time, the IRS came calling. Essentially, they wanted to know: How is it that you went from growing your business three successive years to declining your business the next three years with pretty similar expenses? They asked questions. Physically, I could not provide what they needed, so I hired an attorney.

The legal team didn't understand my condition and eventually lost interest in the case. What they didn't tell me was that the IRS called them multiple times and they didn't call the IRS back. So, when I called the IRS to check on things, I got an unpleasant surprise. Because they were ignored, they filed a lien against me. I had no idea. Preparing to protect myself and do right with the IRS only put me in a hotter pool of water.

I found a CPA who did handle things well and was ethical with the process. It took almost five more years to get everything settled correctly. I'm in good standing now.

Listening to Your Body Is Sage

Back when I first started having symptoms of this illness, three signs revealed to me that something was wrong. The first occurred while I was a groomsman for my college friend's wedding. I would never want to take away from my friend's special day, and I kept my drinking modest at the reception, but the alcohol inexplicably hit me hard. I stopped by another friend's for the evening and became violently sick. I slept on a couch in his basement. I awoke in the morning still sick. It did not make sense. Everyone thought I drank too much—some losing respect for me—but I knew something else was occurring. I just had no clue what or why yet. Combined with my other symptoms, this prompted me to go to visit the doctor and get my initial diagnosis. Looking back, had I not been persistent in action and listened to what my body said, I believe if I was even alive today, my quality of life would be absolutely diminished, with most of the accolades achieved and memories enjoyed never being realized.

The second big clue for me was about a month later when I missed the early morning setup for a training class my team was running for a client. That morning, I physically could not get out of bed. I woke up and for two hours lay there feeling like someone was pressing on my shoulders. It bothered me deeply. Because I was late, the training started late, which created a bit of a situation. I explained everything to the client and attendees, imploring them to not dock the team for the short window of chaos. Fortunately, the class proceeded successfully. Upon returning home, I visited another medical specialist.

The third clue and the final straw for me was about six weeks later after a celebratory business dinner with a subcontractor. We shared a nice bottle of wine. Two glasses each. After a joyous evening, I was incredibly sick in the morning. A week later, the fog set in. I needed help.

Another six weeks elapsed in which I visited additional medical specialists to no avail. My then-girlfriend suggested a different route, and I went to a naturopathic doctor (ND). I'm not arguing for or against an ND over an MD, but I realized I needed to do something different and get a new perspective. This doctor was in demand, and it took nearly three weeks to see her. During that time, the fog got worse and worse.

When I finally got to meet the doctor, she knew exactly what I had. She ordered tests that would confirm the diagnosis, and I left with medicine I could start taking as soon as the results were returned. Unusual, but given the severity of the infection consuming me from the inside, prudent.

I was told it would be a three-month recovery and made a three-month adjustment in my business for projects and cash flow. After three months, I was nowhere close to being well. It took almost 10 months of visiting several doctors to resolve the infection. Additionally, several new health complications appeared, each needing a specific treatment and doctor. The last doctor was a gem and became a close friend of 20 years I still see today. The truth is though, that extra recovery time crushed me financially.

With knowledge from my college finance class, I kept myself afloat. Many times over the years I've told of how much respect I have for my college professor and his toughness. If he was soft, I would never have survived this chapter of my life with my credit score and much of my business reputation intact. Professor St. John was an active duty Colonel in the Reserves who hammered into my brain quality financial knowledge and accounting practices that saved me. Thank you, Professor.

Around this time, I had the chance to make amends with my friend at whose wedding I had become sick. After the wedding, the groom and I communicated, but the bride maintained her distance for a few years. Then, my friend gave me a window to explain. I met them at a large train station for a food court meal.

It was one of the most difficult conversations I have ever had, but I knew I was speaking with good people, and I spoke directly from the heart with integrity and respect. I offered a factual explanation of my illness combined with a heartfelt apology. That was a powerful moment for me. Their friendship remains important to me. Getting this situation corrected meant a lot—perhaps more than I could ever explain. I could continue on my healing journey with an inner calm and a sense of wholeness.

Due to the infection, my diet had quickly devolved. Many foods fed the infection and had to be eliminated. But it was also diet that allowed me to heal and regain my strength. Advanced nutritional knowledge became compulsory for me. Several years later, my dietary discipline permitted increased choice and I regained the 40 pounds I had lost during my health decline. My distance runner's point of view provided a long-term perspective and holistic approach which aided in my recovery.

"Strive Not to Be a Success, but Rather to Be of Value."

I really appreciate that Albert Einstein quote. An eternal optimist, I knew the illness and succeeding events would help me help others. My purpose in life was revealed: stop focusing on how much money I will make and focus on how much value I can add. If done properly, one can have both. This mental transformation changed me in ways I could never have imagined.

Intrinsically, adding value became my model post-recovery. It took many years to get the fundamental systems executed, but I evolved into a solution architect and now help my clients solve business challenges around technology. My resume includes some amazing opportunities I've had working with incredible people. Each project helped me grow.

Part of any transformational journey is having the confidence to continue down an unfamiliar path toward your goal. A lack of confidence or lucidity creates mental barriers. Having a clear goal allows clarity of vision and for action steps to appear. Getting to that point is not always easy but is certainly worth the commitment.

Every few years, my approach to what I offer clients evolves further. The work I do now is very different from when I started my business. Some changes are directly correlated to changing market conditions, whereas others are a result of situations forcing my hand, as with my illness. In the end, seeing the opportunity in every challenge lends itself to greatness— or at least a better outcome than if you focused on the negative (in the moment).

Despite being incredibly challenging, testing my integrity, patience, drive, and creativity over many years, the illness became one of the best things to happen to me. Perhaps divine intervention is at play, but this extended chapter in life shifted my focus to being healthy first then adding value to others. If you live a life with an abundance mindset, it is easier to find the opportunity in any challenge.

To learn more about how Bill Malchisky can help your business thrive through effective technology solutions, to invite him to present, or to ask a question, please contact him at 203.374.2973 or book@effectivesoftware.com. Bill enjoys sending the elevator back down, helping small business owners solve problems so they too can achieve success.

Quotable: A solution architect sees the opportunity in every challenge. If you live with an abundance mindset, it is easier to find a way to add value. First, be healthy for you, then add value for others.

 Tech Teasers

GINA SHIN

Escaping Financial Illiteracy
How Grit and Determination Changed My Life

Gina Shin is a real estate investor, top-producing mortgage lender, and board member obsessed with creating win/win scenarios. She invests with the purpose of creating positive impacts for the community she serves. She is the founder of Shin Equity Partners and a board member of the Dreams Come True Foundation, a non-profit focusing on attainable homeownership for the underserved.

Mom's Abacus

I wasn't a military brat, but it used to be normal for me to move every one or two years. My dad was a pastor, and that required our family to move around constantly. Aside from the moving, I had a typical life of a working-class, Asian immigrant kid. My parents were frugal so my closet was full of hand-me-down clothes and toys. It wasn't fancy, but we had all our necessities covered. Even so, there was one thing that I think made me different from other kids: my subconscious fixation on our finances.

I remember back when I was four. My dad was aspiring to be a pastor and in seminary school, and my mom worked as a bank teller and went to community college in the evenings to study English. In the evenings, my parents were typically busy with church-related duties. Every now and then, when my parents didn't need to go out, we'd cross the Golden Gate Bridge to pick my mom up from the bank, stop by the local video rental store, and come home with tapes of Korean cartoons. It was a simple, but good life.

There were many nights when I didn't see my parents before I went to sleep. So, sometimes, I would stay up until my parents got home and then hang out in their room while they coordinated schedules and discussed the happenings of their days.

One night, I was laying on my parents' bed while my mom sat on the floor with open, white envelopes in piles around her. She had her wooden, brown abacus in front of her with a bright red, crocheted cover next to it. I knew that meant that she was doing math and paying something called "bills." I think she was exasperated. She looked me in the eyes and said,

"Gina, we have no money." It was almost as though she desperately needed to vent her pent up feelings out loud when she looked at me and said that, not because I was her child, but because I was the only person there.

Being four years old, all I knew was that money was the reason we did or did not do something. If we didn't have money, we weren't buying clothes or treats and I wasn't enrolling in activities that my schoolmates were doing. All I knew was that it wasn't a good thing if we didn't have any money, and that scared me.

Figuring It Out

"We're moving back to Korea."

My parents made this decision shortly after the housing collapse. They explained that their finances were too tight and they couldn't afford to live in the States anymore—that they had held on for as long as they could so my older sister and I could finish high school with as much stability as possible and make it into college. Now that I had graduated high school and moved out of the house, they felt it was time for them to return to Korea.

I knew our family didn't have a lot of money. It made sense since my parents were lower-earning individuals raising two daughters, paying for a mortgage, expensive music lessons, and a host of other financial responsibilities. I just never realized that this was how little money we had.

I was in community college and in a transitory stage of my life. I wasn't aware of exactly how this change would affect me, but I assumed I would figure it out. My dad moved to Korea first to secure housing and get established over there, while my mom continued to work in the States to financially support the move. A year later, our house was taken back by the bank, and my mom left to join my dad in Korea.

After my parents left, I struggled to find my footing. I casually attended community college without much effort to transfer or excel in my studies. When I realized that my barely passing grades were not going to get me into medical school, or any other school, for that matter, I shifted my focus to working. But, whether it was the recovering economy, a terribly written resume, or bad luck, I couldn't seem to secure even the most basic jobs. I applied for every opening I could find. I even applied to be a security guard for Brink's, an armed armored truck company. Imagine the recruiters' surprise when a five-foot three-inch, 120-pound girl with zero experience in weaponry applied to be a security guard! I'm guessing they laughed and comically appreciated the fact that I was at least willing to get a gun license.

I didn't understand how to budget, and I lived off my financial aid for school—which was insufficient. To cover my living expenses, I rushed into an oppressive living situation that was unhealthy, but stable; my mental and emotional health deteriorated, and my confidence plummeted. This time was the lowest point of my life. It was a lonely and difficult time, but I stubbornly, and somewhat miraculously, was able to trudge through it.

My Mortgage Career

When I was 21 years old, a few days before Christmas, I visited my sister in Southern California. While I was visiting, she asked if I had any interest in relocating and living with her. One month later, I had my car packed up and was driving to Orange County. My sister knew I was unemployed and offered to cover my portion of the rent and utilities while I searched for a job. I assumed that would be a while since I had no luck securing work in Northern California.

Much to my surprise, I received a job offer within a month. I applied to be an office assistant and received an offer only days after my interview. I didn't even know what industry the job was for, but I desperately needed the opportunity and instantly accepted the offer. I knew I was underqualified, so I was thrilled for the opportunity.

My first week on the job, I was scanning and uploading documents to the cloud server. Within a few months, I was learning how to process mortgage loans and was able to learn about real estate and personal finance along the way.

Growing up, I never learned how to manage personal finances. I knew you needed to have a high credit score, but didn't know what went into determining this score or how to increase it. I made several mistakes and mismanaged credit extended to me. Late payments and collections accounts dropped my score down to the 500s.

Getting this job gave me so much more than a paycheck. It certainly allowed me to pay my bills, but it also opened a part of me that I never knew existed. I learned about financial literacy, to think big, and to think beyond my immediate needs. I gained confidence in my ability to work well and thrive in high-stress situations, and more importantly, it provided me with a financial glimpse into my parents' life and how they lived.

My parents asked me to look into something for them, and I had to pull their credit report in the process. I had developed the skills to read a credit report and interpret it as a story, but I wasn't prepared for the story that their reports told.

I learned how they maxed out their credit cards and then opened new cards for balance transfer offers. I learned how they cashed out the equity of their house over and over. I learned how expensive it really was to raise a family in the States. I learned how difficult it can be to understand finances as an immigrant who grew up with an entirely different credit system.

I imagined the fear they must have felt when their creditors told them they had maxed out their cards. I imagined the anxiety they must have felt when their 0% APR promotions ended. I imagined the stress they must have felt when they started receiving default notices from the bank. And I started to feel remorseful for the year that my 18-year-old self was an authorized user on my parents' credit card: for the times my mom said I spent too much money and I ignored her, or the times that I would buy groceries and share them with my friends, or the times that I drove around aimlessly just because I could refill my gas without a care in the world.

The resentment that I felt about my parents' move back to Korea slowly turned into sadness and regret. I wish I had better understood the situation.

COVID-19 Boom and Bust

Once I started working, I realized my acumen for all things numbers. I went back to school and juggled being a full-time employee and a full-time student for six years. During that time, I started my career with mortgages, briefly flirted with other fields I was interested in, and ultimately, came back to the mortgage industry.

Then, in March 2020, I thought my career was over. I thought my entire industry might have been destroyed. The impact of COVID-19 ravaged our economy, and in the midst of the heightened uncertainty, it felt like banks had shut down overnight. The loans I was working on got canceled, mortgage loan programs were discontinued, and entire banks closed for future business effective immediately.

A few months later, just as quickly as the economy had shut down, the government slashed interest rates in favor of reviving the economy. And immediately, work resumed. In fact, it poured in. In the eight years since I had started in the industry, I had never seen so much work, and money, coming in.

This was a once in a lifetime opportunity. The general unpredictability of commissions combined with an extreme desire for financial stability led me to workaholism. I justified this by repeating the narrative that this was a once in a lifetime opportunity and continued to work 80-100 hour weeks. I relished in the surprise people expressed when they received emails from me at 3:00 a.m., and I savored the praise of my worth ethic and attention to detail.

The fruits of my labor paid off. I had the privilege of making income that I had once only ever dreamed of and my savings rate exceeded that of most salaries. As far as money was concerned, I felt like I was on top of the world—I had made it!

Eventually, I was forced to come to terms with the fact that what goes up must come down. The work slowed down almost as quickly as it had come. More importantly, my health, which I had neglected for so long, caught up to me. It was undeniable that my body was deprived of basic care. I was lucky that the waning flow of work forced me to slow down.

Real Estate Investing with a Mission

Partway through the COVID-19 pandemic, I began syndicating commercial assets. A syndication is a group investment where funds are pooled to purchase a larger asset for stronger returns. I had always been curious about real estate, and now that I had this newfound wealth, I decided to start investing for myself. I assumed that I would obtain financial security, then time freedom, and ultimately, amass wealth, which could be donated and redistributed to the causes I was passionate about.

As I began networking and learning more about the complexities of commercial real estate, I noticed a handful of people who donated a percentage of their profits to charity. They didn't become multimillionaires before they began giving back to their communities. Seeing this, I started pondering my values and ambitions.

My analytical brain loved value-add proposition deals. The idea of optimizing the finances and subsequently forcing appreciation on a property was intriguing to me. My altruistic side loved finding motivation beyond the numbers and the money. Ever since I was a child, I believed in volunteering and giving back to the community in whatever capacity I could. So, I started to think about my business model and ways I could integrate these.

I reflected on my childhood and my family life: *If we had more money would life have been easier? How would my life have changed if there had been someone willing to educate my parents on financial literacy?*

My family was unable to get out of debt due to both systemic and socio-economic reasons, and this has left a deep and lasting impact on me today. I am still working to reconcile my feelings and experiences with this intergenerational trauma.

I realize I am one of the fortunate ones who escaped financial illiteracy. I had the privilege of learning valuable skills on the job that grew my knowledge, and ultimately, my financial stability and wealth. For those who have not been able to break the cycle, I vow to take part in that reconciliation. My life mission has shifted to providing knowledge and opportunity to those who have not yet experienced it.

My company's fundamental mission is unchanged. I will continue to provide quality investment offerings to our investors with competitive returns while creating win/win/win scenarios for everyone involved.

Rather than waiting 10 years to make a significant impact, I'm working to create real change today. My goal is to create housing developments specifically designed for those who are still learning financial literacy and to help them purchase their first home. Statistically, those who grow up in a parent-owned home have fewer behavioral problems, higher educational accomplishments, and a greater likelihood of generational wealth.

I want to empower people like myself with the belief that they can think big, no matter where they are starting from. I started with a 560 FICO score and zero understanding of how to make money. Through the kindness of those around me and access to financial education, I am able to lead a financially successful life. I want to pay it forward and lend a helping hand as I invest with the purpose of leaving a lasting impact.

Contact Gina Shin to learn about investing with impact and to live your life on your own terms with the power of passive income. For the latest updates on her journey, tips for financial wellness, and insights about real estate, follow her on social media @investwithgina. Subscribe to her newsletter, inquire about speaking engagements, or interview requests at Hello@ShinEquityPartners.com.

Quotable: My family was unable to get out of debt due to both systemic and socio-economic reasons, and this has left a deep and lasting impact on me today.... I realize I am one of the fortunate ones who escaped financial illiteracy.

 Scan to invest with Gina.

LANDON SCHLABACH

From a Dream to Reality
Achieving Success Through Patience

Landon Schlabach is the CEO of BNB Breeze, a vacation rental management business, and an entrepreneur with a deep passion for real estate. He went from furniture store employee, to house flipper, to CEO of a successful multi-faceted real estate business that he is still growing today. Through total faith in the Lord, he is living the dream!.

The Desire

Growing up, my parents encouraged us to start investing our money wisely, not just throw it away on movies or something we wouldn't get anything out of. (Don't ask my mom what she thinks of $5+ coffee drinks). So, they encouraged us to raise dogs! It went well. We learned to put in the work ourselves and start a small business, which to us was big at the time.

Right after high school, I moved to Sarasota, Florida, to learn the restaurant business in hopes of creating a family restaurant back home in North Carolina. During my two years there that idea ended up falling through. I did meet my wonderful wife in Sarasota, so the move was well worth it.

After moving back home, I found myself working in sales at a furniture store and working with a multi-level marketing company. This allowed me to dive deep into the world of sales, which is a very important trade to learn in the entrepreneurial world. My time with the multi-level marketing company was great. It allowed me to grow a small business and gave me a platform to speak at events, which I enjoy doing.

The furniture business was where my life really seemed to change. My boss would give us books on sales and also focused on training each of us in how to relate with clients. Around this time, I started feeling the need to focus on my personal growth and realized there had to be a better way to spend my working hours than working for someone else in the normal, nine to five, rat race job.

The first personal development book I read was SO eye-opening: *Rich Dad Poor Dad*. It got me hungry to learn more. I love to learn and ask questions of people. If you want to increase where you go, you must increase what you know. I have since spent thousands of dollars on my personal development and will continue to do so.

A big part of personal development is recognizing the influence others have on you. I love surrounding myself with like-minded thinkers and, more importantly, friends and mentors who are further along in their personal journey than I am in mine. One of my favorite proverbs is "Show me your friends and I will show you your future."

I enjoyed the customer relations at the furniture store but realized I didn't want to be an employee forever. I wanted to own the business! For years, this desire grew in me, but I didn't know how or where to start.

The Learning Stage

When our family was in negotiations to purchase the furniture store, I thought, There! This will take us to the next level financially.

When the deal fell through, it left me and my family devastated.

I told my wife I thought it was time to leave the business. Too much was going on with it, and I just knew I couldn't stay an employee there any longer. In three months, we were expecting our first child, so a sudden career change was a great idea. Right?!

I've always had an interest in the real estate market, so I decided to jump in and see what I could make of it. Shortly after leaving the furniture store, I bought my first house with an investor and flipped it. By the way, it was nothing like they make it look on HGTV. It took me six months, but I completed the renovation and made a little bit of money. So, we did it again and then again.

In all, we flipped about 10 homes using other people's money (OPM). This made us a little bit of money but never really took off like I envisioned. However, during this time, I gained a wide expanse of knowledge about homes and what exactly goes into them—from electrical wiring to toilets. I was able to apply all of these lessons in future real estate ventures.

Additionally, during this time, I got my real estate license, thinking I could learn more about real estate and crush it in sales by helping others find their dream home and find more flips to do. But my heart wasn't in it.

I've since learned, if something doesn't make you excited and you can't see yourself thriving in it, it most likely is not for you.

The Promise Coming to Life

A few flips later, a trip to Pennsylvania would change my life. In Pennsylvania, there was, and currently still is, an incredibly close-knit friend group that meets once a month for book club. A close friend of mine was a part of this group and invited me to their book club meeting one night.

I had been very intrigued with the short-term rental (STR) industry and was looking for confirmation from the Lord on this potential industry opportunity. At this book club meeting in 2018, I got that confirmation! The next day, I hit the ground running. I bought a course for $1,000 and started learning.

Our company, BNB Breeze, began managing other people's vacation homes. We took the first property from doing $440 as a short-term rental in March to $4,400 in April. The owners were thrilled with what we had done. So, I set out to find more properties. Now, we are managing 80 homes across 10 states.

What started as a side hustle quickly turned into a full-time business. So, I stopped actively seeking flips and went into full-time STR management. Today we have an amazing team that helps us manage these homes, which provide great vacations for many guests and positive returns for our investors. I can't speak highly enough of our team. I am big with aces in their places. Put people in a position where they come alive and enjoy, and the business has a good chance of taking off. Having a great team where we set people up to maximize their potential allows us to do way more than I could do by myself.

We own several vacation homes, including our Florida investment property that we have named Living the Dream. The goal is to build out more legacy properties in areas where we want to vacation ourselves. We have even had the opportunity to build our own unique stays, including two shipping container homes called The Green Creek Shipyard, which I own with my brother and sister. These unique stays really get me fired up. The sibling trio will continue to build out more creative and unique stays. The returns on these types of homes are fantastic, and we love the challenge of creating them.

"Find your gift then serve it to the world: That is how you will affect this world with the Kingdom." I truly believe I am right where God wants me in this season in life. You only live once. I figure I might as well do something I enjoy doing. The lifestyle we now have is absolutely amazing. I get to spend time with my wife and three boys, traveling all over, seeing so many amazing sights, and spending time on my favorite hobby—golfing.

I truly believe, when God speaks to your heart, stand on that promise, no matter what. He told me that I will eventually have a thriving business, real estate I'm proud of, and financial independence by the time I turn 30. I also set a goal to own a Tesla by 30 and eventually a jet. The Tesla did happen before I turned 30 and while I am still waiting on the jet, I am in partnership on a smaller plane already. "If you're faithful with what's in your hands, God will give you what is in your heart."

The Lesson

In anything you do, do it with excellence.

This is a point my dad has driven home to me ever since I was little. I have never forgotten this. It has even gone into my personal well-being, including what I eat and how I exercise. I hate running, but I know it is good for me. I do a daily cold plunge in sub-50-degree water every day because I know it is good for me, even though I hate doing it. Getting in cold water is most likely the hardest thing I will face for the day, and if I can conquer that, it makes everything else seem way easier.

My life very much feels like the parable of the Chinese Bamboo Tree. Like any plant, the Chinese Bamboo Tree requires nurturing—water, fertile soil, and sunshine—to grow. In its first year, we see no visible signs of activity. In the second year, again, we see no growth above the soil. The third year, the fourth year, still nothing. Our patience is tested. We begin to wonder if our efforts (watering, caring, etc.) will ever be rewarded.

And finally, in the fifth year—behold, a miracle! We experience growth. And what growth it is! The Chinese Bamboo Tree grows 80 feet in just six weeks!

Does the Chinese Bamboo Tree really grow 80 feet in six weeks? Did the Chinese Bamboo Tree lie dormant for four years only to grow exponentially in the fifth? Or, was the little tree growing underground, developing a root system strong enough to support its potential for outward growth in the fifth year and beyond? The answer is obvious. Had the tree not developed a strong, unseen foundation, it could not have sustained its life as it grew.

The same principle is true for people. People, who patiently toil toward worthwhile dreams and goals, building strong character while overcoming adversity and challenge, grow the strong internal foundation to handle success. Eventually, your business will bust through, and you will wonder how you got there.

To connect with Landon Schlabach about the short-term rental industry, reach out to Landon at landon@bnbbreeze.co, 828.817.5056. To book a home for your next vacation, check out BNBbreeze.co.

To book a vacation rental, use code Book2023 to receive 15% off at Living the Dream or The Shipping Containers.

Quotable: If you can dream it, you can do it.

Scan to get in touch with Landon.

DR. STORMY HILL

A Radical Breakthrough of Self-Acceptance

Dr. Stormy Hill, OTR/L, owner of two occupational therapy businesses, helps special education students and adults with mental health challenges and is a pioneer in implementing rehab sensory rooms. Stormy is also a certified intimacy coach, founder of Love Deep Lab, and a speaker on relationships, sex, and wellness. She has been featured in the NY Post, Daily Mirror, *and more.*

Letting Go of Childhood Dreams

I wanted to be a doctor since I was five years old. So, like the overachiever that I am, I made my dream come true. With a lot of hard work, I graduated in 2006 with my medical degree.

My childhood dream had come true, but the thing about dreams is that dreams change and grow as we do. We can cling to an outdated dream, or we can let go and create space for a new one. While I wanted to be a doctor so much and had become one, there was one thing I wanted more, and that was to be a mother.

A Journey of Life and "Death"

For me, motherhood was not an easy journey, and it took several rounds of in vitro before I finally became pregnant. On a snowy January day, I gave birth to my son. It was as serene as a 36-hour natural birth can be, until something went terribly wrong.

A bit of placenta remained in my uterus, so I started hemorrhaging profusely. I was in and out of consciousness and excruciating pain as they attempted to stop the bleeding by compressing my uterus from the inside out.

At some point, I left my body. I witnessed the bloody scene from above, and I was no longer in pain. I saw, from my new vantage point, my son laying in his bassinet with no one tending to him. They were all tending to me. My husband was nose to nose with me as I was fading away.

I then had an all-encompassing desire to come back. I kept hearing, *I need to come back. I need to feed my son.*

Eleven blood and platelet transfusions saved my life, and I snapped back into my body in intense pain. But the pain was welcome because it let me know I was alive. I demanded to nurse my son, not knowing if I was back for good or only for a short time. My near-death experience did not include a profound meeting with God, a movie reel of my life, or a white light calling me. It was simply a deep desire and obvious choice to come back and be my son's momma.

To this day, the role of mother is my deepest gift, honor, and adventure. My son is my greatest teacher on this earth and being his momma is my greatest joy. When you become a mother, your prior notion of love is so small compared to the all-encompassing love you experience with your child. This was the beginning of my life as a momma and the force of nature that motherhood is.

His "Too Big" Heart

I believe one of the superpowers of a mother is her intuition. When my son was three months of age, mine started speaking up loudly. Something just did not feel right with my baby, despite my being reassured by doctors and family. After demanding a chest x-ray, we found out that my son was in heart failure. In the cardiac care unit, with his heart quivering more than beating, he fought for his life.

My son was diagnosed with dilated cardiomyopathy, a rare and often fatal heart disease that affects 12 in one million children in the United States. With the late stage of his heart failure, we were told that our son's life expectancy was not likely long.

To care for my son, who was in and out of heart failure for the next 18 months, I decided to discontinue my medical residency in psychiatry and pediatrics. I did not want to miss a moment with him. My childhood dream of being a doctor was replaced by my deep calling to be a mother. While those roles are not mutually exclusive for many, for me, they were.

So, a stay-at-home mom I became as well as his caretaker, case manager, patient advocate, and nurse. I took on a volunteer position as physician/family liaison for the Children's Cardiomyopathy Foundation and worked with families who had lost children to the disease my son was battling.

During my long days in medical school, I had only dreamed of being a stay-at-home mom. And again, my dream changed as I did. I adored being with my son but realized that I was a better mom when I was also helping others. I learned that we cannot hoard moments, we can just learn to cherish them whether they are few or many.

My son is now 19 years old and thriving at college on his own. He's living proof that miracles do exist. Science and research would say that he should likely be dead, and yet he is very much alive, living with his own "too big" heart, and driving me crazy in all the best ways.

Moving from Regret to Power

One night, in prayer, I said, *Okay, God. What is next? If I am not going back to my medical training, what am I going to do?*

An insightful question raised by a family member was, "Who has been the most important person in saving your son's life?" The answer was his occupational therapist. I had seen the impact she had on my son and my family, and it was profound.

Right then and there, I chose to return to graduate school and this time pursue a master's in occupational therapy. That decision has led to a massively fulfilling career as a mental health occupational therapist for the last 13 years.

In occupational therapy school, guided again by intuition, I chose to focus my studies on autism and sensory processing. Just a few months later, my son was officially diagnosed with autism, and my professional world and my mom world deeply collided. While my book knowledge of autism was vast, being a mom to a kiddo with autism was a whole different arena. Not only was I getting to know my toddler son, I was also getting a crash course in autism, its joys, and its challenges.

Catalytic Change

I was also in the process of a divorce. My son's father is an amazing dad, but we were not amazing at being married. We struggled in many arenas, including our sex and intimacy. After painfully navigating the infidelity between my husband and my best friend, we initiated divorce. We did so amicably because our desire to successfully co-parent our son far outweighed any bitterness we had.

I consider my divorce a failure because I made vows before God and family, and I broke that commitment. I accept that failure. We all fail, and embracing failure makes us more whole. My ex-husband continues to this day to be an incredible father, and we co-parent almost seamlessly. I am grateful for my divorce and for what it showed me about myself, my strength, and how I wanted to live.

My divorce was my catalyst for learning everything I could about sex and intimacy. I chose to create passion, aliveness, and joy, in all aspects of my life. That became my personal mission and continues to be my mission today.

Relationship Darkness

While my professional world was in a state of flux as I moved from graduate student to working professional, my personal world entered what I call "the dark night of my relationship soul." As my mother curtly put it, "My chooser button was broken."

I was a single mom and living on maxed-out student loans. Seeking solace, I pursued love in all the wrong places. First, it was a long-term relationship I broke off with a cheating narcissist. Then, it was a relationship with an emotionally and physically abusive man with severe PTSD. Infidelity and abuse are non-discriminating and can happen to anyone. And they happened to me.

Once I finally freed myself from that last unhealthy relationship, I tenderly and shockingly realized that I was the one common denominator in all my failed relationships. The men and the challenges changed, but I was the common thread. I decided to dive into conscious celibacy and do deep, interpersonal work with an amazing therapist to be sure I would never tolerate an unhealthy relationship again.

I learned the life-long, daily practice of truly loving myself. The quote "We accept the love we think we deserve," was very true in my life. So, I moved on with a deep knowing that I deserve a passionate, safe, kind, powerful love…. We all do!

Entrepreneur on the Fly

I was making $33K per year in an occupational therapy job I hated. It was punch in, punch out day after day to barely make ends meet. Again, I said my prayer which was becoming a bit of a mantra…. *Okay, God. What is next? This can't be it. I am listening.*

Soon after that, on my morning drive to my dead-end hospital job, I received a call from a special education teacher who was looking for an occupational therapist. He asked me if I did this sort of work, to which

I replied "yes" before I could doubt myself or the fact that I had never actually done contracted, school-based work.

He asked me the name of my company, which I invented spontaneously at that moment! That night, I was up until 4:00 a.m. getting my first business tax ID and operating license and buying an online contract template. It was a mad dash to get my ducks in a row. In his office the very next day, my first business was launched and my entry into entrepreneurship began.

Fourteen years later, that business is still going strong, is growing, and financially supports me. I often think back to that morning commute. What if I had let doubt or fear stop me from saying yes? What if I had shrunk back rather than leaned in? I am so grateful I did not. My company and staff have helped more than 3,000 special education students to succeed.

A few years later, I was asked to consult a group of clinicians in a rehab facility for substance use disorders. I thought, *What can I consult on?... I work with children and autism....* But, as I began to witness the patients, I realized that the overarching struggle, whether in the autistic brain or the substance-abusing brain, is self-regulation: the ability to handle life's hurdles with success.

For the next 10 years, in both of my occupational therapy businesses, I studied and taught how change, healing, and integration lie first in the alignment of mind and body and second in the mindfulness needed to reflect, self-confront, and grow. I learned how much we still don't know about the brain and how this thing that rests between our ears and its connection to our body is the biggest player in the quality of our life, the depth of our pleasure, and the intimacy of our relationships.

Living as Parts

I realized one day that so many of us, particularly in long-term, committed relationships lose touch with passion, stop cultivating intimacy, and settle for a tepid love partnership rather than the loving, passionate, sexy relationship we all deserve. We settle for mediocrity in one of the most important relationships we have on this earth. So, to be able to help couples and deepen my clinical toolbox, I embarked on a one-year certification to become a sex and intimacy coach. Along with being a mom, this work is my passion on Earth.

I was living my purpose, and so I was perplexed to find myself SO exhausted. I was still running my other two businesses, single parenting, and now creating a third business as a sex and intimacy coach. I struggled to see how my life journey, my degrees, and my businesses all contributed to the me I was becoming.

I judged my journey and regretted my choices. I was frozen in moments of victim mode. I looked at my businesses as roadblocks rather than roadways. The exhaustion came from the lack of integration of these seemingly separate parts of myself.

It's All Connected

In time, I began to see the connections between the science of my doctorate, the sensory and nervous system focus of my occupational therapy practice, and my passion for helping people live intimate lives with themselves and their partners. I moved from living in *I am this OR I am that*, and I began to live in *I am this AND I am that*.

The truth is ALL the roles I play are part of who I am. All your roles are part of who YOU are.

With this new awareness, my world started opening in ways I couldn't imagine. My businesses all started to do better. I enjoyed my life, love, sex, and relationships more. And I experienced more pleasure in all aspects of life.

Pleasure is our birthright, and yet, so many are living mediocre lives dotted by overworking, overthinking, overeating, over worrying, and a whole slew of other "overs" that have made us unsatisfied, unhealthy, and unhappy in staggering numbers.

Did you know that you can have a life that is healthy, vibrant, and passionate? While there is no secret to this sort of life, no pill to take or fad to try on, embracing ALL parts of you and your story is essential to help you create that reality.

Cracks of Gold

While we don't get any "do-overs" in life, the important mindset shift is that you don't need any. Instead, learn from mistakes and befriend all parts of yourself to step into the most powerful you. This is a key to living a life turned on by the beauty of life itself.

You are a wondrous composite of all your parts. Not just your refined and best-foot-forward parts but ALL your blundering and misstepping parts too. You are an amalgamation of not just the good things that have happened to you, but also the hard things.

I am not going to tell you "everything happens for a reason," because even though a large part of me knows that is true, the therapist in me finds that invalidating to your pain and your story. And sometimes, life is just hard.

AND every part of your journey from the painful to the priceless has made you YOU. Every part of your story has made you the unique human being that you are.

The metaphor that comes to mind is *kintsugi*, the beautiful Japanese art of putting broken pottery back together and filling the cracks with gold. The cracked pieces, claimed and reintegrated, create a stunning and totally unique piece of art. Similarly, by embracing ALL of who you are, you become the most powerful version of yourself. Anything else is a shrunken facade of your magnificence—a black and white version of your truly technicolor self.

The challenges, traumas, and missteps in your life do not make you broken. They make you art. They are the cracks of your life. You can be shattered by them OR through self-acceptance, you can fill them with gold and become the stunning work of art you already are.

And just like the *kintsugi* bowl is not broken, neither are you. Your cracks ARE your gold.

Learn more about Dr. Stormy's coaching and programs at www.lovedeeperlab.com.

To inquire about speaking engagements, please email stormy@lovedeeplab.com.

Join our monthly newsletter for strategies to add more passion, power, and vibrancy to all areas of your life!

Instagram: @docstormy1 TikTok: @TouchySubjectsss

Quotable: While we don't get any "do overs" in life, the important mindset shift is that you don't need any. Your mistakes, traumas, and errors all make you the magnificently unique human being you are.

 Scan here for your free Wellness Guide.

DENIS WAITLEY

Facing My Biggest Battle
Wisdom from an Iconic Thought Leader

Denis Waitley is a world-renowned speaker. He has written 16 bestselling classics, including Seeds of Greatness *and* The New Psychology of Winning. *His audio album* The Psychology of Winning *is the all-time bestselling program on self-mastery. Denis is the former chairman of psychology for the US Olympic Committee's Sports Medicine Council and is in the National Speakers Association Speaker Hall of Fame.*

Dysfunctional Upbringing

My parents divorced when I was in my teens. They were always arguing about money or my father's drinking, smoking, and socializing. I was always putting my pillow over my head in my bedroom to block out their constant bickering, and my little brother would hide. He was seven years younger than me and my sister was three years older.

My father joined the Merchant Marines at the onset of World War II and left when I was nine. He came into my room and said goodbye instead of goodnight. He returned briefly after the war, however soon left again, and I only saw him once a year thereafter.

Six years later, he came back from World War II as a Lieutenant and said to me, "If I was you, I'd head for the Naval Academy. If you can, get a congressional appointment and take the competitive exams." As a Merchant Marine, he couldn't give me an appointment himself.

During the Korean War, I was a senior in high school. As a kid in the 1940s, I grew up playing with Army helmets, Army men, and rubber guns. Then, as a senior and student body president at La Jolla High School, I believed I was going to go to Stanford on a Naval ROTC scholarship. I would only have to serve a couple of years. But when the Korean War came, my father encouraged me to go to the Naval Academy to become an officer the right way. It wasn't me, but at that time it was the right thing to do for the country.

When I was in the Navy in Washington, I got a chance to tie the Navy into the Blue Angels at the Ice Capades. I got to do Sea Power, sell the

Navy, and see how to promote. I became a Navy department head of media relations. Then I got the opportunity to work with Ampex, who had invented the video recorder in the early 1950s and traveled the world selling the first instant replay videotape recorder. There was a little show biz in that. People were wowed that the device could replay short bursts of video instantaneously without the need to develop the film first.

Early, Iconic Mentors

I then got the chance to work with Dr. Jonas Salk at the Salk Institute for Biological Studies in San Diego. He changed my life. He said to me, "Be careful. You're very bright and very optimistic, kind of like Jiminy Cricket. But don't tell people they can walk on water. They need pontoons." He said, "You're not a scientist. You're a promoter of self-awareness, but you're not magic." Dr. Jonas Salk introduced me to Abraham Maslow who was the head of the American Psychological Association. He introduced me to Carl Rogers at the Center for Studies of the Person. And he introduced me to Viktor Frankl, author of *Man's Search for Meaning*. This connection with Jonas Salk in the 1960s helped me develop into who I would become.

Then the Apollo Program came along. My classmate, astronaut Bill Anders orbited the moon with Apollo 8, the first crewed spacecraft to leave low Earth orbit and the first human spaceflight to reach the moon. I had an opportunity to do simulation project studies and seminars for all the Apollo astronauts. I became friends with Gene Cernan, Wally Schirra, and all the guys that ended up going to the moon and walking on the moon.

Earl Nightingale was also a great influence of mine—*Our Changing World* and *The Strangest Secret*. "We become what we think about most of the time." When I gave my POW talk, I carried a little Sony recorder and recorded every talk I gave, in churches, women's clubs, Lions Clubs, Kiwanis International clubs, and Rotary Clubs. I spoke 500 times before anyone would pay me. Having recorded the first 500 speeches, I knew what made people laugh, what didn't, what they liked, and what was a hot button. I got rid of the things that didn't work and kept the things that did. Then, one day, a little cassette of mine traveled around to somebody and plopped into Earl Nightingale's home recorder.

He listened to it, then called me and said, "Hey, this is Earl Nightingale. I notice you're here in Sarasota, Florida, working for Dr. Jonas Salk. I'm calling you because you have a nice voice and I like your stuff. If you're ever in Chicago, go see my partner Lloyd Conant." So, I took my last $500 with me to Chicago. It took me two years to convince them that I had enough in me to record. I watched all the speakers in those days and became close to Robert Schuller, Norman Vincent Peale, Paul Harvey, and Art Linkletter, real influences in my life.

Nightingale-Conant was also responsible for my becoming chairman of psychology for the Olympics. I met the chairman of the sports medicine council for the United States Olympic Committee at a conference. *The Psychology of Winning* album had just hit it big with AT&T, IBM, General Electric, and more companies who were buying it. William Simon, president of the United States Olympic Committee said, "You know, we really need a guy like that." So, unprepared, never having been a sports psychologist, never having worked in a university in psychology for sports, Bill Simon named me chairman of psychology to enhance the performance of the greatest US athletes for all of America.

My nomination caused a furor. Imagine me going into the Olympic committee of 17 psychiatrists and psychologists, each of whom was also an expert in their sport: figure skating, track and field, fencing, high jumping, all that. They said, "Who do you think you are?"

And I said, "Have you ever heard of the administrator of NASA?"

They said, "No."

I said, "Me neither. I don't know his name. Look at me as that—somebody who's administering the sports psychology programs for the Olympics but who's not going to take any credit. I don't know how to deal with each sport, but you do. You get all the credit. I will help raise the money and work with athletes and teams doing my psychology, but you're the guys."

And they said, "Do you mean you're willing to subordinate your ego to let us do our thing?"

I said, "Absolutely. I couldn't do it anyway. You know that." I learned more from the Olympians than they ever learned from me.

Positively Influencing Others

I have four children, many grandchildren, and now great-grandchildren, some already teenagers. I believe in being a role model, not a critic. If they shouldn't be doing it, neither should you. Values are more likely caught than taught. Be someone worth emulating to your children by setting the example in your life. If you set the example, later on, you'll find that they remembered what they saw. I never got anywhere by preaching. In fact, I remember lecturing my children, and them saying, "Is this your half-hour or your 45-minute version of *The Psychology of Winning*?"

Your children are a reflection of how you live. They may misunderstand the advice you give, but there's no misunderstanding how you and your spouse live. Don't tell them about it, show them by your actions. It's much better to walk your talk. A positive role model does more as a parent than any lecturing could possibly do.

I've made every mistake you can make. In other words, I'm a flawed person who's not impressed with himself. My significance comes from my insignificance. I'm an oboe player in the 12th row of the maestro's orchestra, but I'm not the conductor, and I'm not the guy in front of the cameras.

The older I get, the more I realize it comes down to the few we love, our closest handful of friends, and trying to help young people by passing on everything we've learned. Just like money does you no good when you have it, only when you employ it, if you have knowledge and die with it, it's no good. It's better to pass it on while you're alive.

For me, a widow with a rose garden is as important as a politician, rock star, or superstar athlete. Let's say that you're not interested in entering your roses in the local flower show competition, and the blue ribbon is not important to you, but you love taking care of flowers. The sheer exhilaration of doing something excellent for its own merit—not to prove it to others, not to get the money, and not to get accolades—is its own reward. We all want to be experts in something. We all want to be competitive and beat somebody to make us feel a little better. We all want material things. But the two greatest motivators of all are the sheer exhilaration of doing something excellent, that feels good, and doing it independently without somebody telling us to do it. Those two motivators drive more people to accomplish great things than all the money in the world.

Give More in Value than You Expect in Payment

One of my philosophies is to always give more in value than you receive in payment. If you give more in value than you receive in payment, you'll always be sought after because you're a bargain. If you're a bargain, they'll be attracted to you. My philosophy has always been to push all your marbles, all your chips, over on the other side. You may not get paid, but still, you pay value first. You don't quid pro quo in life. Give it all away. Every time, upfront. It will come back to you, probably more than you ever dreamed.

With my grandchildren, I have a passion project. I ask each of my grandchildren to come to me with their passion. It has to be something that they're so magnificently obsessed with doing that they bring me a kind of business plan. I help them fund their passion so they can get really into it. That's one of the things I'm doing with my estate. I don't want to give people money after I'm dead. What I want to do is make money useful while I'm alive.

I don't do things because of how expensive they are or put on a show. I used to come in close contact with many people like that. They would take me on a tour, showing me all the things they'd accumulated because that was important to them. Status is not important to me. What is important to me is human interaction, nature, and love.

Doing Something That Benefits Life

I wake up happy and ask myself, "What are you going to do with this day? How can you make life breathe easier as a result of your actions today?" Every day, I try to do something that benefits life. I'm much more in tune with nature, flowers, trees, and animals these days. I also still have this longing inside to help people, younger people especially, to not be a redwood tree in a flowerpot. I don't want them to be rootbound.

The digital era creates speed and creates the ability to communicate everywhere, but it is the enemy of intimacy. It allows you a virtual smell, but not the real fragrance of the rose. It allows you to have a romance without love and to go places where you don't get your feet muddy or sand in your shoes. It's the most marvelous tool for communication and the most dangerous thing.

I want younger people to take time. Take time to listen. Take time to look. Take time to smell a rose along the way. Take a hike. Smell the ocean. But don't be so engaged in getting from one place to another that you miss everything along the way.

Age 90 and Looking Forward

My early life consisted of a series of roller coaster events, many of which were negative. I've revealed publicly that my most profitable and noteworthy work, *The Psychology of Winning*, was written during one of my lowest points, while I was losing in nearly every aspect of my life.

However, it wasn't until five years ago that the demand for authentic resiliency paid me a sudden, unforeseen visit. I had just returned from a month-long speaking tour throughout Asia, Europe, and the Middle East. A health checkup revealed that I had inherited a thickened heart valve condition from my mother. In my middle 80s, feeling good, I opted for a new heart valve so I could happily reach my goal of 100 golden years. Unfortunately, a surgical error severed my femoral artery and I nearly died on the operating table.

During recovery, I contracted a life-threatening infection in my new heart valve and spent three suspenseful months in isolated skilled nursing care. Just when I felt I had won this battle, I noticed a chronic sore throat, which was diagnosed as an acid reflux issue. Nearly a year later, a biopsy revealed I had been misdiagnosed and actually was facing advanced-stage throat cancer requiring immediate, massive radiation and chemotherapy to save my life.

I rarely speak about my own pain and suffering, preferring to dwell on desired outcomes. Suffice it to say, it has been the most brutal, indescribable experience imaginable. Internal and external radiation burns. Cognitive challenges from chemotherapy. COVID lockdowns in skilled nursing facilities.

Confined to a 9-foot by 12-foot room, with no visitors for months. Too painful to swallow. Then unable to swallow. Liquid diet only by feeding tube. Taste buds destroyed, salivary glands inoperative. Sleep deprivation, weight loss, and muscle atrophy. And then, the moment of truth. *Dig deep into your resilience reservoir and take charge, Denis! This is no drill, it is reality. Remember, this is a cakewalk compared to what POWs and wounded servicemen and women have endured.*

I converted my hospital room into an office and fitness center: weights, stretch bands, an Exercycle, a desk, a computer, and Wi-Fi. *TV off. Up at 5:30 every morning, make my bed like a Navy Seal, get rid of the hospital gown, and get dressed. Stop complaining, start training. No stewing, start doing.* During that six-month period, I finished writing *The New Psychology of Winning* and nearly completed a draft of a second book, *The Psychology of Loving.* With speech therapy, I got my voice back. With swallow therapy, I learned how to swallow again. With physical therapy, I learned how to walk without a walker.

Is this a miracle? Not really. Just someone being resilient when the chips are down. All those second-hand experiences in which I marveled at the resilience of others and wrote and lectured about them paled in reality; it was not until I, myself, faced my mortality, that I truly practiced what I so often preach.

Just when all seemed bright again, I learned that the cancer had reoccurred in my right lung, although I've never been a smoker. So, the radiation and chemotherapy began all over again.

So, what is my prognosis? Well, I am a happy, grateful father, grandfather, and great-grandfather to a loving inner circle. I am on a permanent, liquid diet, with no taste or desire to eat. But I can smell the fragrance of beautiful lilacs and roses, and my memory is filled with exquisite senses.

Will I become cancer free? As an optimist, I hope so. As a realist, we'll see.

I know there are many keys to a life well lived and one size does not fit all.

In my heart of hearts, I believe that resilience is a fundamental measure of success and fulfillment, especially today with more real-time confrontations with the world's problems than at any previous time in history. We are inextricably connected to every other living being and creation on Earth.

My joy is in pursuing unconditional love and in doing something every day to make life more fulfilling for every living creation I touch. In short, I am planting shade trees for future generations, under which I, myself, may never sit.

To learn more about Denis Waitley and his speaking, books, courses, and teachings, please visit www.deniswaitley.com. Follow Denis on Facebook @OfficialDenisWaitley and Instagram @theDenisWaitley.

Quotable: I believe in being a role model, not a critic. If they shouldn't be doing it, neither should you. Values are more likely caught than taught.

BOOK EDITOR AND WRITING COACH

Takara Sights is the editor of *The Transformational Journey*. She has been publishing inspirational and motivational books with Kyle Wilson since 2015 and revels in working one-on-one with authors as they develop their stories and share their life wisdom. She currently lives with her wonderful partner and fantastic dog in Los Angeles, California.

BOOK PUBLISHER

Kyle Wilson is the founder of Jim Rohn International and KyleWilson.com. Kyle has filled huge seminar rooms, launched and published multiple personal development publications, and produced/published over 100+ hours of programs. Kyle has published and sold over 1,000,000 books including titles by Jim Rohn and Denis Waitley as well as his own books including *Success Habits of Super Achievers* with Brian Tracy, Les Brown, Darren Hardy, Denis Waitley, Mark Victor Hansen, *Persistence, Pivots and Game Changers*, and *Bringing Value, Solving Problems and Leaving a Legacy*. Kyle is the host of the *Success Habits of Super Achievers* podcast and the Kyle Wilson Inner Circle Mastermind.

ADDITIONAL RESOURCES

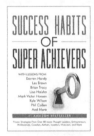

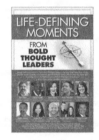

Order in Quantity and SAVE

Mix and Match

Order online KyleWilson.com/books

Praise for *The Transformational Journey*

Transformation is a word we hear, see, and read about a lot. The authors in this book provide real-life examples of the power of a transformation; what it does to your heart, your mind, your relationships, and your life. We get to hear the stories of the what, where, how, and why of these transformations. A must read!

Kevin Eastman, NBA Championship Coach, International Speaker, Author of Why the Best Are the Best

Transformation requires you to start before you have the ability or confidence to make it happen and thus requires courage to take the first step. This book is the perfect dose of courage you need to take that first step!

Tom Ziglar, CEO of Zig Ziglar Corporation

I love the stories and wisdom from the authors in The Transformational Journey! Being a long-time student of Denis Waitley, as well as friends with the publisher Kyle Wilson, it's inspiring to read all the stories of resilience, breakthroughs, and contribution.

Bob Beaudine, Entrepreneur, CEO of Eastman-Beaudine, National Bestselling Author of 2 Chairs and The Power of WHO!

Kyle Wilson continues surrounding himself with brilliant winners—people with real-world experience who are climbing to great heights by contributing value in their unique way. The Transformational Journey affords you an opportunity to immerse yourself in the healthy influence of people like Denis Waitley, Brian Tracy, Chris Gronkowski, Ron White, and more. This book will enrich your life!

TC Cummings, Navy SEAL, Leadership Coach, Founder of Noble Warrior Training

The Transformational Journey is a must-read, as it includes lessons from business, life, and happiness from extraordinary high achievers. This is your opportunity to learn from individuals (artists, athletes, writers, and business owners) who lived transformative experiences, grew to be the best versions of themselves, and now are sharing their transformations with the world so you can do it too!

Olenka Cullinan, CEO, iStartFirst, Executive Coach & Speaker

Find a highlighter because the stories in this book will inspire you to make sure you remember them. You will want to share them with others.

Newy Scruggs, 12x Emmy-Winning Sportscaster, Speaker, Author

The Transformational Journey provides a wealth of wisdom and inspiration from well-known, honored sages along with a myriad of new authors who've also traveled the journey successfully. Each shares a perspective that will assist readers on their similar successful transformation journeys. Read it cover to cover and begin your journey.

Tim Cole, Colonel, US Marine Corps (Retired), Veterans Advocate

I really love the powerful and inspiring stories in The Transformational Journey, a book published by my good friend Kyle Wilson. Many of the authors are friends and some are mentors in the case of Denis Waitley. I highly recommend you invest the time to read each story and take action as needed!

Dr. Tom Burns, Orthopedic Surgeon, Investor, Author of Why Doctors Don't Get Rich